# MARYA HO

## *Madness*

### A BIPOLAR LIFE

## HARPER PERENNIAL

London, New York, Toronto, Sydney and New Delhi

Harper Perennial
An imprint of HarperCollins*Publishers*
77–85 Fulham Palace Road, Hammersmith, London W6 8JB

www.harperperennial.co.uk
Visit our authors' blog at www.fifthestate.co.uk

LOVE THIS BOOK? WWW.BOOKARMY.COM

This Harper Perennial edition published 2009
1

First published in Great Britain by Fourth Estate in 2008

Copyright © Marya Hornbacher 2008, 2009

PS Section copyright © Hannah Harper 2009, except 'Lives Too Often
Kept Dark' by Marya Hornbacher © Marya Hornbacher 2009

PS™ is a trademark of HarperCollins*Publishers* Ltd

Marya Hornbacher asserts the moral right
to be identified as the author of this work

A catalogue record for this book is available from the British Library

ISBN 978-0-00-725064-6

Printed and bound in Great Britain by Clays Ltd, St Ives plc

**Mixed Sources**
Product group from well-managed
forests and other controlled sources
www.fsc.org  Cert no. SW-COC-1806
© 1996 Forest Stewardship Council
FSC

FSC is a non-profit international organisation established to promote the
responsible management of the world's forests. Products carrying the FSC
label are independently certified to assure consumers that they come
from forests that are managed to meet the social, economic and
ecological needs of present and future generations.

*For my parents*

# CONTENTS

# Part II

# Part III

## Part IV

# PROLOGUE

## The Cut
*November 5, 1994*

I am numb. I am in the bathroom of my apartment in Minneapolis, twenty years old, drunk, and out of my mind. I am cutting patterns in my arm, a leaf and a snake. There is one dangling light, a bare bulb with a filthy string that twitches in the breeze coming through the open window. I look out on an alley and the brick buildings next door, all covered with soot. Across the way a woman sits on her sagging flowered couch in her slip and slippers, watching TV, laughing along with the laugh track, and I stop to sop up the blood with a rag. The blood is making a mess on the floor (note to self: mop floor) while a raccoon clangs the lid of a dumpster down below. Time hiccups; it is either later or sooner, I can't tell which. I study my handiwork. Blood runs down my arm, wrapping around my wrists and dripping off my fingers onto the dirty white tile floor.

I have been cutting for months. It stills the racing thoughts, relieves the pressure of the madness that has been crushing my mind, vise-like, for nearly my entire life, but even more so in the recent days. The past few years have seen me in ever-increasing flights and falls of mood, my mind at first lit up with flashes of color, currents of electric insight, sudden elation, and then flooded with black and bloody thoughts that throw me face-down onto my living room floor, a swelling despair pressing outward from the center of my chest, threatening to shatter my ribs. I have ridden these moods since I was a child, the clatter of the roller coaster roaring in my ears while I clung to the sides of my little car. But now, at the edge of adulthood, the madness has entered me for real. The thing I have feared and railed against all my life — the total loss of control over my mind — has set in, and I have no way to fight it anymore.

I split my artery.

Wait: first there must have been a thought, a decision to do it, a sequence of events, a logic. What was it? I glimpse the bone, and then blood sprays all over the walls. I am sinking; but I didn't mean to; I was only checking; I'm crawling along the floor in jerks and lurches, balanced on my right elbow, holding out my left arm, the cut one. I slide on my belly toward the phone in my bedroom; time has stopped; time is racing; the cat nudges my nose and paws at me, mewling. I knock the phone off the hook with my right hand and tip my head over to hold my ear to it. The sound of someone's voice — I am surprised at her urgency — *Do you have a towel — wrap it tight — hold it up — someone's on their way* — Suddenly the door breaks in and there is a flurry of men, dark shadows, all around me. I drop the phone and give in to the tide and feel myself begin to drown. Their mouths move underwater, their voices glubbing up, *Is there a pulse?* and metal doors clang shut and I swim through space, the siren wailing farther and farther away.

I am watching neon lights flash past above my head. I am lying on my back. There is a quick, sharp, repetitive sound somewhere: wheels clicking across a floor. I am in motion. I am being propelled. The lights flash in my eyes like strobe. The place I am in is bright. I cannot move. I am sinking. The bed is swallowing me.

Wait, this is not a bed; there are bars. We are racing along. There are people on either side of me, pushing the cage. They're running. What's the hurry? My left arm feels funny, heavy. There is a stunning pain shooting through it, like lightning, flashing from my hand to my shoulder. It seems to branch out from there, shooting electricity all through my body. I try to lift my arm but it weighs a thousand pounds. I try to lift my head to look at it, to look around, to see where I am, but I am unable to. My head, too, is heavy as lead. From the corner of my eye, I see people watching me fly by.

I am in shock. I heard them say it when they found me. *She's in shock,* one said to the other. Who are they? They broke down the door. Well, are they going to pay for it? I am indignant. I black out.

I come to. I am wearing my new white sweater. I regret that it is stained dark red. What a waste of money. We have stopped moving. There are people standing around, peering down at me. They look like a thicket of trees and I am lying immobile on the forest floor. *When did it happen? What did you use?* they demand, their voices very far away. *I don't remember — everyone calm down, I'll just go home — can I go home? I feel a little sick —* I vomit into the thing they hold out for me to vomit into. *I'm so sorry,* I say, *it was an accident. Please, I think I'll go home. Where are my shoes?*

Am I saying any of this? No one stops. They bustle. I must be in a hospital; that is what people do in a hospital, they bustle. For hospital people, they are being very loud. There is shouting. The bustling is unusually hurried. *What's the rush, people?* My arm is killing me, as it were, *yuk yuk,* though I can't really *feel* it so much, am more just aware that it is *there;* or perhaps I am merely aware that it *was* there, and now I am aware only of the arm-shaped heaviness where it used to be. Have they taken my arm? Well, that's all right. Never liked it anyway, *yuk yuk yuk.*

No one is getting my jokes.

I realize I am screaming and stop immediately, feeling embarrassed at my behavior. I have to be careful. They will think I am crazy.

I come to and black out. I come to and black out. This lasts forever, or it takes less than a minute, a second, a millisecond; it takes so little time that it does not happen at all; after all, how would I be conscious of losing consciousness? Is that, really, what it means to lose your mind? Well, then, I don't lose my mind very often after all. My arm hurts like a *motherfucker*. I object. I turn my head to the person whose face is closest to me to tell him I object, but suddenly he is all hands, and there is an enormous gaping red thing where my arm used to be. It is bloody, it looks like a raw steak, it looks like the word *flesh*, the word itself, in German *fleish*, and the Bastard of Hands has one hand wrapped around my forearm, his fingers and thumbs on either side of the gaping red thing, pressing it together, and he is sticking a needle into the inside part of the thing — *Quiet down! Someone hold her down, for chrissakes* — and he stabs the inside of the thing again and again and I hear someone screaming, possibly me. It does not hurt, per se, but it startles me, the gleaming slender needle sinking into the *raw flesh*. I realize I am a steak. They are carving me up to serve me. They will serve me on a silver-plated platter. The man's hands are enormous, and now the hands are *sewing the cut flesh,* how absurd! Can't they just glue it together? What a fuss over nothing — *Oh, for God's sake!* I yell (perhaps, or maybe only think), *now* I remember, and I scream (I'm pretty sure I really do), *Can you believe I did it? What a fucking idiot! I didn't mean to!* I plead with them to understand this, *I was only cutting a little, didn't mean to do it, sorry to make such a mess, look at the blood! And my sweater!* I black out and come to and black out again. *You're in shock. Can you hear me? Can you hear me, Maria? She's completely out of it,* one says to the other. They tower like giants. They can't pronounce my name. *It's MAR-ya,* I say, stressing the first syllable. *Yes, dear. It is,* I say, *it really is. Yes, dear, I know. I'm sure it is. Just rest.* Fuming, I rest. How can they save my life if they don't even know how to say my name? They will save someone else's life instead! A woman named Maria! Why, I suddenly think, should they have to save my life — oh, for God's sake! I remember again. I've gone and actually done it! Moron! How on earth will I explain this? The pair of hands has sewn the inside flesh together and is beginning another row on top of it. One row won't do? *Stupid,* says the Bastard of Hands. I look at him, shaking his head, disgusted, stitching quickly. *So damn stupid.*

I want to say again that I didn't mean it so he will not think I am stupid. I watch blood drip from a bag above my head into a thin tube that leads, I think, to me. I black out. I come to. There is a giant belly in front of me. It touches the edge of the bed. I follow the belly up the body to a very pretty face. Aha! Pregnant! Now I understand. However, why is there a pregnant woman standing next to me? Where is the hand man? *Do you think you need to be in the psych ward?* God, no! I laugh at the very idea, wanting very badly to seem sane. I prop myself up, forgetting about the arm, and collapse back on it, screaming in pain. Note to self: don't use left arm. *Why don't you think you need to be in the psych ward?* she asks. *I didn't mean to!* I cry. *It was a total accident, I was making dinner, accidentally the knife slipped, not to worry, I wasn't attempting* (I cannot say the word) (there is a hollow between words, which I fill with) (nicer, safer words). I am incredibly dizzy and I wish she would go away so I could go home — who lets a woman who's just sliced her arm in half go home? *Can you contract for safety?* the pregnant psychiatrist asks. Who knew psychiatrists got pregnant? *I can,* I say, very earnest. *You can agree that you will not hurt yourself again if you go home? Absolutely,* I say. *After all,* I joke, *I can't very well cut open the other arm — this one hurts too much!* I laugh hysterically, nearly falling off the bed. She doesn't think this is funny. She has no sense of humor.

She lets me go home. Hospital policy is to impose the least level of restriction possible. If they think you can keep yourself safe, if they can keep one more bed open in the psych ward, they let you go home. And I'm very convincing. I *contract for safety*, swearing I won't cut myself up again. I call a cab and climb into it, dizzy, my arm wrapped in thick layers of bandages. I return to a bloody mess, and as dawn fills the room, I tell myself I'll clean it up in the morning.

I HAVE BEEN in and out of psychiatric institutions and hospitals since I was sixteen. At first the diagnosis was an eating disorder — years spent in a nightmare cycle of starving, bingeing, and purging, a cycle that finally got so bad it nearly killed me — but I've been improving for over a year, and it's all cleared up (brush off hands). They think I'm a little depressed — that's the assumption they make for anyone with an eating disorder — so they give me Prozac, new on the market now, thought to cure all mental ills, prescribed like candy to any and all. Because I'm not, in fact, depressed, Prozac makes me utterly manic and numb — one of the reasons I slice my arm open in the first place is that I'm coked to the gills on something utterly wrong for what I have.

I am probably in the grip of a mixed episode. During manic episodes or mixed episodes — which are episodes where both the despair of depression and the insane agitation and impulsivity of mania are present at the same time, resulting in a state of rabid, uncontrollable energy coupled with racing, horrible thoughts — people are sometimes led to kill themselves just to still the thoughts. This energy may be absent in the deepest of depressions, whether bipolar or pure depression; the irony is that as people appear to improve, they often have a higher risk of suicide, because now they have the energy to carry out suicide plans. Actually, an alarming number of bipolar suicides are unintentional. Mania triggers wildly impulsive behaviors, powerful urges to push oneself to the utmost, to go to often dangerous extremes — like driving a hundred miles an hour, bingeing on drugs and alcohol, jumping out of windows, cutting, and others. These extreme behaviors lead, often enough, to accidental death.

Who knows, really, what leads to my sudden, uncontrollable desire to cut myself? I don't know. Is the suicide attempt accidental or deliberate? It certainly isn't planned. Manic, made further manic by the wrong meds, I simply do it, unaware in the instant that there will be any consequence at all. I watch my right hand put the razor in my left arm. Death is not on my mind.

No one even thinks *bipolar* — not me, not any of the many doctors, therapists, psychiatrists, and counselors I've seen over the years — because no one knows enough. Later, this will seem almost incredible, given what a glaring case of the disorder I actually have and have had nearly all my life. But how could they know back then? With so little knowledge about bipolar disorder, or really about mental illness at all, no one knows what to look for, no one knows what they're looking at when they're looking at me. They, and I, and everyone else think I'm just a disaster, a screwup, a mess. On the phone, my grandfather demands, "So, have you got your head screwed on right yet?" *Yuk yuk yuk,* funny man, raging drunk. But you can't blame him for the question. It's the one everyone's been asking since I was a kid. Surely she'll grow out of it, they think.

I grew into it. It grew into me. It and I blurred at the edges, became one amorphous, seeping, crawling thing.

# Part I

# The Goatman

*1978*

I will not go to sleep. I won't. My parents, who are always going to bed, tell me that I can stay up if I want, but for God's sake, don't come out of my room. I am four years old and I like to stay up all night. I sing my songs, very quietly. I keep watch. Nothing can get me if I am awake.

I sleep during the day like a bat with the blinds closed, and then they come home. I hear them open the door, and I fling on the lights and gallop through the house shrieking to wake the dead all evening, all night. *Let's have a play!* I shout. *Let's have a ballet! A reading! A race! Don't tell me what to do, get away from me, I hate you, you're never any fun, you never let me do anything, I want to go to the opera! I want opera glasses! I'm going to be an explorer! I don't care if I track mud all over the house, let's get another dog! I want an Irish setter, I want a camel! I want an Easter dress! I'm going ice-skating! Right now, yes! Where are the car keys? Of course I can drive! Fine, go to bed! See if I care!*

And I slam into my room, dive onto the bed, kick and scream, get bored, read a book, shouting at the top of my lungs, *"I don't care," says Pierre!* And the lion says, *"Then I will eat you, if I* may." "*I don't care, says Pierre!*" It is my favorite Maurice Sendak book. I jabber to my imaginary friends Susie and Sackie and Savvy and Cindy, who tell me secrets and stay with me all night while I am keeping watch, while I am guarding the castle, and there are horrible creatures waiting to kill me so I talk to myself all night, writing a play and acting it out with a thousand little porcelain figures that I dust every day, twice a day, I must keep things neat, in their magic positions, or something terrible will happen. The shah of Iran, who is under my bed, will leap out and carry me away under his arm.

I have to get dressed. So what if it's black as pitch outside. I go to the closet, I take out a jumper and a white shirt, and from the dresser I get white socks and white underwear and a white undershirt, and I get my favorite saddle shoes, and I suit up completely. I must be very quiet or my parents will hear. I tie my shoes in double knots so I won't fall out of them. I get on my hands and knees and crawl all over the room, smoothing out the carpet. Finally I make myself stop. I lie down in the center of the floor, facing the door in case of emergency. I cross my ankles and fold my hands across my middle. I close my eyes. I fall asleep, or die.


"MOM," I WHISPER loudly, pushing on her shoulder. It's dark, I'm in my parents' bedroom, a ghost in my white nightie. "Mom," I say again, shaking her. I bounce up and down on my toes and lean over her, my mouth near her ear. "Mom, I have to tell you something."

"What is it?" she mumbles, opening one eye.

"The goatman," I whisper, agitated. "He's in my room. He came while I was sleeping. You have to make him leave. I can't sleep. Will you read to me?" I hop about, crashing into the nightstand. "Can we make a cake? I want to make a cake, I can't go to school tomorrow, I'm scared of Teacher Jackie, she yells at us, she doesn't like me, Mom, the goatman, do you have to go to work tomorrow? Will you read to me?"

"Marya, it's the middle of the night," she says, hoisting herself up with her elbow. Next to her, the mountain of my father snores. "Can we read tomorrow?"

"I can't go back in there!" I shriek, running around in a tiny circle. "The goatman will get me! We could make cookies instead! I want to buy a horse, a gray one! And I want to go to the beach and collect seashells, can't we go to the beach, I promise I'll sleep —"

My mother swings her legs off the edge of the bed and holds me by the shoulders. "Honey, can you slow down? Just slow down."

Out of breath, I stand there, my head spinning.

"What did you want to tell me?" she asks. "One thing. Tell me the most important thing you want to tell me."

"The goatman," I say, and burst into tears. "But Mom, I can't —"

"Shhh," she says, picking me up. She carries me down the hall. This is how she fixes it. She holds me very tight and things slow down a little. But I'm too upset. I set my chin on her shoulder and sob and babble. *Everyone's going to leave, you'll forget to come get me, I'll get lost, I'll get stuck in the grocery store and they'll lock me in. What if there are snakes in my bedroom? Why won't the goatman go away? What if it isn't perfect? What if it's scary? What if you and Daddy die? Who will take care of me? What if you give me away? I don't want you to give me away, I want to be a policeman, why do policemen wear hats —*

"Marya, hush. It's all right. Everything's going to be all right."

*I want to see Grandma, let's go see Grandma, I want to go outside and play in the yard, why can't I play in the yard when it's dark, I want to look at the moon —*

We pace up and down the hall. I get more and more agitated, swinging moment by moment from terror to elation to utter despair, until finally I wiggle my way free and start to run. I race around the house, my mother trailing me, until I stumble on my nightgown and sprawl out on the floor, sobbing, beating my fists on the ground. "I'm here," she says. "Honey, I'm here."

I snuffle and drag a hiccupping breath and heave a sigh. She is here. She is right here. She picks me up. She carries me into the bathroom and turns on the bathtub. While it runs, I squirm on her lap, kicking my legs, shrieking, laughing, crying, *I can't ever go back in my room, the goatman, I want to have a party, when is it Christmas, I want to live in a tree house, what if I fall in the ocean and drown, where do I go when I die* —

She pulls my nightgown over my head and sets me in the tub. I am suddenly quiet. Water makes it better. In the water, I am safe. She kneels next to me where I sit, only my head sticking out of the water. She tells me a story. Things are slowing down. I am contained. I bob in the water, warm, enclosed. My limbs float. The noise and racing of my thoughts wind down until they yawn in my head as if they are in slow motion. My head is filled with white cotton, and I hear a low humming, and my skull is heavy. I am aware only of the water and my mother's voice.

Back in bed, she wraps me tight in my quilt, my arms and legs and feet and hands all covered, kept in so they won't fly off. The goatman has gone away for the night. She sits on the edge of my bed, smoothing my hair. I am wrapped up like a package. I am a caterpillar in my cocoon. I am an egg.

She stays with me until, near dawn, I fall asleep.

## What They Know

1979

They know I am different. They say that I live in my head. They are just being kind. I'm crazy. The other kids say it, twirl their fingers next to their heads, *Cuckoo! Cuckoo!* they say, and I laugh with them, and roll my eyes to imitate a crazy person, and fling my arms and legs around to show them that I get the joke, I'm in on it, I'm not really crazy at all. They do it after one of my outbursts at school or in daycare, when I've been running around like a maniac, laughing *like crazy,* or while I get lost in my words, my mouth running off ahead of me, spilling the wild, lit-up stories that race through my head, or when I burst out in raging fits that end with me sobbing hysterically and beating my fists on my head or my desk or my knees. Then I look up suddenly, and everyone's staring. And I brighten up, laugh my happiest laugh, to show them I was just kidding, I'm really not like that, and everyone laughs along.

I AM LYING on the bed. I am listening to my parents scream at each other in the other room. That's what they do. They scream or throw things or both. *You son of a bitch!* [*crash*]. *You're trying to ruin my life!* [*crash, shatter, crash*]. When they are not screaming, we are all cozy and happy and laughing, the little bear family, we love each other, we have the all-a-buddy hug. It's hard to tell which is going to come next. Between the screaming and the crazies, it is very loud in my head.

And so I am feeling numb. It's a curious feeling, and I get it all the time. My attention to the world around me disappears, and something starts to hum inside my head. Far off, voices try to bump up against me, but I repel them. My ears fill up with water and I focus on the humming in my head.

I am inside my skull. It is a little cave, and I curl up inside it. Below it, my body hovers, unattached. I have that feeling of falling, and I imagine my soul is being pulled upward, and I close my eyes and let go.

My feet are flying. I hate it when my feet are flying. I sit up and grab them with both hands. It's dark, and I stare at the little line of light that sneaks in under the door.

The light begins to move. It begins to pulse and blur. I try to make it stop. I scowl and stare at it. My heart beats faster. I am frozen in my bed, gripping my feet. The light has crawled across the floor. It's headed for the bed. I want it to hold still, so I press my brain against it, expecting it to stop, but it doesn't. The line crosses the purple carpet. I want to scream. I open my mouth and hear myself say something, but I don't know what it is or who said it. The little man in my mind said it, I decide, suddenly aware that there *is* a little man in my mind.

The line is crawling up the side of the bed. I tell it to go away. Holding my feet, I scooch back toward the wall. My brain is feeling the pressure. I let go of my feet and cover my ears, pressing in to calm my mind. The line crests the edge of the bed and starts across the flowered quilt. I throw myself off the bed. I watch the line turn toward me, slide off the bed, follow me into the corner of my room.

I want to go under the bed but I know it will follow me. I jump up on the bed, jump down, run into the closet and out again, the humming in my head is excruciatingly loud. The light is going to hurt me. I can't escape it. It catches up with me, wraps around me, grips my body. I am paralyzed, I can't scream. So I close my eyes and feel it come up my spine and creep into my brain. I watch it explode like the sun.

I drift off into my head. I have visions of the goatman, with his horrible hooves. He comes to kill me every night. They say it is a nightmare. But he is real. When he comes, I feel his fur.

I don't come out of my room for days. I tell them I'm sick, and pull the blinds against the light. Even the glow of the moon is too piercing. The world outside presses in at the walls, trying to reach me, trying to eat me alive. I must stay here in bed, in the hollow of my sheets, trying to block the racing, maniac thoughts.

I turn over and burrow into the bed headfirst.

I HAVE THESE crazy spells sometimes. Often. More and more. But I never tell. I laugh and pretend I am a real girl, not a fake one, a figment of my own imagination, a mistake. I never let on, or they will know that I am crazy for sure, and they will send me away.

This being the 1970s, the idea of a child with bipolar is unheard of, and it's still controversial today. No psychiatrist would have diagnosed it then — they didn't know it was possible. And so children with bipolar were seen as wild, troubled, out of control — but not in the grips of a serious illness.

My father is having one of his rages. He screams and sobs, lurching after me, trying to grab me and pick me up, keep me from going away with my mother, but I make myself small and hide behind her legs. We are trying to leave for my grandmother's house. We are taking a train. I have a small plaid suitcase. I come around and stand suspended between my parents, looking back and forth at each one. My mother is calm and mean. The calmer she gets, the more I know she is angry and hates him. She hisses, *Jay, for Christ's sake, stop it. Stop it. You're crazy, stop screaming, calm down, we're leaving, you can't stop us.* My father is out of control, yelling, coming at my mother, grabbing at her clothes as she tries to move away from him. *Don't leave me,* he cries out as if he's being tortured, choking on his words, *don't leave me, I can't live without you, you are the reason I even bother to stay alive, without you I'm nothing.* His face is twisted and red and wet from tears. He throws himself on the floor and curls up and cries and screams. I go over to him and pat him on the head. He grabs me and clutches me in his arms and I get scared and try to push away from him but I'm not strong enough. I finally get free and he stands up again, and I stand between them, my head at hip level, trying to push them apart. He kneels and grabs my arms, *Baby, I love you, do you love me? Say you love me* — and I pat his wet cheeks and say I love him, wanting to get away from him and his rages and black sadness and his lying-on-the-couch-crying days when I get home from preschool, and his sucking need, and I close my eyes and scream at the top of my lungs and tell them both to stop it.

My father calms down and takes us to the train station, but halfway there he starts up again and we nearly crash the car. We leave him standing on the platform, sobbing.

"Why does he get like that?" I ask my mother. I sit in the window seat swinging my legs, watching the trees go by, listening to the clatter of the wheels. I look at my mother. She stares straight ahead.

"I don't know," she says. I picture my father back at home, walking through the empty house to the couch, lying down on his side, staring out the window like he does some afternoons, even though I tell him over and over I love him. Over and over, I tell him I love him and that everything will be okay. He never believes me. I can never make him well.

CRAZY IS NOTHING out of the ordinary in my family. It's what we are, part of the family identity, sort of a running joke — the crazy things somebody did, the great-grandfather who took off with the circus from time to time, the uncle who painted the horse, Uncle Frank in general, my father, me. In the 1970s, psychiatry knows very little about bipolar disorder. It wasn't even called that until the 1980s, and the term didn't catch on for another several years. Most people with bipolar were misdiagnosed with schizophrenia in the 1970s (in the 1990s, most bipolar people were misdiagnosed with unipolar depression). We didn't talk about "mental illness." The adults knew Uncle Joe had manic depression, but they didn't mind or worry about it — just one more funny thing about us all, a little bit of crazy, fodder for a good story.

This is my favorite one: Uncle Joe used to spend a fair amount of time in the loony bin. My family wasn't bothered by his regular trips to and from "the facility" — they'd shrug and say, *There goes Joe,* and they'd put him in the car and take him in. One day Uncle Frank (who everybody *knows* is crazy — my cousins and I hide from him under the bed at Christmas) was driving Uncle Joe to the crazy place. When they got there, Joe asked Frank to drop him off at the door while Frank went and parked the car. Frank didn't think much of it, and dropped him off.

Joe went inside, smiled at the nurse, and said, "Hi. I'm Frank Hornbacher. I'm here to drop off Joe. He likes to park the car, so I let him do that. He'll be right in." The nurse nodded knowingly. The real Frank walked in. The nurse took his arm and guided him away, murmuring the way nurses always do, while Frank hollered in protest, insisting that he was Frank, not Joe. Joe, quite pleased with himself, gave Frank a wave and left.

# Depression

*1981*

Maybe it begins when I am seven. I'm in bed. It's too sunny outside, I can't go out. The blinds are drawn and yet they let in a little light, and the little light pierces my eyes. I turn my face into my pillow. It's cool and safe in my sheets. My father comes in.

*Time to get up, kiddo.*

(Silence.)

*Kiddo.*

(I pull the pillow over my head to block the incessant light.)

*Kiddo, are you getting up?*

No.

*Why not?*

*I'm skipping today.*

*What's the matter with today?*

I sigh. I despair of ever getting up again. I cannot move. I will not move. Everything is horrible. I want to go to sleep forever.

*I can't go to school,* I say.

*Why not?*

I bang my head on the mattress and let out a shriek. I sigh and flop onto my back and shade my eyes.

*There's an art project.* I burst into tears.

*Oh,* my father says, unsurprised. *Is it complicated?*

*It's very complicated,* I wail. *I can't do it. I don't want to do it. So I'm sick.* I wipe my nose and let the tears fall into my ears.

*Okay,* my father says.

*I'm staying home.*

*Okay.*

Okay. Okay. Now I will be okay. No crowded classroom, no scissors, no paste, no other kids, no cafeteria lunch, no recess, no wide sky and too much sun.

The world outside swells and presses in at the walls, trying to reach me, trying to eat me alive. I must stay here in the pocket of my sheets, with my blanket and my book. I will not face the world, with its lights and noise, its confusion, the way I lose myself in its crowds. The way I disappear. I am the invisible girl. I am make-believe. I am not really there.

I don't come out of my room for days. Days bleed into weeks. I lie in bed in the dark.

# Prayer
## 1983

On my knees. Praying. Pleading. The basement floor is cold beneath my knees. I come here to hide, to hide my prayers. My mother would mock me. God is merely a weakness for people who need to believe. She wouldn't understand that I am chosen to speak for all the sorrows of the world.

I'm not crazy. God has called me and I have no choice but to answer, or I will be sent to hell. It all depends on me. And so I pray myself to sleep, and pray the second I wake, and pray all day, terrified that God will catch me slacking off and punish me severely.

My knees grow sore and my heart beats a million miles an hour. I panic. I practically pant. My mind spins with the things I am forgetting to pray for, things I have done, there is a light flashing in my brain, like the headlight of a train in the dark, the dark is my mind, which teems with sins, which torment me with their noise. I can hear the sins whisper; are they inside my head or outside my ears? Are they in the basement? Coming from the water heater, the washing machine? God answers at last. *You may get up*, I hear him say. His voice reverberates against the concrete walls.

Halfway up the stairs, I hear God call me to prayer again. I kneel and pray. He calls me in the kitchen. Calls me in my bedroom. Calls me at school. I raise my hand, hurry into the restroom, kneel on the floor of the stall, the restroom empty and echoing with my rapid breath, echoing with the shrieking, pounding in my head. I pray in class. I pray in the car, after dinner, all night long — hours after silence has settled around the house, my mouth moves with manic prayers.

God watches me, sees my every mistake, every sin. God's voice booms in my head, now praising me, his chosen one, now spitting at me, sending the snake into my mind. It curls itself around itself, its body pressed against the walls of my skull. I lie in bed, rocking, my head in my hands, the snake flicking its tongue at the backs of my eyeballs. It sinks its teeth into the gray, wet brain. I press my open mouth to the mattress and scream.

# Food
## 1984

God has left. My mind is spinning. I'm out of control, unable to contain myself. I am propelled forward, toward something drastic. I'm going to hurl myself into *anything that will stop the thoughts*. Suddenly I find a focus. It's incredibly intense. I must, I *must* fill myself to bursting, then rid myself of that fullness. Food. It's all about food.

My body disgusts me. I stand naked in my bedroom in front of the mirror. I pinch the flesh, the needy, hungry, horrible flesh, the softness that buries the perfect clean bones. I pinch hard; red welts appear on my skin. The body revolts me, its tricks, its betrayals, its lies. I starve and starve, and then it happens — the black hole in my chest yawns open, and suddenly I'm in the kitchen, standing at the counter, stuffing food into my mouth, anything I can find, anything that will fill me up. Food covers my face, my cheeks bulge with it, but I still can't stop, my hands move back and forth from food to mouth. I hate myself for it. I want to be thin, I want to be bones, I want to eliminate hunger, softness, need.

Every day I come home from fourth grade and try to avoid the kitchen. I sit in my bedroom, clutching the seat of my chair. The empty house echoes its silence around me. I sit, gritting my teeth, and then the hum of compulsion drives me into the kitchen. I eat. Leftovers, frozen dinners, whatever I can stuff in my mouth.

I lean over the toilet with my fingers down my throat. I throw up, body heaving, until I'm spitting up blood. I straighten up. I am empty. Clean. I run my hands over the flat of my stomach, play the xylophone of my ribs. Satisfied, absolved, I open the door, walk calmly down the hall to the kitchen, and do it again.

It's my secret and my savior. It's reliable. It saves me from the unpredictable mind, where the thoughts are a cesspool, swirling, eddying with rip tide. When I starve, the sinking, pressing black sadness lifts off me, and I feel weightless, empty, light. No racing thoughts, no need to move, move, *move*, no reason to hide in the dark. When I throw up, I purge all the fears, the paranoia, the thoughts. The eating disorder gives me comfort. I couldn't let it go if I tried.

It is what I need so badly, a homemade replacement for what a psychiatrist would prescribe for me if he knew: a mood stabilizer. My eating disorder is the first thing I've found that works. It becomes indispensable as soon as it begins. I am calm in starvation, all my apprehensions focused. No need to control my mind — I control my body, so my moods level out. I live in single-minded pursuit of something very specific: thinness, death. I act with intention, discipline. I am free.

My parents wonder where all the food is going. I say I'm a growing girl.

## The Booze under the Stove

*1985*

Nothing is going fast enough. At school, the teachers are talking as if their mouths are full of molasses. Their limbs move in slow motion. Pointing to call on someone, the teacher lifts her arm as if it is filled with wet sand. I swear to God I think I am going insane, *it is so slow,* while my thoughts whistle past like the wind, so fast I can barely keep up. I turn my mind inward to watch them. They move in electric currents, crackling, spitting, sending out red sparks.

The other students are slow, stupid, asleep. In the hallways, they move like a herd of slugs, wet and shapeless, inching toward the door. I explode out of school, dancing as fast as I can across the playground, whipping in circles around the tetherball pole, dashing off across the yard, trying to shake off this incredible *energy*, this amazing *energy*. I'm ten years old and I might as well be on speed.

My parents are on their way out the door. *Eat dinner!* they call, but I am too fast for them, their voices recede in the distance as I race through the house, bouncing off the walls. I've been pleading with them to let me stay home by myself, and so they do, heading off to their meetings or dinners or places unknown. Maybe not a great idea to let a ten-year-old stay home alone, but I've twisted their arms, and they're immersed in work and in their own nightmare marriage, avoiding each other, avoiding the fights, thinking up reasons to be gone. They work compulsively, and when they're not working they see friends, putting on the face of the happy couple. Everything's fine. We're the perfect little family. People tell us that all the time.

And I am home alone with a raw steak on the counter, hopping up and down, my mind jetting about. Time for homework! I reach into my bag and throw my books and papers up in the air, *ha ha! Watch this, ladies and gentlemen, the amazing Marya! Look at her go! Can you believe the incredible speed?* My homework covers the kitchen floor, and I crawl around picking it up, talking to myself: *Hip-hop, my friends, never liked rabbits, must get a tiger, it will sleep in my bed, take it for walks, I need new shoes, fabulous shoes, I will show all of them, hark the herald angels sing! Christmas is smashing! Love it, people, just love it* — I hop up, slap my hand to my chest, salute the refrigerator, click my heels, make a sharp turn, and walk stiffly over to the kitchen table, where I whip through the papers, laying them out perfectly in a complex system, the most efficient system, each corner of each page touching the corner, exactly, of the next. Having arranged the papers, I gallop up and down the hallway, slide into the kitchen as if I'm sliding into third, yank open the refrigerator, pull out some mushrooms, chop them up, my knife a blur, toss them into the frying pan, sauté them — but they need a little something. A little *zing*. I pull open the cupboard beneath the sink, pull out the brandy, splash it in the pan. But now that I think of it, what are all those bottles?

I turn off the burner, bouncing up and down, and open the cupboard again.

Booze.

I pull out a jug of Gallo, stagger underneath its weight. *A little wine with dinner, the very thing, don't you think?* I pour it into a giant plastic Minnesota Twins cup and collapse with my mushrooms and tankard of wine at the dining room table.

I get absolutely shitfaced. I am shitfaced and hyper and ten years old. I am having the time of my life.

I lope up and down the hallway, singing Simon and Garfunkel songs, juggling oranges. I do my homework in a flurry of brilliance, total efficiency, the electric grid of my mind snapping and flashing with light. I am in the zone, the perfect balance between manic and drunk, I am mellow, I'm *cool, cool as cats*. I've found the answer, the thing that takes the edge off, smoothes out the madness, sends me sailing, lifts me up and lets me fly.

It's alchemy, the booze and my brain, another homemade mood stabilizer, and it stabilizes me in a heavenly mood. I am in love with the world, gregarious, full of joy and generosity toward my fellow man. My thoughts fly, but not up and down — they soar forward in a thrilling flight of ideas, heightened sensations, a creative rush, each thought tumbling into the next. It's even more perfect than eating and throwing up.

My future with alcohol is long and disastrous. But at first, it works wonders for me. No longer low, not yet too high. Just on a roll, energetic, inspired. I truly believe the booze is helping. I'll believe this, despite all evidence, for years.

Eventually I stagger into bed and, for once, fall asleep.

# Meltdown

*1988*

My moods start to swing up and down almost minute to minute. I take uppers to get even higher and downers to bring myself down. Cocaine, white crosses, Valium, Percocet — I get them from the boys who skulk around the suburban malls hunting jailbait. I'm an easy target, in the market for their drugs and willing to do what they want to get them for free. The boys themselves are a high. They have something I want. They are to be used and discarded. The trick is to catch them and make them want the girl I am pretending to be. Then twist them up with wanting me, watch them squirm like worms on a hook, and throw them away.

I find myself on piles of pillows in their basements, pressed down under their bodies, their lurching breath in my ear. They are heavy, damp, hurried, young, still mostly dressed. I don't know how I've wound up here, and I want it to end, and I repeat to the rhythm of their bodies, *You're a slut, you're a whore,* and I want a bath, want to scrub them off, why does this keep happening? Why don't I ever say no? There's a rush when they want me, and they always do, they're boys, that's what they want, and once they've got me half lying on the couch, each basement, each boy, each time, my brain shuts off, the rush is over, I'm numb, I want to go home. The impulsive tumble into the corner, the racing pressure in my head always ends like this: I hate them, and I hate myself, and I swear I won't do it again. But I do. And I do. And I do.

And then I am home in my bedroom, blue-flowered wallpaper and stuffed animals on the bed, stashing my baggies of powders and pills. If I hit the perfect balance of drugs, I can trigger the energy that keeps me up all night writing and lets me stay marginally afloat in junior high, accentuating the persona I've created as a wild child, a melodramatic rebel — black eyeliner and dyed black hair, torn clothes, a clown and a delinquent, sulking, talking back. In class, I fool everyone into thinking I'm real.

But then I come home after school to the empty, hollow house, wrap into a ball in the corner of the couch, a horrible, clutching, sinking feeling in my chest. Nothing matters, and nothing will ever be all right again. I go into rages at the slightest thing, pitching things around the house, running away in the middle of the night, my feet crunching across the frozen lake. I cling to the cold chainlink fence of the bridge across the freeway and watch the late-night cars flash by, my breath billowing out into the dark in white gusts.

DAY YAWNS OPEN like a cavern in my chest. I lie in the dimness of my room, the blinds shut tight and blankets draped over them. I weigh a million pounds. I can feel my body, its heavy bones, its excess flesh, pressing into the mattress. I'm certain that it sags beneath me, nearly touching the floor. My father bangs on the door again. *Breakfast!* he calls.

I crawl out of bed and slide out the drawer from the bed stand, turn it over, and untape the baggie of cocaine underneath. Kneeling, I tap lines out onto the stand, lean over, and snort them up with the piece of straw I keep in the bag. I sit back on my knees and close my eyes. There it is: the feeling of glass shards in the brain. I picture the drug shattering, slicing the gray matter into neat chunks. My heart leaps to life as if I've been shocked. I open my eyes, lick my fingers and the straw, and put the straw away, replacing the drawer. I lift off, the roller coaster chattering on its tracks, me flying upside down.

Humming, I take a shower and dance into a ridiculously short skirt with a hole that black tights, a ripped-up shirt. I pass another baggie, pills this time, from drawer. I select a few and put them the day, a gorgeous day, a good day to be alive. *Good morning!* I call, sitting down at the table, bouncing my knee at the speed of light.

*You're in a good mood this morning.*

*I am! I am indeed.* I watch my father scramble eggs, and then panic: what am I thinking? I can't eat that. I leap to my feet. *Gotta go! Can't stay to eat!* I punch my father on the arm as I run out the door.

*But you need to eat!* he calls after me. *Get back here! You can't leave dressed like that!*

*Bye,* I call, setting off down the street, my book bag banging against my leg. The trees are in bloom. The sun is pulsing. I can feel it touching my skin. My skin is alive, crawling. Suddenly I stop. My skin is on fire. I drop my book bag, start rubbing my skin. *Get it off!* I am dancing around in the middle of the road. There are bugs on my arms, crawling up my neck, crawling on my face and into my hair, *Get them off me! Where the hell are they coming from?* I fall onto the grass at the side of the road, rolling, trying to get them off. My hair tangles and dirt grinds into my clothes. Finally the bugs are gone. I stand up, smooth my hair, and, much better now, skip down the road to school. It's so annoying when that happens. But I'm not about to give up the cocaine.

No one knows about the powders, the pills, the water bottle filled with vodka that I keep in my bag. My friends are good girls. I am a tramp. I don't know why they bother with me. I slouch in my seat in the back of the room, my arms folded, hiding behind my hair. The teachers are idiots. I hate their clothes, their thick, whining Minnesota accents, the small-town smell that clings to them: dust and tuna casserole. This whole town is a bunch of suburban clones, blond, blue-eyed, dressed in tidy matching clothes. Everyone looks the same. Everyone will wind up married, living in a ... with a sprawling, manicured lawn. There'll be cute little identical children, and the men will golf and drink and slap each other on the back, *old chum,* and the women will lunch at the country club and listen to lectures about the deserving poor, the homeless children downtown. They'll shake their heads with concern and volunteer for the PTA and at the Lutheran church, collect bad art and vote Republican, and hate people like me.

I have to get out of this town.

After lunch, I lean over the toilet in the bathroom stall and throw up. I wipe my mouth, scrub my hands, sniffing them to make sure they don't smell, wash them again, wipe them dry, look in the mirror, reapply my lipstick, study my face. I brighten my eyes, paste on a smile, and go back out, where the kids teem down the hall.

These are supposed to be the best years of my life.

I fail home economics. I refuse to sew the stuffed flamingo. I question the necessity of learning to make a Jell-O parfait. I blow up an oven — I forget to put the nutmeg in a baked pancake, and when it's already in the oven, I toss in a handful as an afterthought, setting the entire thing on fire.

I persecute the art teacher. I sit in detention until dark, day after day. When I'm not in detention, I'm running around the newspaper room, putting together what I'm sure is an incendiary tract that's designed to infuriate everyone who reads it. I am ducking under my desk every half-hour, sucking up the vodka in the water bottle. I am in the library, snorting cocaine off Dante, back in the stacks.

I gallop down the hall at school in a state of absolute glee, dodging in and out between the other kids, shouting, "Hi!" to the people I know as I pass. They laugh. I am hilarious! "You're crazy!" they call. I am crazy! I'm marvelous! I'm fantastic! The day is fantastic, the world!

"Slow down!" a teacher shouts after me. "No running in the halls!"

I turn and gallop back to him. "Not running!" I shout joyfully. "Galloping, as you can plainly see!" I gallop off.

At the end of the hall, I crash into the wall and bounce back into the circle of my friends who are clustered around my locker. "Isn't it *wonderful*?" I cry, flinging my arms wide, picking them up in the air.

"Now what?" Sarah laughs.

"Everything! Absolutely everything! You, today, all of it, wonderful! Amazing! Isn't it grand to be alive?"

"Weren't you, like, all freaky and twitchy this morning?" asks Sandra. I pound down the stairs, my legs are faster than speed itself! Tremendous! Spectacular speed, splendid speed, splendiferous speed! I reach the bottom of the stairs and go skidding across the hall. My friends are laughing. I make them happy. I make them forget their horrible homes. I love them, I love them hugely, they are absolutely *essential,* I would absolutely *die* without them.

"No!" I shout, "I wasn't freaky! Well, if I was, I'm certainly not anymore, *obviously!*" I skip backward ahead of them as we go to lunch. I grab an ice cream sandwich and a greasy mini-pizza. I will be throwing these things up after lunch, *obviously,* wonderful! I laugh with delight, pleased with myself. "Aha!" I shout, and the people in the line ahead of me crane their necks to look. "Hello, all of you!" I shout, waving, "it's a beautiful day!" Someone mutters, "She's crazy," and I don't even care, everyone's entitled to his opinion! That's the way of the world! We are a world of many opinions, many beliefs! To each his own!

My friends and I move in an amoeba-like cluster over to an open table near the windows and sit down. We munch away on our lunches, chatting, and I chatter like a ventriloquist's dummy, and all of us laugh, and then I start crying, but right myself quickly. "Enough of that!" I say, wiping my nose, making a grand gesture, "all's well!" And everyone is relieved, and I have a brilliant idea! I pick up my personal pizza and whip it across the room like a Frisbee! And it lands perfectly in front of Leah Pederson, whom I hate! *"Yes!"* I shout, triumphant, and the entire lunchroom is laughing, and it's time to go back to class. I gather my books and my friends and walk calmly down the hall and fling myself into my chair with an enormous sigh.

This time I will be good, I promise myself. This time I won't make a scene. My heart pounds and I feel another round of hysterical laughter welling up in my chest. I press my face between my hands. I will hold it in. I won't get detention. I won't get kicked out of class. I won't punch Jeff Carver. I won't turn over any desks, or throw any chairs. I sit up in my chair, open my notebook, click my pen. I stare straight ahead at the teacher who is shuffling papers and handing them out. I will be good. I will, I will, I will.

I SIT IN THE OFFICE of my mother's shrink. The air circulates slowly in the room. I turn in circles in my swivel chair. To my right, through the window, two floors down, is the parking lot and the sunny, empty afternoon. A small man with square black glasses and gray hair sits kicked back in his leather office chair, watching me.

"What would you like to talk about today?" he asks.

I keep turning in circles. I shrug. "What do you want me to say?"

"What would you like to say?"

I look out the window, count the red cars in the parking lot, then the blue. "I don't have anything to say."

We sit in silence. The minutes tick by.

"What are you thinking right now?" he asks.

"Nothing particular." I turn to face him. He scribbles something on his yellow notepad.

"What are you writing?" I ask.

He gazes at me. "What do you think I'm writing?" he asks.

"I haven't the faintest idea," I say.

He scribbles some more.

"Are you supposed to be helping me?" I ask.

"Do you think you need help?"

I turn to face the window again. "I don't know." From the corner of my eye, I see him write something down.

"You seem very upset," he says thoughtfully.

Startled, I look at him. "I'm not."

He tilts his head to the side. "You're very angry, aren't you?" he says.

I laugh. "You're very perceptive, aren't you?" I say. He writes it down.

Seven red cars, six blue. The day is still. The branches of the trees don't move. We sit in silence. I turn circles in my chair.

HE'S A FREUDIAN therapist. When he speaks, he asks me about my mother, about my dreams. I wait for him to tell me what's wrong with me, why I snap into sudden, violent rages, and shut myself in my room with the dresser backed up against the door for days, and disappear in the middle of the night, and stay in constant trouble at school. Why is it that my moods are all over the goddamn map? How come I'm terrified all the time? He sits silently, watching me, saying nothing, fixing nothing. I give up.

He isn't looking for eating disorders or drinking or drug use. He isn't looking for mental illness. In truth, he isn't looking for much at all. One day he slaps his notebook shut. *What's wrong with me?* I ask. *Am I crazy?* I don't ask that. I think I know.

His wise and considered opinion is that I'm a *very angry little girl.*

WORD GETS OUT at school that I'm seeing a psychiatrist. My friends avoid the subject. But other kids whisper about it when I come into the room, kids I don't like and who don't like me, the

rich kids and the snobs. One of them, egged on by the others —
*Go on, ask her* — comes up to me: *Is it true you're, like, crazy?*

*No*, I say, looking down at my desk.

*Then why are you seeing, like, a psychiatrist? Isn't that for
crazy people? Isn't it? Come on, admit it!*

I don't answer. I scribble so hard in my notebook that my ball-
point tears the page. They laugh. I'm a freak, and everyone knows
it, including me.

Then suddenly it hits, a massive, crippling headache. My mi-
graines are coming on nearly every day. I stagger into the nurse's
office and collapse on a cot, curled up in a ball with a pillow
over my face. The nurse calls my parents. Back home, I lie in the
dark, blinds drawn, rabid thoughts and images zipping through
my brain, flashes of blinding color and light. I lie there, shivering
and sweating as the pain clenches my skull, nearly paralyzed with
fear at the fierce throbbing behind my eyes.

My father opens the door slowly, shuts it quietly behind him. I
wince at the deafening noise. The bed sags and he leans over me.

"Here," he says softly. He lays a wet washcloth over my eyes.
"How is it?" he asks.

"Horrible," I whisper.

"I'm sorry," he says. He lays a hand on my shoulder. "It will go
away soon."

The bed squeaks as he gets up. The door thunders shut behind
him. I press my hands to my head.

They take me to doctor after doctor. No one knows what's
wrong. They give me medication, try biofeedback, tell my parents
they don't know. My parents tiptoe through the house, confused,
scared. They don't know what this onset of violent headaches
means. Neither do the doctors. Neither do I.

DEATH WOULD BE so quiet. I hide in the bathroom with an X-
Acto knife, making tiny cuts, crosshatch patterns in my thighs.

Nothing deep. It helps relieve the pressure, focus the thoughts. I take a sharp breath and breathe out slow. The blood beads along the cuts. I sop it up with Kleenex, the red spreading out over the tissue. I bleed. I'm alive.

AND THEN it's dinner and my father's screaming, and my mother's cold and icy and cruel, and they're yelling at me and I'm yelling at them — the crazies rise up in my chest and I run away from the table, the rage welled up so far it presses at the back of my throat. I can taste it. My father chases me, hollering. I shriek and run away. We stand face to face, screaming, his face is twisted and I can feel that my face is twisted and I hate him and his craziness and I hate myself for mine, and my mother gets up, walks down the hall, and slams the bedroom door.

My father and I scream each other down until we are exhausted, completely spent. We stand there panting.

"Say," my father says brightly, perking up. "Want to play Yahtzee?"

"Sure!" I say. And we sit down to play, laughing and having a wonderful time.

AFTER SCHOOL, I open our front door and step inside. The first thing I see is my father, lying on his side on the couch. Light streams in through the long windows, and it takes my eyes a moment to adjust.

I drop my book bag. "What's wrong?" I say to him from across the room. I don't want to know what's wrong. I'm tired of this. You never know which father is going to show up.

He curls up and wraps his arms around his knees.

"I don't know, Marya," he says, and starts to cry. "I really don't know."

I stare at him flatly. I want to run over there and kick him and pound him until he gets up. When he gets like this, I feel like I am drowning. The hands of his sadness close around my throat and I can't breathe. I have run out of the enormous love he needs to be all right.

"You know those afternoons," he asks, drawing a shaking breath, "where you're just going along, doing fine, and then afternoon comes and it feels like you just got the wind knocked out of you and everything is wrong?" He sighs and slowly pushes himself up so he's sitting upright. His shoulders are slumped. "That's all," he says. "It's just one of those afternoons."

We are silent for a minute. Then he lies back down on the couch.

I should say I love him. I should say it will all be all right. But it won't.

I walk down the hall to my bedroom. I lie down on my side and stare at the wall, the blue-flowered wallpaper next to my nose. Despite my best efforts, I start to cry.

I know those afternoons.

# Escapes
*Michigan, 1989*

I'm sitting in the study lounge, it's five A.M., and I have no idea how many nights or days have gone by since I last slept. I'm starving, I'm writing, I can't stop, don't want to stop, don't want to eat, I am possessed by words. I'm at boarding school, an art school where students not yet eighteen spend ten hours a day, six days a week, training, practicing, studying harder than even seems possible, possessed by a desire to *make it,* to succeed, and I'm surrounded by open books on the study lounge table, my typewriter pouring out a short story, a paper, another, another. I am no longer a fuckup, I'm going to make it, I'm going to ace my classes, I'm going to stay awake forever if I have to, just so long as I write this, whatever it is.

Through the window that looks out over the snowy campus, the light is coming up. The snow is lit a violet-blue, the horizon's a red-orange line. I sit back in my chair, my body buzzing, this heavenly hum in my head. Paper in stacks on the table. I'm ready for workshop, a fistful of stories in my hand. I've read everything for class that I was supposed to and then some. Physics thrills me, math confounds me, the German teacher despairs, but the English teacher, the writer-in-residence, the staff writers who pound us with work, they pull me aside and say: Read it, write it, don't stop, you've got it, *you're going to make it*. The magic words, the promise. The hope.

I just give up sleep. I've noticed by now that maybe my moods get a little crazier with sleep deprivation. Never mind. The deprivation unleashes a chemical reaction that feeds on itself, so that the less I sleep at night, the less I can sleep the next night, and the next. Night and day reverse themselves — but I'm not going to sleep during the day either. My body clock is no longer keeping time.

I don't care. The future is unfurling ahead of me. I'm going to be a writer if it kills me. I will kill myself trying, I will get there, I've got to learn it, train for it, write it until the writing is perfect, until I get it, until I make it, I'm going to be real. This time I won't fuck it up. I won't fail.

The sun crests the horizon halfway, a winter sun, a blinding white. I stagger from the study lounge, carrying my piles of papers and books, and stumble down the stairs and into my room. My roommate is still asleep, the room still in shadow. As she mumbles in her sleep, I pull on my running shoes, go out into the cold, head across campus to the classroom building with the half-mile-long hall.

I run. Time stops. Thoughts stop. The never-ending pounding

of my blood, the energy that surges through me all the time these days, it never runs out, I feel as if I will explode with it, I run. Up and down the long hall, compulsively touching the cold metal door on each end, must touch it or it doesn't count, one mile, five miles, ten miles, chanting *thinner, thinner, thinner,* I am killing myself with the running, the starving, but I am *alive,* I run in the morning, between classes, during lunch, after school, during dinner, after workshops, before bed, and when I stop, I panic, afraid that until I run again, the flesh will creep back on my body. I've got to burn it off, get down to bones, a running, writing, starving skeleton, I eat only carrots and mustard, drink gallons of coffee, chatter with my friends, who tell me to stop, who worry, but they don't understand, the flesh is always encroaching, trying to drown me, I will be thin, clean bones.

## Minneapolis

*1990*

I am caught. I pace up and down the hospital halls, the eating disorders ward back home, refusing to believe I'm half dead. These doctors are fools, my parents' terror unfounded. *Let me out!* I holler. *Leave me alone!* I scream as the nurses chase me with Dixie cups of Ensure, the evil drink, all calories and fat. They're trying to make up for what I'm burning while pacing, pacing, pacing the halls, panicked, hyper, locked in. I beat on the doors, crying, yell at my parents, stare at the food they put in front of me six times a day, *Get it away, I won't eat it, you can't make me.*

The doctor tells my parents I'm depressed. *I* know I'm not. Something else entirely is wrong. But doctors always say people with eating disorders are depressed. His diagnosis ignores my agitation, the fact that I sail up and crash down minute by minute. I guess he has his reasons: the extremity of my anorexia and bulimia is, to say the least, distracting. I have a life-threatening condition. No one — not my parents, not the therapists, and certainly not the doctors — has time to focus on the mayhem of my moods. Their primary goal is keeping me alive. But they're missing the forest for the trees. (That happens to this day to patients with eating disorders. Doctors zoom in on the havoc that starving, bingeing, and purging wreaks on the body; and while it's certainly true that some people with eating disorders have depression, the doctors assume that all of them do. So in people with eating disorders but without depression, the symptom is treated, but not the cause, and the physicians end up ignoring the mood disorders that the patients may actually have. The real underlying mental illness runs wild, advancing steadily, irreparably damaging the mind.)

*Fuck this!* I shout at my parents. I stand up from my chair and say again, *Fuck this!*

*Marya, sit down.*

*No!* I shout. I pace in circles around the room. The other patients and their families watch me from the corners of their eyes. My brain is burning. I stand over my parents, waving my arms. *You can't just keep me here!* I scream. *What about my civil rights?*

*You have no civil rights,* my mother points out. *Not until you're eighteen.*

*I'm moving to California,* I say.

*What are you talking about?*

*I'll live with Anne* (she's my father's first wife), *and I'll go to school and everything.*

They stare at me.

*It will be totally good for me,* I say, honing my argument — this plan has just occurred to me in the last three minutes, but now it is essential, *imperative,* that I go. It is the most important thing ever in my whole life.

I perk up, suddenly loving and cheerful. *It will be totally* healing *for me,* I say. *I will totally get better. You won't have to worry about me. I'll totally* take in the sea air. *It's very* centering *out there.*

California will be perfect. No one will watch me.

*I'll totally take long walks on the beach,* I say. *I'll walk in the sunshine and celebrate the rain. I'll get back in my body. I'll do yoga. I'll totally blossom. You see? It's perfect. It's just the thing.*

My parents look at each other.

A few weeks later, they let me out of lockup, and I'm sitting on a plane.


# California

*1990*

Here I am, healing. Centering. By now I'm convinced that my eating disorder is entirely sensible, necessary, that I'm completely sane and everybody else is nuts. Obviously I had to get out of there.

I rattle through the salt-air night in the back of a pickup truck, heading for Bodega Bay. The bottles of booze, the baggies of pot, the friends from school. We trudge through the dunes, lie on our backs, stare up at the ocean of sky. I am in heaven. This is my hideaway. Here, I can starve without anyone stopping me. I can drink myself high, smoke myself into a steady drifting down. Here, I can write all night. If I can just make it through high school, I can escape to college in some city far away. I'll be a writer and show them all that I am *not a fuckup, I can make it,* I am real.

The moods are steady, sky-high. My mind is racing ahead and I chase it, writing as fast as I can, failing heart stuttering, body disappearing. I can do anything. Nothing can stop me.

I'm a flurry of motion, sitting on the floor of my bedroom, arms flying, shuffling papers into piles, brain racing, reading snippets of writing, hopping up to get something on my desk, making rapid little red-pen marks on the pages, cutting and pasting, short of breath, pulse pounding, I am back in my element, where I can do a thousand things at once, fueled by the rabid energy triggered by the booze, no food, no sleep, I stand up and compulsively do three hundred leg lifts, balancing on the back of the chair — and I leap onto the chair and pierce my nose with a safety pin — and I climb out my window onto the roof, flinging my head back to look at the glorious blanket of stars and their halo, and the round-bellied moon — and I spin around in circles, arms out, teetering near the edge, dizzily gazing out over the dark, thick woods that surround the house — and I hop back in the window, grab my jacket, and dash down the stairs and out the door.

I walk down the long driveway onto the winding dark road that runs nearby, the Spanish moss hanging in heavy swags from the cypress and eucalyptus trees. I walk down to the strip mall in town, the neon signs fizzling in the night. I am violently alive. Every snap and spit of the neon pierces my eyes. A few cars go by, the *whoosh* of their tires making a hollow echo in my ears. This is my secret life, these nights I prowl and hide in shadows in the dark, walk the roads near their guardrails, the hills dropping sharply from the road to the valley below. Eventually, the lights, the noise, become too much, and the frenzied intensity begins to fray, tearing at my brain, slicing through my body like razor blades, and I walk down the road to my boyfriend's house. He is older, stupid, stoned, and he passes me the joint and I take a deep drag and pass it to his sister and get up to get myself a drink. I flop belly-down on the carpet, watch the interior of my mind as it empties of thoughts. The agitation begins to subside, and I slide into a rocking, gentle nothingness. We watch idiotic reruns on TV. I am starving, and the hunger pinches at my gut. My head lolls. I lay face down on the carpet, the laugh track on the television rolling over me. I fall asleep.

I am lost, a satellite orbiting the world. The energy is turning dark, the sunshine of the early months here in California fading. The starving and the drinking and the disembodied sex — all my methods for stilling my thoughts are starting to fail me. I tell myself it's not happening. I tell myself I'm all right. I can stay here. I can stand this. Surely, this will stop.

But a part of me knows I'm going to die, and doesn't care. In fact, I wish like hell I would. I'm seventeen, and I've had enough.

## Minneapolis

*1991*

Caught again. Yellow-eyed, skeletal, bitchy, I am hauled back to Minnesota by my parents. Hospital, take two. Organs failing, deathly low weight, sick as a dog, but I'm fine, *I'm fine, I'm fine.* I sit on the floor, head nodding, nothing but static in my brain, my mother trying to get me to talk, speak, show some signs of life, my father making desperate jokes, trying to make me laugh. He cries and my mother cries, and through my fog I hate that they cry, and hate myself for making them cry, and, trying to form words, I tell them they don't need to worry, I'm fine, *please just leave me alone.* Desert Storm plays a weird soundtrack to my days, fiery explosions on the TV screen, tanks barreling over entire towns, screaming people, that world far away — and I am far away too, lost in my own mind. The other patients hang limply over the arms of the couches and chairs, or stand in corners pretending to look at something, pacing in tiny, rapid circles, bouncing up and down, trying to burn off the calories that are keeping them alive. I lie awake at night, the bed bruising my bones, and listen to the wild, endless chatter of voices in my head.

Hospital, take three. Then the doctor's had enough, tells my parents to put me in a state institution and leave me there. Instead, they find the last resort, a locked institution for kids as crazy as me. My last chance.

I am standing outside a square, two-story brick building. It's ten degrees below zero, no flesh to keep me warm, and my mother grips me tight until the staff of this new place pulls me away. I look over my shoulder at my parents, they cry, I hate myself, I look forward, go away. Three triple-locked doors close one by one behind me as I follow the staff person inside, up the stairs, down the hall.

We are all crazy, under eighteen, the dregs of the system, the failures, the rejects of families, foster care, juvenile hall, we have been removed from society, a danger, a blight. We are a twelve-year-old car thief, a rapist, a sociopath, two cutters, a violent mute. We careen from pitching chairs and tables, to throwing our own bodies against the walls, to moments of calm that still the mayhem for a little while. We are in here for years, the shrieking girl, the roaring, crashing boys, the suicide attempts, the abused, the tortured, the troubled, the insane. I am here, wrapped in my coat, curled up in a ball, silent, afraid, disoriented, skinny, sick. I scream at mealtimes, pitch my food across the room, refuse to eat, they weigh me, I hate them, I swallow their fucking pills.

They are trying to kill me. Make me stupid, make me fat. They take my books, the only things I need to survive. If I can have my books, they'll disappear, I'll be safe, but they lock my books away, I scream and swear and cry and pound the walls, collapse on the floor, they say, *Marya, you have a time-out,* I go to my room and lie face-down on my bed, they come in with my *treatment plan, you are assigned to play, you will play one hour a day, you will eat what you are told, you will not scream, you will make your bed, you will go to therapy, you will engage with other people, look me in the eye, you will not be allowed to push us away with your books.* We spend our days in therapy groups, *Marya, how are you feeling right now?* I chew my nails until they're bloody stumps, I stare at the floor, I have no books, I cannot starve, they're pumping me full of pills, their kindness encroaches, surrounds me, suffocates me, *Marya, it's all right to feel, you will not die of feelings, why don't you color your feelings on a piece of paper? Stop pushing them away, get out of your head, it's safe out here.* It is not. I am trapped.

We shuffle through our screaming, crying, silent, laughing days, frightened, angry little kids cared for inside of and made safe by these thick walls. The bedroom doors don't close. The windows are three-paned Plexiglas, unbreakable, we cannot cut ourselves on them, or escape. I am sitting in the bathroom sink with scissors, chopping my long hair off, it falls around me, I'm cutting it so close it nicks the skin. I am bald as a baby. I lose control, fight, I lie in bed all day, staring at the ceiling, until they haul me out and make me talk and *feel my fucking feelings,* eat my fucking food, take the Prozac — *you're depressed!* — that's making me more insane. But gradually, despite myself, I really start to try to get better. The pressing kindness and care of the people here gets to me, and after a few months, I'm *trying* to get well, I really am. I talk, I play, I work out my *issues,* I participate, I give hugs, I make the effort, take responsibility, share the love.

But it's not enough. I'm still so sucked into the eating disorder, and so racked by the wild, roaring moods that no one can explain, that no amount of trying is going to work. As tempting as this health thing is, the idea of going back to my familiar obsessions is more so. I want out. I want my bones and my books back. I become the star patient. I talk them into letting me go to college, and they finally agree. I want to be rid of who I am, go back to the place where I wasn't a fuckup, where I was good at something, instead of a place where all I do is talk about how fucked up I am. I've got to get out.

I AM SHIVERING at the bus stop. They let me out each morning to go to the university across town. I am on fire with the classes, writing like mad, hunched over my desk, my underused, overanalyzed brain coming to life again, who cares if I'm an institutionalized freak? All I can think about is when I will get a job writing. I have to make up for this hideous failure. I'll never tell anyone. This will disappear in my past. I'll be a new person, *soon, soon.* When class lets out I avoid the other students, *Come have coffee!* they call after me, *I liked your paper, let's talk! Can't,* I mutter, hurrying off, can't very well tell you I have to get back to the loony bin before they give me a time-out.

# Washington, D.C.

*1992*

Sophomore year. I've won a scholarship and am completely nuts. I'm at the office, editing for a wire service, racing through the pages, assigning, working, I'm finally a success, I'm taking five classes and getting all A's, now I can be up all night again, this starvation is better than speed, I'm nearly dead and don't believe it for a minute, I'm on my sixth pot of coffee, my fingers are blue, my hair is falling out, I'm winning awards, people stare at me with disgust, I couldn't care less, I sit at my desk all night, how many nights now? The nights become days become nights and I am working, working, working, starving myself to death.

I am nineteen years old. I am lying in a hospital bed, hooked up to a tangle of IVs. My heart monitor barely moves. I weigh fifty-two pounds. I am almost perfect. I lift my arms and admire them, bones covered in gray, dry skin. My fingers run their course over my body: the thin ridge of my collarbone, neck and chest sunken far beneath; the hollow of my cheeks, the way I can run my fingertips along the teeth underneath; the cavern in the center of my body, the way the cage of my ribs curves around the hollow, and my hipbones jut up, the way I can feel my internal organs through the skin. I wrap a fist around each thighbone. My thighs are no longer round. They are just right. They don't exist. I've done it. I've erased myself. I've won.

I pass out.

THE FIRST CLEAR thought in years: *I refuse to die.*

## 1993

The feeling of health, as I slowly gain the sixty pounds I need to keep me alive, is foreign, weird. My body morphs as I stare at it in the mirror. I am going to stay alive. Finally I have grasped that I cannot feed my mind and starve my body to death. Finally, from somewhere, comes this visceral urge to survive. And so here I am, living. I'm working again — I'm going to school, and getting grants, and I get a job teaching undergrad classes, and I make friends, and stay up with them all night talking about books, and I'm going to parties, and learning to eat, and I suddenly have a life. A normal life. I walk tentatively through my days, afraid of breaking the spell, afraid I'll fuck it up, I'll fail.

Afraid I'll go mad again, and lose it all.

## 1994

I am writing a poem. I am only vaguely aware of myself: the point is the poem. To the effort I contribute the mechanism of my mind: the cogs and wheels groan and begin to chug along. They move faster, sending out a conveyor belt of neatly packaged words. A story, a poem begins to take shape. Pages pile up. I scribble and gnaw on my fingers, getting blood and spit on the paper. The pages are a product of my body. I can touch them. I can eat them if I want. I worry their edges, rip at their corners, throw them to my right as I finish each one, the letters running up to the edge and spilling off onto the desk until I get another piece of paper and continue recording the automatic generation of language from my mind. As the sky outside my window turns from black to midnight blue, as thin clouds stretch across the indigo sky like someone lying on her side, I hurry: morning is almost here. I race to get down the last of the words. The light comes up. I push myself away from the desk, unclench the fist that held the pen, stagger off to bed, fall into a thick, drunken sleep.

I wake up an hour, a few hours, half a day later. I wince at the light. I am a bat. I dangle in the corner of my room, my leathery wings folded over my face. I look at the clock. Did I call in sick to work? What day is it? Do I have class? Am I teaching? Oh, Christ. I let my head fall back on the pillow and stare at the ceiling. I am silent. I do not exist. I am merely a pair of eyes, looking around at the room. The rest of me is invisible. I won't be visible again until someone sees me. If a woman stands in a kitchen rubbing her eyes and pouring coffee with no one there to see her, does she exist? I will not register in the world until I speak.

I stumble out the door, hop the bus to the university, my head bobbling as we drive over ruts in the road, listening to the slow milling of arbitrary words around my head. The words displease me. They are not in order. Everyone is talking at once. I sit in silence, staring out the window, watching the city go by.

An hour later I find myself standing in front of a classroom with chalk in my hand. They will drop a nickel in me and I will begin to talk.

MY BODY CLOCK is completely screwed up. I'm drinking again. One minute I'm flat on my face in the living room, crying and deep in despair, the next I'm tearing back up, moving so fast my head is spinning, trying to do a million things at once, trying to keep up with the rocketing, plummeting moods.

I can't so much as clean my apartment. My bills pile up, unpaid. The phone gets turned off. I'm so broke I'm feeding my cat cans of beans. The only things in my refrigerator are a bag of wilted carrots and beer. I guzzle coffee all day and vodka all night.

What's wrong with me? Nothing. I'm fine. I've just become a lazy slob. Get ahold of yourself. Now.

But I can't. And soon enough I snap.

## Full Onset

*1995*

The cutting helps. I'm cutting every day. I stand in the bathroom, slicing patterns in my arms. They'll scar. My arms will, for the rest of my life, be covered with scars. I clench my teeth. Cut more. Cut deeper. The thoughts stop.

The pain is perfect. It's precise. My mind, for one blessed moment, is aware only of the pain. The pain makes me feel alive. My heart beats steadily in my chest. I picture the blood pumping through me, reaching the cuts, spilling over, running down my arms.

Morning comes. I'm passed out on the floor. I try to lift my head. A thick and pressing sadness lies on me like a dead body. I roll over on my stomach, lay my face on the floor, close my eyes. I can't move.

By night, I feel like I'm on speed. The moods carry me up and down, up and down. I fly and fall, crashing and sailing and crashing again.

The therapist's office: she leans back in her chair. She's lovely, and out of her depth. She keeps increasing my Prozac. It's making me insane.

"I don't know what's going on," I say, trying to sound calm but grappling with a desperation that clutches at my chest. "I don't think things are going very well."

"What makes you say that?" she asks kindly, tilting her head. Sometimes her kindness gets to me. It's excessive and saccharine, almost a parody of itself.

"I'm acting a little crazy," I say. "One minute I'm flying around and the next I'm, you know, lying on the floor."

"But don't you think that's progress? That you're really feeling your feelings? I think you've finally reached a special place in your life, a place of real balance, where you're able to fully *respond* to those feelings. You're not just locked up in your head all the time, intellectualizing, pushing those feelings *away*."

"Maybe," I say, hesitant. "It just seems like maybe it's a little much. You know, like really *extreme*. It seems like the feelings are taking over my entire life."

"Well, consider this — how's the eating going?"

"Pretty well."

"Now, I want you to really *take that in*. Stop for a moment and really *appreciate* the significance of that. How different is that from ever before? You've never really been *in a space* where the eating disorder was under control. I feel like you're really using the *tools* we've been working on, the *mindful eating*, the *being in your body*. You should really bear *witness* to the progress you've made in that area. I think you've finally, really, truly made the decision to stay alive. That's just enormous. Can you see that? Can you be proud of yourself?"

"I'm cutting my arms up every night."

"Have you been journaling?"

"Yes."

"And what are you finding?"

"When I read it over, it's like two different people are writing it. One of them's a maniac and one of them's completely depressed."

"Do you think you're depressed?"

"Not when I'm flying around."

"I think, honestly, that you're in much better shape than you're giving yourself credit for. I think maybe that you are still just so *angry* at yourself for all the years of being sick, and so *unfairly judgmental* of yourself for finally breaking away from the past and finally *feeling your feelings,* being *true* to yourself, that you just aren't *allowing* yourself to appreciate how well you're really doing."

"I really would rather not be cutting. I'm getting scars all over my arms."

"Well, I think that's a matter of doing some *self-soothing.* Have you been trying out the self-soothing techniques I suggested? Take some real *time* for yourself. Just sit down at night, make yourself a cup of tea, and be quiet *in yourself.* Wrap yourself in a warm, fuzzy quilt. Put on lotion. Splurge on some perfume. Take yourself out to lunch. Turn on some soothing music and try self-massage. Take a warm, comforting bath. Light a candle and really *feel* the water surrounding your limbs. Do you think you could begin tonight? Do you think you could try taking a bath?"

I take a fucking bath.

Night comes. It finally happens. It's the scene in the bathroom of my apartment in Minneapolis. I'm twenty years old, drunk out of my mind. I am cutting patterns in my arm, a leaf and a snake. And then, without thinking, on blind, unstoppable impulse, I slash my left arm with a razor so hard I hit the bone.

NOW I'M SOMEONE else. Now I'm someone who's tried to kill herself. I've opened my artery and not even felt it. Has it gotten that bad?

No problem. A blip on the screen of my usual nuttiness. I'll simply start over. No more of that. Out with the cutting. Out with the Prozac. Out with the old me, and in with the new.

Obviously, the next thing to do is to skip town.

I head off for California in my rattling car. I'm getting out of here. I'm going to go be a *real* writer. I take only some books, a ratty blue bandanna, a few clothes, and my cat.

And the five-inch purple scar on my forearm, which looks like a terrible worm.

# Part II

# The New Life
*1996*

Suddenly, I'm writing a book about my years with eating disorders. I don't really know how that happened — a writer I know talked me into it, insisted I should — but I sit at my desk all day, pounding it out. The sun crosses the floor of my one-room apartment in Oakland as I race through the pages, barely aware of the world, trying to forget the crazies, the razor, the cut.

Now I'm drinking in earnest. At the end of the day, each day, I head down the street to the liquor store to buy the night's supply of vodka. I go home, add a splash of orange juice to an eight-ounce tumbler, fill the rest of the glass with the vodka, and spend the evening at my desk writing poetry, then stay up all night reading every secondhand book I can afford. I stagger around my apartment, completely unaware that I am quickly crossing the line from binge drinker to alcoholic. It happens overnight.

And here's the kicker. On impulse — it just occurs to me — I stop by Julian's house. Julian is a friend from my adolescent California days, the only semi-sane friend I had. He is a nice guy, kind, a port-in-a-storm kind of fellow. And he is also a little boy, aimless, easy to sweep away. He has no life — now he can have mine.

I pull up to his house, my hair in a crewcut, wearing a tank top, old jeans, and a beat-up pair of boots. He opens the door. His jaw drops. I grin.

We spend a year in a particleboard apartment, drinking constantly, playing grownups. My new life is complete. I've abandoned the crazy years, the crazy self, and here I am with a book deal, a future, and a fiancé. We spend the nights in Melendy's Bar, pool balls cracking, Patsy Cline on the jukebox, swimming in smoke. We talk nonstop, laugh our heads off, plan an extravagant wedding, an extravagant life.

Our families and friends are alarmed, wondering where the hell we got this idea, urging us to wait, but we ignore them — it's perfectly reasonable that two twenty-two-year-olds who knew each other as kids and have now been living together for all of a year are completely prepared to begin a life together.

Idiots.

WE MARRY in July, and the next day, because this is perfectly obvious, we get in a moving van and head back to Minneapolis. I want to be near my family, my friends, my cousin Brian, who's been my closest friend since we were kids, the one sane point in the whirlwind of my chaos, the voice on the phone long-distance, the writing on the letters, the hand that held my string as I bobbed and wove in the breeze.

So Julian and I go sailing forward at a breakneck pace. We're grownups now. I am spending money as fast as I make it, and we jet around the country to lavish hotels in cities, anywhere, everywhere, eating fabulous meals, blowing thousands of dollars, making drunken fools of ourselves, collapsing on endless king-size beds. At home, I careen from parties at friends' houses to Brian's downtown apartment, where I talk a mile a minute and we cackle with laughter. He's the dearest person to me in the world, a person of substance, solidity, sanity, and a deep and abiding gentleness, and he is what I rely on, even if I'm not entirely aware of it, to give my life some semblance of sense. As much as we laugh, he gets me to sit still for a minute, tries to tell me I'm going too fast, that I'm going to crash, but I ignore him, that's the old me, I'm a different person now. I go racing through the mall, buying everything in sight, staggering under bags and bags of things I've bought, who cares what they are? I want it, *I have to have it,* it's perfect! It's gorgeous! I can't stop shopping, our house fills up with china, crystal, expensive sheets, mountains of books, gourmet cookware, every kind of booze you can think of, paintings, clothes and more clothes and more clothes. We're like little kids. We *are* little kids, but don't tell us that—we're having a *fantastic* time. We have our little house, and live our little life. We are the perfect young husband and wife. We have nonstop dinner parties — the glorious food, the fabulous friends, the gallons of wine.

I sometimes feel as if I've raced off a cliff and am spinning my legs in midair, like Wile E. Coyote. But I'm fine. It's fine. It's all going to be fine. Crazy people don't have dinner parties, do they? No.

We go to concerts and plays, and never once do I let on that sometimes the music turns colors in my mind, veering toward me, making me flinch. I laugh at the funny parts and clap when everyone claps, even if I'm confused, disoriented, scared.

When I get lost as I drive through the streets of my city, I tell no one. Every night, after a day of writing, I open the bottle of wine, and Julian and I settle in for an evening of drunken glee. I make the fancy meals and wash the wedding dishes and write the thank-you notes for all the million wedding gifts on stationery stamped with my married name.

Crazy people don't have stationery, do they?

The wineglasses will stave off the madness, surely, or the breakfast nook will, or the husband himself. I'm not going crazy.

Not again.

IT SEEMS TO HAPPEN overnight: one day I am calm, and the next I am raging. It's very simple. Happens like you're flipping a switch. Julian and I are going along, having a perfectly lovely evening, and then it's dark and I am screaming, standing in the middle of the room, turning over the glass-topped coffee table, ripping the bathroom sink out of the wall, picking up anything nearby and pitching it as hard as I can. The rages always come at night. They control my voice, my hands, I scream and throw myself against the walls. I feel like a Tasmanian devil. The room spins, I run up and down the stairs, I can't stop. Julian tries to grab me, holding my arms until I scream myself out and collapse, exhausted, in tears — but there are nights I manage to squirm free and run out the door. Sometimes I just run as far and as hard as I can, until I can't breathe, until my heart is about to explode, or until, stumbling drunk, I fall and hit my head on a tree stump or the curb and lie still.

Sometimes, though, I get in my car.

I peel out of the driveway, roaring up Thirty-sixth Street, away from my pretty house and sleepy neighborhood. *Slow down!* I am screaming at myself, *Marya, slow down!*

And the madness screams back, *I won't!*

It slides under my skin, borrowing my body without asking: my hands are its hands, and its hands are filled with an otherworldly strength. Its hands feel the need to lash out, to hit something, so it tightens its white-knuckled fists on the wheel, its bare foot slamming the gas. My head jerks back. Half in abject terror, half in awe, I watch the lights streak across the sky, bending as I careen around corners, up Hennepin, down through the seething nightlife of Lake Street, past the spectrally brilliant movie theater marquee, the crowds a blur, *stoplights are not for me!* Streetlights smear behind me like neon streamers. I hurtle forward. The only thing that matters is motion, *forward motion, propulsion,* I veer onto the freeway, playing chicken with the cars. The road comes at me full speed, it looks as if it will hit me dead between the eyes, but then it swerves around me just in time. The other cars, the median, the guardrail flash around my face, and I in my roller coaster am clattering and screaming along. I wind up in some unknown neighborhood, over by the river or on the north side of town. I turn the car around and, my rage spent, find my way home.

Rage swings into a stuporous sleep, and sleep swings into the awful morning sun. My head slides off the edge of the bed, and my mood plummets from shrieking high to muffled low, my heart beating dully on the inside of my ribs. I fall out of bed and stumble down the stairs, heading for coffee, but get too tired on the way and lie down on the living room floor, a painful hole yawning open in my chest. This old, familiar ache does not feel so much like sadness as it does like death, if death is blunt and heavy and topples into you, knocking you flat.

Julian comes in, carrying a cup of coffee. He sees me there on the floor. "Do you want help up?"

I mean to shake my head no, but my face is pressed into the carpet, and it would be too hard to shake it anyway. He picks his way through the wreckage of the night before, clears a chair of debris, and sits down, crossing his legs, an action I find futile and absurd. Slowly, I lift myself up. I'm dizzy — I always am after a rage — and I try to focus my eyes. I look around me at the mess: there's a jagged-edged half of a wine bottle, a pile of green glass shards nearby. There's a circular stain of wine on the wall, streams running down as if it leaked blood, and a puddle-shaped stain on the carpet below. There are the remains of a couple of smashed glasses. The bookshelf is cockeyed, leaning precariously on the back of the couch. Books everywhere. The couch has moved across the room from where it's supposed to be. I peer at what looks like a hole in the wall. I look at Julian.

"Lead crystal clock," he explains.

I nod, still looking around the room. "This is bad," I finally say.

"Not good," he agrees.

"Sorry," I say.

"It happens," he says.

"It does," I say, bewildered. "I don't know why."

He leaves — does he even understand what's happening? I certainly don't — and I stand barefoot, alone in the mess. I go over to the hole in the wall and stub my toe on the aforementioned lead crystal clock. I pick it up and turn it over in my hands. Wedding present. Ugly. I marvel that it didn't break. I set it down on the table and look out the window. My shoulders slump.

I shake the fog out of my head. *Get a grip,* I think. I'm fine. It's little-boy Julian who's making me crazy. No one could cope with his dependency, his lack of drive. It's stressing me out, this game the two of us play, his kicking back, jobless, using my money, embracing the identity of kept man.

No, I correct myself. He's my savior, companion, the *husband,* the rock. Our life is normal, balanced. We're just like everyone else.

I cling to the persona of the good wife, the disciplined writer, the hostess, hanging on with both hands. But even I wear down eventually: the constant fighting, the afternoons crashed out in bed, the sudden spells of ruthless energy — they're just too much.

I give in. I call for help.

# The Diagnosis
*April 1997*

I page through the phone book surreptitiously, looking out the window to make sure Julian hasn't pulled up to the house yet. For some reason, I don't want him to know I'm calling a psychiatrist. Maybe that would confirm the incredibly obvious. Or maybe he hasn't noticed that I've gone completely nuts. I run my finger down the column and stop at one Richard Beedle, M.D. I like his name. A man named Beedle can't be all bad.

I sit in the waiting room, paging through an old *Time*. It's the same *Time* they keep in every waiting room. There is only one, and everyone has it, and it is sorely out of date. Bored, I slap it shut and study the painting of flowers on the opposite wall. It looks like every other painting of flowers on every other wall of every office of every psychiatrist, psychologist, nutritionist, behaviorist, et al. that I've ever seen.

He calls me into his office. I take my usual place in the usual chair on the usual empty afternoon. I study him the way I always study them. Some of them are mean, some very smart, some idiots, most a little hurried, but some just plain old nice — your usual cross-section of humanity. This Beedle looks to be okay. He has one wandering eye and wears a brown suit. I watch his eye while he settles into his chair. Does he get to see two whole scenes at once? Is one part of him having a conversation with me while another is looking out the window at the new green leaves on the trees?

He mispronounces my name and I correct him, as usual. This is how all psychiatric visits start. He looks friendly enough, so I decide to give him a chance.

"What brings you here today?" he asks.

"I'm going crazy."

"Well, don't beat around the bush," he says. "Jump right in."

"I'm going nuts. I mean, I am nuts. I've always been nuts. They've been telling me I have depression for years, but they're wrong. I used to have an eating disorder. They're always giving me Prozac. I know, I know, you'll probably give me Prozac too, which, okay, I understand, you have to give me *something,* though I should mention that if you had something *other* than Prozac I would be open to trying it, just so you know. In fact, I'm open to pretty much anything, at this point. I'm kind of desperate." Weirdly, I laugh. "I mean, kind of *really* desperate. Not to make a fuss or anything. I don't want to overstate my case. I don't want to be malingering. Do you think I'm malingering? Once a nurse told me I was malingering when I told her the Prozac was making me crazy." I pause. "What exactly *is* malingering?" I ask.

"It's when you're making a big deal out of nothing. Making symptoms seem worse than they are."

"See?" I say, and throw up my hands. "Exactly. I don't want to be malingering. I definitely don't want to make something out of nothing."

"You're not malingering."

"Well, that's good. But anyway, really, now that I think of it, this really is nothing. It's not such a big deal. I mean, I'm not *crazy* crazy. I'm not wandering around with a grocery cart full of newspapers and cans talking to myself. I mean, I talk to myself a little, but not in a crazy way — doesn't everybody talk to themselves?" He nods. He sits with his hands folded on his desk. He hasn't written anything on his notepad and appears, oddly, to be listening. I appreciate his attention; it's very courteous of him. "By the way, oh my gosh," I say, suddenly flustered, "I'm going on and on. I know you're busy. I know you must have a million patients. Have I already used up my time?" I ask, a little panicked.

"No."

"How much time do I have?"

"As much as you want. This is a private practice. I'm not an HMO, so no rush."

"*Well,*" I sigh, collapsing back in my chair — I notice I've been sitting bolt upright the whole time — "thank goodness." I take a little breather.

"May I ask you something?"

"Sure," I say, feeling magnanimous.

"Do you always talk this fast?"

"Yes."

He nods. "Okay," he says. "Go on."

"What was I saying?"

"Feeling crazy, but not *crazy* crazy."

"Right," I say. "So I guess that's it. Do you mind if I look around?"

"Not at all," he says, so I get up and go over to his bookcase and read all the titles and look at the framed photos and laugh at the little framed cartoon — a man is lying on a couch, yammering on, and the doctor's writing *TOTALLY NUTS!!!* on his little pad — and I go over to the window and hop up on the sill and swing my feet a little, then hop back down and come back and sit in my chair.

"All better?" he asks. I laugh. "Has anyone ever mentioned the word *mania* to you?"

"Nope," I say, folding my hands across my middle.

"They haven't," he says. "I find that a little odd."

"I mean, I've heard the word, obviously," I say. "I've just never heard it applied to me. Is that what you're saying?"

"It was, yes. Out of curiosity, what *does* mania mean?"

"Mania — well, going around like a maniac, I guess." Now that I think about it, that doesn't sound so far off.

"Sort of," he says. "Anyway, you're right, you don't seem depressed right now. You seem like you've got lots of energy."

"I do indeed," I say. "Indeed I do."

"An unusual amount of energy," he replies.

I shrug. "Pretty typical for me," I say. "I like to keep busy."

"What do you do to keep yourself busy?"

"Oh, working, mostly. Or seeing friends. Cleaning, laundry, things like that. I like to have a clean house. Very clean. Unusually clean. Spotless, in fact. I'm an extremely good housekeeper. Most of the time."

"Except?"

"When I'm not. I go through stages. Sometimes I don't clean the house for months. But usually," I say, not wanting to give the impression that I'm a lazy slob, "it's pretty clean."

"What else happens when you go through those stages?"

I furrow my brow. "I don't know. Nothing. It happens in the afternoon, usually. I just want to crawl into bed and hide from the entire world and stop thinking. My brain empties out. It's kind of an effort to breathe. It's like time slows down. It feels like I'm flattened. I don't want to do anything. I can't concentrate. I feel like a failure. I sort of hate myself." I shrug. "It goes away. Then I get energetic again." I fiddle with my ears, not wanting to tell him about the rages. I feel like I've said too much already and come off as crazy. Can't have that.

"Is there a pattern to the swings?"

"Swings?"

"What did you say? Stages. Do you have any idea when the stages come and go? I mean, you know when they happen during the day, right? Do you see any pattern over, say, a few months?"

"No. Sometimes they happen, sometimes not. I'm just kind of moody. Which," I say, "is kind of the issue. I'm really insanely moody right now. I mean, I'm out-of-my-head moody. I can't stand it. I'm going nuts. As I said."

"What's happening?"

"I'm having these rages," I finally confess, embarrassed. "I kind of go into these insane rages and wind up smashing all kinds of shit and throwing things and hollering and crying."

"Any particular reason?"

"No. That's the thing. It just happens. It comes out of nowhere.

Well, it happens at night, usually. At night I'm crazy, in the morning I'm flat. So at night I have these rages and destroy all this shit and am horrible and awful, and then in the morning I wake up and look at it and kind of want to die. I mean, not *die* die," I say. "I never want to really die." I lean forward, wanting to set the record straight. "But I'm not *depressed,* for God's sake. You said so yourself. They've always said I was, but that doesn't make any *sense.* I'm usually pretty happy," I say, sitting back in my chair, waving my hand, suddenly aware that that sounds a little ridiculous at this point. "I mean, seriously. It's not like I lie around all *day.* How could I get up every morning and work, and do all this stuff, if I was *depressed?*" I laugh in disbelief.

He nods amiably. "Ever wish you were dead?"

I consider it. "I wish I wasn't crazy."

"Ever attempted suicide?"

"Not exactly."

He raises his eyebrows, then skips on. "Let me ask you a couple of questions."

The questions are endless, and with each one, I feel a little crazier. But I also start to feel like he might know what's going on. Which means there might be something he could do.

"You say you had an eating disorder? How long ago?"

"Started when I was nine. I finally started getting a handle on it a couple of years ago, when I was about twenty."

"What about cutting, any history of cutting?"

"A little bit. Ages ago." I'm torn between wanting his help and not wanting to seem crazy. The cutting was crazy. I don't care to elaborate.

"What about drinking? Drugs?"

"Drinking? I suppose so, yes. But not too much. Nothing that would cause concern." I'm thinking, *Drinking? All the time. Until I can't see. Until the crazies go away. I drink myself sane.* I'm not about to tell him that. That's the last thing I want him to know. I'll tell him anything he wants to hear except about the drinking. It's my last hope to keep myself from going totally over the edge. "No drugs," I say.

"Do you have a habit of being impulsive? Things like shopping, making snap decisions? Taking sudden trips?" The more he asks, the less I can answer. Snap decisions? Always. Shopping? Until I've nearly gone broke. Trips? I just took a trip. Lit off at night, drove six hundred miles to see an old friend, on a whim.

"What about sex?" I slept with the friend, too, without thinking about it, then felt like shit. "Not to pry, but would you say you sleep with a lot of people? More than you mean to? Sometimes it feels like you don't want to but can't stop?" For as long as I can remember. I can't begin to count the beds, the nights when it felt easier just to close my eyes than to get myself home.

"Do your thoughts race?"

I sit up. "That's it," I say. "That's what I mean when I say crazy: I can't get the thoughts to stop. It's torture. It's hell."

"Do you ever feel like you're not in your body, like you're numb?"

"Yes."

"When?"

"Sometimes during the rages. Sometimes when I get really happy. It comes and goes."

"Does it bother you?"

"I don't know. It's just weird. It feels like I might just go flying off."

"Does anything make the feeling go away?"

"I pinch myself."

"Does it work?"

"Not really."

"Do you ever cut yourself?"

"Not anymore."

"When you did, did it help?"

"Yes," I say flatly.

"Good for you for not doing it anymore."

"I slipped once. Nearly killed myself. I'm not interested in doing it again."

"Slipped?"

"Slipped."

He lets it slide.

"How far apart are the mood swings?" He keeps saying that! What's he talking about? "Every few months, weeks, days?"

"I wouldn't know about mood swings," I say. "It's nothing that specific. It's just, I don't know —" Now that I think about it, it's *obviously* fucking mood swings. "More like I just go flying around, up and down. Sometimes days. Hours. Minutes. So fast I can't keep track. I'll be going along in a perfectly good mood and suddenly I'm pitching shit all over the house. I'll be lying in bed feeling like I'm dead when suddenly I'm up and running around. It's maddening. I'd give anything to be *just normal* for an entire day. Just a day. That's all I'm asking."

"What about sleep, do you sleep? Can't fall asleep or can't stay asleep? Wake up early even when you don't want to?"

"I would sell my soul for one good night of sleep. I lie awake for hours, then prowl the house all night. By morning everything feels surreal."

"Nightmares?"

"When I sleep."

"What about work, what kind of work do you do? Do you find it hard to work? Easy? Can you stop working? Or do you just keep going?"

"I'm a writer. I write and write. I would write until I was dead, the way some dogs will keep eating and eating until they die. I can't stop. And then, suddenly, I have nothing to say. It goes away. The words are gone."

He's studying my face.

"Do you ever feel hopeless?"

The word yawns open in my chest. "Not really," I say, looking out the window.

"But sometimes?"

"Sometimes."

"When?"

I still don't look at him. "When I stop to think about it."

"About this?"

"About any of it. About being crazy." I chew my thumbnail and look at him. "It's getting worse," I say. "It's getting harder not to think about it."

"Does anything help?"

I snort. "A drink?" He doesn't laugh. "Not really," I say. "No." Nothing. Nothing makes it go away.

He finally scribbles something on his notepad and clicks his pen. He looks at me.

"You don't have depression, that's for sure."

"No shit." What a relief.

"You have bipolar disorder."

I sit there. "Is that the same as manic depression?"

"The very same."

"You're joking."

"I'm serious."

"That's crazy. I mean, manic depression: that's *crazy*."

He shrugs. "Depends on how you look at it. I wouldn't say it's crazy. I'd say it's an illness."

"Bipolar disorder," I repeat. "Do you take Prozac for that?"

"Not a chance," he says. "You're right that the Prozac makes you feel crazy. I'm going to prescribe a mood stabilizer. It should help."

My chest floods with a mixture of horror and relief. The relief comes first: something in me sits up and says, *It's true*. He's right, he has to be right. This is it. All the years I've felt tossed and spit up by the forces of chaos, all that time I've felt as if I am spinning away from the real world, the known world, off in my own aimless orbit — all of it, over. Suddenly the solar system snaps into place, and at the center is this sun; I have a word. *Bipolar.* Now it will be better. Now it has a name, and if it has a name, it's a real thing, not merely my imagination gone wild. If it has a name, if it isn't merely an utter failure on my part, if it's a disease, *bipolar disorder,* then it has an answer. Then it has a cure. At least it has something that *should help.*

And then the horror sets in. All that time I wasn't crazy; I was, in fact, *crazy.* It's hopeless. I'm hopeless. *Bipolar disorder. Manic depression.* I'm sick. It's true. It isn't going to go away. All my life, I've thought that if I just worked hard enough, it would. I've always thought that if I just *pulled myself together,* I'd be a good person, a calm person, a person like everyone else.

I think how impossible it seems that I have never connected the term *manic depression* — I guess they're calling it *bipolar* — to myself. For that matter, it seems impossible that *they* would never have applied it to me.

What if this Beedle fellow is right? What if my good moods are the same thing as mania? And what if, God forbid, the lows are the same as depression? And what if manic depression means crazy? Well, obviously, it does.

So. I'm crazy as a coot. Mad as a hatter. End of story. That's all, folks, now you can all go home. I'm sure, sitting here in the doctor's office, that there's no final *cure* for the truly insane. I am no longer young, wild, crazy, a little nuts. I'm a crazy lady.

I knew it all along.

"WENT TO THE DOCTOR today," I say, yanking the cork from a bottle of wine. Julian is sitting in the breakfast nook, reading the paper.

"Are you sick?" he asks, taking the glass I hand him and glancing up at me before looking back at the front page.

"In a manner of speaking," I say. "He says I have bipolar disorder. It's the same thing as manic depression."

"Is it serious?"

"I don't think so. But it sort of explains the last few months."

"How so?" He sets the paper down and takes a swallow of wine.

"The rages," I say, stirring something on the stove.

"This was a psychiatrist you went to?"

I nod. "Named Beedle."

"Beedle," he muses.

"Right," I say. "Anyway, he gave me a prescription."

"For rages? What do they prescribe for that?"

"Mood stabilizers." I look at the prescription slip in my back pocket. "Depakote. I think it's supposed to help, you know, sort of all around. With the moods. And things."

"Ah yes," he says. "The moods. And things."

"So I should be a little less crazy."

"All right," he says, and bites into an apple. "When's dinner?"

By the end of the evening a miracle has occurred, and I'm feeling fine. All those years of *changing my thoughts! improving my attitude!* have suddenly become very useful. By my second glass of wine, I have *chosen a new perspective!* as follows:

Bipolar? Kind of an overstatement, but whatever. Just another name from yet another shrink. Interesting, but not really relevant to my day-to-day — after all, it's not like I'm *sick*. I'll take the meds, though — they'll get rid of the rages, and the afternoon lows. Back to normal in a jiffy, back to my usual *good mood*. And surely no one needs to know; why focus more on what a fuckup I am? They'll take it wrong and make a fuss. This is really no big deal. I'll be good as new.

I'm immensely pleased with myself for *changing my thoughts* in this so-healthy way.

*

MY INSURANCE doesn't cover Dr. Beedle, so he refers me to someone it does, a Dr. Lentz. I like him — he's mild, cheerful, seems awfully concerned. He asks how things are going; I've got to get rid of the rages and lows, so I tell him about those and he fiddles with my dose. He asks me, for some reason, how much I drink, and tells me if I drink a lot, the meds won't work, but since I'm not an alcoholic or anything, his question has no relevance.

I'm delighted with these meds, and I usually take them. When I feel bad, anyway — that's what they're for, right? To cheer me up? It's those depressions I hate, and the rages, and the spinning thoughts — what I want is to hit that perfect high. That's my normal self.

And I'm getting happier and happier all the time, working constantly, keeping the house spotless, throwing parties that feature gales of laughter and me at the very top of my game. These meds are a miracle! I tell him how much they're helping. Perhaps I'm a little too happy? Why, no! He raises an eyebrow as I babble on about how inspired I am, so I tone it down — obviously not *too* happy, I say, dismissing the thought with a wave of my hand. I'm just back to normal! It's summer, after all. This is the way I'm *supposed* to be! I'm always high as a kite in summer!

I WONDER what difference it might have made in my life if I'd taken my bipolar seriously right then. If I had, in fact, stopped to think about it. Maybe read up on it. Maybe learned something that might have changed the way I lived, something that in turn might have altered — maybe dramatically — the way the following years played out. I sit here now, writing these words, just out of the hospital for the umpteenth time this year. My vision is blurry, my speech is slurred, I can hardly keep my fingers on the keys. I'm not safe to drive, I can't make a phone call; I woke up the other day in a hospital bed, staggered out to the nurses' desk, and demanded to know how long I'd been there. "Eleven days" came the calm reply. "Eleven days?" I shouted. "What have I been doing this whole time?" The nurse looked at me. "Well, you've been sick," she said. That means I've been sleeping for days on end, when I wasn't running around like a demon possessed, and getting electroshock, and being wheeled through the ward with my head lolling onto my chest, and downing Dixie cups full of pills, and slurring through the haze of medication and chemical malfunction to my hospital psychiatrist (who is nothing short of a saint and who makes a regular practice of saving me from the vicissitudes of my mind), and falling back into bed again, and launching myself out, and running around; eleven days, twelve days, fourteen. It happens like clockwork, every few months. Hospitalizations lately: January 2004. April 2004. July 2004. October 2004. January 2005. April 2005. July 2005. December 2005. January 2006. July 2006. September 2006. October 2006. November 2006.

IT'S APRIL 2007. I haven't been in the hospital in six months. Okay, I was completely out of commission, living in my pajamas, moving from my bed to my office, sitting with my head in my hands, trying like hell to have one coherent thought, for February and March. But I stayed out of the hospital. I'm doing fucking *great*.

For years after I was diagnosed, I didn't take it seriously. I just didn't feel like thinking about it. I let it run rampant, and these are the results. But what does it matter, what might have happened? What might have happened didn't. This is what did.

# The Break
*July 1997, Nine A.M.*

One hot, sunny morning, three months after I first hear *bipolar disorder* from Dr. Beedle, I am suddenly, floridly mad. Just like that. *Mad.* I am going along, minding my own business, when I find that I have gone completely over the edge. Why today? Who cares? I am not thinking a bit about that, because, as I said, I've gone insane and couldn't possibly care less *why*. You don't wonder, when you've completely lost it, *how*. You were going about your morning, and now you are mad, and you can't remember what it was like before. You will never really remember. Your life breaks in half, right there. Sure, I've been crazy before. I've been crazy all along. But this is different. This is *fucking nuts*.

Because I haven't told Lentz about the suicide attempt in 1994, he's diagnosed me with bipolar II. Bipolar II is a little milder than bipolar I (though it's still hellish); bipolar II has more depressive episodes than manic ones, and when the manic episodes occur, they're not as severe. I don't know it yet but I'll soon find out: what separates bipolar II from bipolar I is a manic break. Bipolar I is harder to manage, harder to treat, and often, because of the extremity of the disasters caused by full-blown mania, more likely to mess up the patient's life. On this summer morning, I experience that defining break. I go from bipolar II to bipolar I just like that. A doctor might put it this way: I go from sick to really, really sick. For the average Joe, I go from having an illness "just like diabetes!" to being flat-out crazy.

But I, cheerfully mad as a hatter, am entirely unaware that something has snapped and will never be put back together. Here we are: it's Tuesday, and now we are quite mad. Not *mad* as in *moody*. *Mad* as in *under the impression that I am God*.

I am driving through the city. I am speeding. It seems that I have had a good deal to drink, to calm my nerves, for I am *just a touch* nervous. I woke up this morning and things were a little off. I went to the kitchen for a cup of coffee and stopped in the doorway. Glass covered every surface. I vaguely remembered throwing the coffeepot at my husband's head. Hell. No coffee. There was blood on the floor; I checked my feet, which were covered with shallow cuts that were more or less painless. I wondered absently if they really were painless, or if I was numb.

It occurred to me that I had to leave immediately, and I went upstairs to collect my purse and shoes. I made it as far as the car when I noticed that I wasn't wearing any clothes. *Oh, for goodness' sake,* I thought to myself, and went back into the house shaking my head. I put on my blue-flowered sundress, and then realized I ought to shower, so I took a shower, and stepped out soaking wet, my dress clinging to me, and then there was a fold in time and now I am driving, very fast. I am downtown. I am speeding through a parking lot, honking at nothing. I run inside a building and find I am at my husband's place of work. I kiss everyone hello, despite their surprise (perhaps they are surprised because I am all wet?), and I babble excitedly and my husband calls Dr. Lentz and kindly escorts me back to my car and sends me on my way, and it is very important that I put on lots of lipstick, it's always good to look nice for an appointment with a shrink, it makes one look much more *sane,* and I am pacing in his office, *Please sit down, Marya, really, would you sit down? Have you taken your meds? Are you suicidal? Have you been drinking? Does your husband know where you are? Did you drive here? No, you certainly* cannot *leave —*

Inexplicably, I am in the car again. From out of nowhere, Julian is here and is driving and I am bouncing up and down in my seat, we are going on an adventure! We're going to California! I want to move to California! Or New York, let's move to New York! I find a bottle of vodka under the seat and drink most of it because I am clearly a little agitated and shouldn't be seen like this, it's embarrassing. And now we are at a hospital. Why are we at the hospital?

My husband looks worried. I am sitting on a gurney and they are taking my blood, which apparently I don't care for because I bat them away and shriek that they are invading my privacy and this is still America and they can't just do whatever they want. Then, for no reason I can see, I am being wheeled along a corridor. I say I can walk perfectly well and hop up and wheel the chair myself, though the person in the blue pajamas declines to get in; and they unlock a large door and we are in a safe place and they take my shoes.

I sit here in the hospital room painted the shade of pink that is supposed to make people calm. I examine, enchanted, my feet in their blue hospital footies, while someone speaks in soft tones to me and says I am psychotic, but it's going to be all right. I put on my hat, unperturbed, and ask for some crayons.


# Unit 47
*Same Day*

"For all is well in our little tiny town," I sing, my hands a blur as I deal out the millionth game of solitaire of the night. I stand up in my chair, sit down in my chair, hop out of my chair, do a little Snoopy dance, my hospital gowns flapping about me like wings — I've grown inordinately fond of these gowns and am wearing several at once, "for dramatic effect" — and I sing the Snoopy song, stand on my chair again, imitating Snoopy as vulture, plop down. "I never did like *Peanuts* much," I remark to the catatonic man who sits across from me, "but when I was little my parents took me to see the *Peanuts* musical, and I liked that, but I thought it was kind of ridiculous that all the kids were played by grownups." I look at the man, who is just off an unfortunate suicide attempt, and, feeling bad for him, I climb onto the table and deal him a game of solitaire too, very pleased with myself for doing so upside down. I spit tobacco juice in a little cup, this nice man having loaned me some chewing tobacco since I am not allowed to smoke. "I don't mind that stuff," I say, my lower lip full of chew. "Here," I say, climbing off the table and coming around to the back of his chair, "old chum," I say, banging him on the back, "you play like this. You pretend that all the face cards are aces, and so when you get a face card you put it *here,* and then you go through the deck looking for all the *twos* or *fours,* which you use as wild cards, and when you *do* get an ace, or a joker, we're playing with two jokers, see, then when you, like I said, *do* get an ace, you turn the face cards upside down on it and call it a *double ace,* and after that you flip the cards upward, like regular solitaire" — I am leaning over him, my hands flying over the table like a blackjack dealer's, my arms on either side of his head, and I'm stacking the deck and shuffling the deck and stacking it and shuffling, and flipping up the cards — "and you start going for a flush or a full house." I fan out my hand, the result, apparently, of the above machinations, say, "See?" and pound him on the back. "It's very grand!" I cry, and go skipping down the hall, am shushed (nicely) by the very nice night staff as I skip by, skipping backward back to the desk; "You're *very* nice," I say, "I like you *very* much," and I skip on, skip straight on till morning.

Dr. Lentz has explained to me that I'm having the good kind of mania, a euphoric mania. Everything is beautiful, simply gorgeous, I am talking a blue streak and what I'm saying is nearly incomprehensible, seeing as I'm dashing through a thicket of random thoughts so quickly no one can follow (it's called flight of ideas). I am grandiose, delusional, I'm flinging my body about; I am, to the casual observer, clearly possessed.

It would seem I'm a textbook case. Every symptom of mania I could have, I have, in force: the extreme, minute-to-minute mood swings, rapid speech, the grandiosity, the impulsivity, the delusions, the feeling of complete invincibility, and the absolute conviction that certain untrue things are true. I can hear my thoughts zipping and whistling through my head, and see them snap and sizzle in streaking red lines on a complex grid that was designed by God and given to me personally; I am a millionaire high-society lady and should be treated with the utmost respect due to my superior station; my car can fly. These and various other ideas flash through my head, passing as quickly as they arrive. What causes them? I'm guilty of every precipitating factor you can think of — no sleep, gallons of booze, not enough effort to stick with my medication, a complete inability to grasp the seriousness of my diagnosis — and, it turns out, I have a disorder that has gone untreated for too long. But from my perspective, a manic break is a fine, fine thing, and I can't for the life of me imagine why everyone is so upset.

The staff of this hospital, at least, is experienced and trained (and did I mention that I like them very much?), so my batshit state is nothing new to them. I'm on Unit 47, where they put patients who aren't capable of being responsible for themselves — the suicidal, the very manic or profoundly depressed, the schizophrenic during a severe episode of delusion, and the variously psychotic. They dose me with a powerful antipsychotic, probably Zyprexa. It's a stopgap to get me down off the ceiling while, over the next few days, Dr. Lentz works on figuring out what kinds of meds and how much of them I'll need long term. I don't mind taking it, not at all — these people are lovely, absolutely lovely, and so nice! I'll do whatever they say.

Dr. Lentz makes his rounds in the morning. He sits on a chair in the center of the room and I sit on the edge of the bed, bouncing up and down. I come in and out of the conversation. I stop bouncing and fall back on my bed. I sit up again. I fall back, sit up, and keep finding him still there, sitting on his chair. I leap to my feet and start striding in purposeful circles around him, studying him from all angles, walking in and out of the stream of light coming through the window.

And still, here sits Dr. Lentz. Amazing. He has not moved. He is a compact, square sort of man, and his pants are hemmed too short and show his socks when he crosses his legs, and his hair is gray and dense like a thick-haired poodle's shorn short, and he wears dated glasses and has an almost beatific look of kindness on his face. He is completely calm as I whip around the room in a frenzy, babbling, questioning, wanting to know what the hell is going on. Elated as I am, I am also mightily disoriented, and Lentz's calm manner — *Marya, it really is going to be all right. Would you like to sit down? No? Well, perhaps you could hold still for a moment while we talk. That's better. Now, I know the mania is lots of fun, but here you are in the hospital, and you don't care for that. So perhaps you should try taking your medication all the time? Just to see how it works? Here's what I'm going to give you* — is comforting, and gives me some sort of compass with which to navigate the truly weird waters I'm in.

I do understand that I am locked in, but I am feeling particularly magnanimous about it. Maybe I'll stay. Every time I can get myself to hold still, as I am practically levitating, I again tell everyone — Lentz, the staff, the other patients, all my visitors — how very much I like them, and how much I appreciate their concern, and that I am sure we will get this whole thing sorted out soon. Then I expound on my theories, of which I have not a few, and they are elaborate, extremely logical theories evidencing the sheer scope and connectivity of my thoughts, which, I explain, exist as a complex web in my head, in 3-D, that turns on an axis, thus showing more clearly the precise connections between, and activity of, my thoughts.

Psych wards these days are a far cry from *One Flew Over the Cuckoo's Nest*. The staff has assured me that there will be no lobotomies. They don't seem to mind me; they explain everything, no matter how many times I ask, and forget, and ask again. They make every effort to treat people as if they are completely sane. You are sane until proven crazy. And when you are proven crazy, they know you'll come around again.

The outside world — "real" people — might treat me as if I'm a lost cause, hopeless, but the staff treats me as if I'm still human, still conscious, and that makes an enormous difference. I'm not completely removed from the world that you and I agree is real. My perspective is off, certainly, but I'm not totally gone. I'm not off the planet. I know what the world would think if they came onto the unit, what they would think if they saw me. The staff simply refuses to make those sorts of judgments.

Eventually I slow down to a frantic, cheerful agitation, in which state I spend several days — no sleep, extreme motor activity, rapid, continuous speech, but no hallucinations or delusions. I am no longer a millionaire, and I have no private jet; regrettable, but so it goes. Now, instead, I'm terrified, my chest churning with unspecified, wretched fears. Any thought that whips through my somewhat slowed but still speeding mind is cause for panic. I race up and down the hall trying to outrun the terrors, reciting under my breath, *It will all be all right, I will be all right, it won't all fall apart* — I pop out of my room twenty times a night, come padding down the hall in my hospital footies, hopping up and down with my latest question for the staff — What if my husband keeps me here? What if I stay in here so long I can't go on book tour? What if the doctor doesn't like me, what if he can't help me, what if morning never comes?

*Marya, sit down. Well, all right. I'm going to give you something for the anxiety. It should help. No, it won't turn you into a zombie. It'll just take the edge off. It's called Klonopin.*

THE SUNLIGHT STREAMS through the window in my room in a single ray. Dr. Lentz's face is half hidden by shadow, and periodically I forget who he is.

*Marya, I need you to hold still and listen to me.* He puts both laced-loafer-shod feet on the floor and leans forward. *You need to start taking this seriously. From what you've told me, you're not doing the first thing to manage your mental illness. That's going to get you in trouble. Look around you. This is what you can expect to see, more and more often, if you don't work with me to treat it.*

I leap out of my chair, irritated, agitated, dimly aware that what he's saying is important but not wanting to hear it. I fold my hands behind my back and start loping in circles around the room. Dr. Lentz is in the center and his head swings around to follow me as I go.

He clarifies my diagnosis — the manic break changed it from bipolar II to bipolar I, and he adds the term *rapid cycle. The way you cycle up and down all day, and the way the moods come close together? That's what rapid cycle means.*

He watches me lie face-down on the bed.

*I honestly can't believe you weren't diagnosed sooner. That's one of the reasons your illness has gotten as bad as it is. But that's just the way it is. You're really going to have to work with me. You need to completely change the way you're living. You need to stay on your meds. It's going to take a while for us to get the right combination, and you need to do your part to control this.*

Like what? Do what?

*Don't drink, for starters. It will just neutralize the positive effects of the meds, and with the specific meds you're on, it can cause serious liver damage, seizures, and some other very unpleasant side effects. Sleep. Every night, seven to eight hours. Stay away from caffeine. Avoid situations that make you agitated. Marya, there's a lot you can do to make this better for yourself. You need to educate yourself about the illness and what you can do.*

I leap off the bed and gallop around the room. I may be nuts, but I can take this in. Holy shit. If I go by his definition, if the symptoms he's talking about mean I'm having an episode, then how long have I been having them? I think of the suicide attempt three years ago. It must have been going on for at least that long. Does that mean that everything that's happened since then wasn't, somehow, real? Is my entire life going to be defined by being crazy?

*No, no, Marya. Not at all. You're a writer, right? All the things you've written in that time, they're real. And the people in your life are real, and your memories are real. It's all real. It's just that it was all probably a little painful. Wasn't it? A little hard to get through the day?*

I press my head with my fists, as it seems the thing to do if I am not going to cry. Far away, out in the hall, I can hear people shouting and talking, the calm voices of the staff saying, *Maybe you could get dressed? How about you come into the day room and eat some breakfast? Come back here! Harry, you need to come with me. Sue, slow down, please. Stop shouting. It doesn't help the rest of the patients,* and I hear the rapid chatter of some patients, and the slow, slurred speech of others. The voices come near my door, a body flashes or shuffles past, and then the voices fade away. I see the sound in waves, and put my hand out before me, tracing the waves in the air.

*So the point is that now we can treat it, and make it a little less hard.*

Always? Will it always be less hard, then? Will I stop acting crazy for good?

He smiles gently at me. *No.*

Then what?

*Things will still be hard. You've had this a long time. It probably won't ever be easy. But we can make it livable.*

Livable? I think. That's it?

But I have to admit, livable is better than nothing. Depending on what it entails.

Dr. Lentz tells me that once I've had a major manic break, I'm likely to have one again, and the more I have, the more I will have. He tells me the bipolar has already progressed quite a ways. *No, it's not going to go away. No, there's no cure. Yes, you'll always have to take the meds. Yes, always. Yes.*

Now I am crying. What will happen to me? I ask.

He raises his eyebrows and shrugs. *That depends,* he says. *It's up to you. You can treat the illness, and you can arrest the progression, and your outcome will be better. It's possible, though unlikely, that you'll never have another complete break. You'll have fewer of them, though, if you are vigilant with your medication, and if you start living in a much healthier manner than you are right now — you've got to stop trying to do everything, you've got to learn how to rest. You've got to get some balance in your life.*

I roll my eyes. Balance. They've been telling me that for years. It doesn't mean anything, and even if it did, I'm not capable of it.

*That may be true.*

I look sharply at him. Well, what if I'm not? What if I can't balance?

*Then you'll get sicker.* He closes my file and stands up. *I think it could be more a matter of you don't want to balance,* he says.

Wait — so what you're saying is that I could go crazy for good.

*Not likely, with treatment.*

Does the treatment always work?

*Not always. Usually.*

So you can't promise me I won't go crazy and wind up on the street. (This has always been my greatest fear, that I will become a muttering bag lady, talking to the voices in my head, people staring at the ground as they pass me, avoiding my eyes.)

*I can't promise you anything. Although I think that's very unlikely.* He looks at me. *It really is up to you.*

Okay! Okay okay okay, I yell. I flap my arms around and climb up on my bed. I stand here in my many gowns, mind spinning with information I can barely grasp but that makes me extremely afraid. Dr. Lentz smiles at me and tells me he'll be back tomorrow. I leap up and crash back on the hospital bed.

Upside down, I watch the clouds scud across a blue, blue sky. Lentz is gone. Well, never mind all that. It's not really so bad. I just take my meds, and I'm cured.

I lie on my back, still for a moment. I am at peace.

*

NOW, THIS IS the part of the book where I emerge from the hospital into the July sunshine, fresh-faced, rosy-cheeked, eyes a-twinkle, and gung ho to embark on my journey, the obvious journey, the recommended journey, the acceptable journey from sickness to health, from dark to light, from inside the locked door to outside it, freedom! How dear a price we pay! Here is me, mellowed and medicated, smiling mildly, like the Madonna, with that touch of knowing sorrow in my brow, but overridden now by the hope of new life.

Here I am, striding with newfound purpose into my house, collecting the bottles off the bar, out of the wine rack, out of the tank of the toilet, out from under the bed, behind the desk, in the washing machine, the garage, the spice cabinet, the bucket of cleaning supplies under the sink — shocked, just shocked to realize how much I'd been drinking, but full of strength, the strength of the totally sensible sane, strength enough to dramatically flush all the booze down the toilet, and here I am going to bed by ten and waking up at six every day, exactly right, and I'm taking my meds in the morning and taking them at night, and I begin yoga, and kickboxing for good measure, and in the interest of balance, I become a Buddhist and meditate while perched on the silk pillow in my little temple, formerly my husband's office, and my husband is part of my support system and totally supports my hijacking of his office for the higher purpose of sanity and balance, and I decorate the room with all sorts of meaningful little knickknacks, Buddhas and the like, knickknacks not purchased, oh no, in any kind of manic spending spree.

Well, no. That's not exactly what happened. Just kidding. Really, it embarrasses and frankly baffles me to write this, but the next part of the book is where I'm at my house, knocking back my meds with a beer. I'm working twenty-four hours a day. I'm having parties, going to parties, staying up all night. I'm acting exactly as I did before.

You may be asking at this point, Why? Or more to the point,

What the fuck is wrong with you? Are you completely dense? Are you — ha ha! — insane?

Ladies and gentlemen, yes I am.


# Tour
*January 1998*

I'm standing in front of a crowd of people in New York the first time it happens: I'm on book tour, giving a reading from my book *Wasted,* and suddenly I come to, as if I've been away, and I don't know how I got here. I'm terrified, and I hear myself talking, and then people clap and praise my book, which I have apparently been reading from, and then they take me to a hotel and I stand in the middle of the hotel room, paralyzed and confused. Where am I? Where am I going tomorrow? What if I fuck up? What if I make a fool of myself? What if I just go crazy and start to scream? That's what scares me, because I feel as if I'm just about to do it, every minute of the day. I sit in television studios, in radio studios, the crazies welling up in my chest. I sit in coffee shops with reporters and recite the correct answers (What are the correct answers?), still feeling it. And then, at night, the switch trips and I am *on,* in front of a crowd, *questions, more questions! Bring it on! I'm on top of the world!* My speech comes out in rapid fire, I fling my hands around in sweeping gestures, my brain races along at the speed of light, and I love it, the heat, the crowds, the way I get so fucking high each night I think I'll never come down.

At first, it's just mania, which isn't so bad when you're on book tour. You're flying from one interview to the next, guzzling coffee, off to a reading, to a dinner, back to the hotel for a few hours of sleep, and up early to get on a plane to go do it again. I keep going as fast as I can. Day after day, I have endless energy. I'm always cheerful, never get tired, never need a break, will take any number of interviews; the publicists who drive me around are amazed. And, okay, I'm a little nuts, and they laugh at my constant stream of chatter, my loud laugh, my wildly gesturing arms. But no one mentions it because I'm a writer, and everybody knows writers are crazy (or maybe she's on cocaine?).

Might as well be. I hardly sleep. That in itself is enough. But I've forgotten everything Lentz told me about sleep, and everything else — the bipolar body clock is readily startled, he told me over and over, trying to get it through my head that I can't just go careening around all night. He warned me that the tenuous balance that exists in my brain is easily set off kilter, but like everything else he said, that has slipped my mind. I've thrown myself into the insane schedule of book tour, possessed with the need to do it perfectly, I have to do it *right*, what if I fail? I can't say no, I can't slow down, I have to keep going or they'll find out I'm a little kid in grownup's clothes and a fraud. The lack of sleep is one thing, and the airplane rides and time changes another, the erratic, unpredictable daily schedule, the back-to-back events and interviews, the poor nutrition, the continuous state of heightened awareness, the fact that I'm drunk almost around the clock — if Lentz were here, he'd tell me yet again: there's no way my system can maintain the homeostasis it requires to keep my chemistry on course. My brain becomes highly "brittle," thinks it's in a fight-or-flight situation. It's primed for collapse.

I fly back to Minneapolis for a weekend break from the tour. I get in around midnight and collapse into bed. I have forty-eight hours to get some sleep into my bone-tired body. But it's in these forty-eight hours, by some freak chance, that the worst that could happen does.

At five o'clock in the morning, the phone rings. It's just getting light. I pick it up.

My beloved cousin Brian is calling. I knew this phone call would come one day. His muscular dystrophy has been slowly killing him since the day he was born. The last two years in Minneapolis, I've been able to talk to him at all hours, see him nearly every day, have dinner, go to movies, spend time with all our friends as often as I wanted; and as close as we've been since we were little kids, now he's the most important thing in my life. I made myself forget he was sick. I knew, but I ignored it. I knew in the back of my mind I would lose him. I just didn't think I'd lose him so soon. Not yet. Not today.

We rush him to the hospital. His mother, father, and sister are there, and so are my mother and father. We race after the nurse who has cared for him when he's been hospitalized these past few months, who runs toward ICU, pushing Brian's gurney, Brian is howling in pain as his vital organs shut down, the nurse is crying and saying, *I promised him this would never happen,* and we finally reach the room and the nurse turns up the morphine and Brian's wails slow and then stop. He dies at 8:23 A.M.

His mother cries, *My child, my child.*

I turn into Julian's chest and slide down him to the floor.

I delay tour for a few more days to stay with my family and our friends for the memorial. We planned the service this winter while Brian was in the hospital. He made us swear they wouldn't play "On Eagle's Wings." He made his mother promise there would be no Jesus. There were to be two eulogies: he ordered our old friend Chris to make everyone laugh, and me to make everyone cry. He gave us his credit card and told us to go out after the wake and blow his entire credit line on a party at a bar, since he wasn't going to have to pay anyway. He made me promise to wear a red dress. Furious, I wear a red dress.

The night of his memorial, we drink ourselves half to death at Benchwarmer Bob's, laughing and crying and telling stories until last call. Julian drives and I stare out the window at the freeway lights and passing cars as we head for home, feeling like my guts have been ripped out.

I shut down. The next day I get on a plane bound for London

to do what I'm supposed to, show up for the still-long list of radio, TV, and newspaper interviews, the panels and dinners and readings, another month on the road while it's taking everything I have not to scream. Shock. Grief. Jet lag. The booze I inhale on the plane. The pot of black tea I drink when I arrive. Enough to make anyone crazy. And more than enough for me.

I am triumphant. I have arrived. I am torn apart with grief. Brian is dead. BBC London loves me. The book critic loves me. I hold court at a publication party, pouring wine down my gullet like a pelican, the table littered with bottles, everyone laughs.

Then it hits me: they're laughing at me. They've found me out. They see what I actually am.

You can almost hear it: a little tiny *snap*. Here's my tiny scream as I go down.

I AM SITTING at a table in a hotel bar in London, wrapped in a black wool thing. I am watching my hand, in fascination, as it lies on the table and trembles like a paper napkin in the breeze. My hand absorbs me completely. The bar is enormous, then tiny. I am sitting in a brass-tacked, leather-upholstered chair. I myself am enormous, like Alice, my legs and arms everywhere. But then I am minute, tucked back into the corner of the overstuffed, regal, genteel chair. They are watching me. Especially the barmaid — she hates me. She speaks to me only in French. My ashtray is the size of Montana. My cigarette burns in it slowly. The sound of the paper spitting as the red cherry creeps down the cigarette is deafening. I look around the room. The barmaid turns her head away in a haughty gesture. I note that things have taken on a particularly tactile, vivid, saturated look. The leather chairs are oxblood. They are very, very fine. There is a businessman in the bar, leaning back in his chair, smoking his cigar and reading the London *Times*. I panic. I remember there is an article about me in today's *Times*. I shrink in my chair. I know he will see it, see my picture, and he will swing his head in slow motion toward me and fix me with his beady, foxlike stare. *"I don't care," says Pierre,* I chant in my head. *But I will let you fold the folding chair! "I don't care!" says Pierre.* I will show that man I don't care. I am Pierre!

A desperate situation has arisen: I am out of wine. There is nothing left for me in this world. I look pleadingly at the bar, behind which the French barmaid stands, ignoring me as if she were an elegant cat. Two men enter the bar. Shit! More knees to navigate in my path to the bar. Everyone's shirt pleases me: they are all superbly ironed and have excellent cuffs. Eventually I manage to stand. I take deep, calming breaths. I take my wineglass and tiptoe up to the bar and point to the bottle of burgundy I like. In mortal shame, I lower my head as the barmaid pours me a glass. I want to tell her I am sorry I don't speak French. I feel horrible about it. She puts the bottle back and I crawl away like the bug that I am. I crawl up the leg of my chair, carefully balancing my fine crystal wineglass in my hand. I crawl across the seat. I crawl up the arm of the chair and sit perched there. I am a millipede. Elegantly, fooling everyone, I cross my million legs and sip my wine.

I am outside and lost. I hunch over, pulling my black wings over my shoulders. I stay close to the buildings. I duck around corners, searching. There is a crepe stand around here somewhere, and I shall find it. I put my head in my hands and lean my back against a stone wall. I note the puddles running off into the gutter. I take a deep breath and *carry on, old chap, buck up, old chum, tallyho, sally forth,* and I continue skulking through the narrow alleyways of London. There is one safe place; that place is the crepe stand. There they do not humiliate me as they do in the other places.

I am in a square. There are people all around, and thousands of pigeons. Mary Poppins! *"Feed the birds, tuppence a bag! Tuppence, TUPPENCE, TUPPENCE A BAG!"* I may have shouted it aloud. I have been walking through the square for years, never getting closer to the other side. Perhaps it is Trafalgar? Where is Trafalgar? *Where is my bloody crepe stand?* Where they give me a ham and cheese crepe and don't ask any questions and leave me to huddle into my plate, keeping an eye out for the watchers? My mother went to London once, and brought me the Mary Poppins hat when she returned. There is a picture of me holding an umbrella and wearing a fine little blue wool suit and my Mary Poppins hat. I am grinning my horrible grin. I hate the child. She is hideous. Her blue wool suit fit poorly. See someone about it.

Trafalgar becomes Knightsbridge, *Excuse me, where am I?* I remain very polite so nobody knows. Occasionally I stop in a bar to refuel. The wine in London is highly satisfactory. If they knew who I was, they'd hasten to help me. But I dare not disclose myself. I cover my mouth with my hand, and demur. Piccadilly Circus, Mayfair, Harrods! Heavenly Harrods! The excellent people, the fine, fine people there! I make many purchases. I trot through London, hailing cabs, carrying my packages, *Where to, Miss?* Take me to the theater! No, *take me to my hotel,* and I recite the name and street number, which I have written down on the back of the business card of a literary critic with whom I recently had dinner, and behaved spectacularly well, and got hilariously bombed. I mutter my way up the stairs of my little hotel, my black thing over my head.

I am on the phone to my agent, sobbing, pacing, *I'm lost, I'm lost, I can't find the crepe stand, what am I going to do? I can't go out like this*—I have fleeting moments of clarity during which I realize I am not doing well, and moments of abject terror as I pace around the hotel room, crying my head off.

Then the escort comes and drives me off to the BBC for radio interviews. I comport myself appropriately. I sit in my little sound studio wearing headphones, being interviewed by BBC London, BBC Leeds, Belfast, Dublin, Manchester, Edinburgh, Wales. Their accents are fascinating and I can't understand them at first but then I catch on and have to restrain myself from taking on the accent, which I like very much.

I am running down a rainy street in one shoe. I dash into a shoe store, shouting, *U.S. size six! Black heels! I'm about to be late for BBC TV!* Which, absurdly, is true — it's just come to me, and I am running around trying to find my hotel, where the escort will be waiting to take me to the studio — the girls in the shoe shop are incredibly helpful, and hurry to find me the very black shoe — they urge me to take both, though I say I need only one — I arrive, somehow, at the hotel, and the escort, looking alarmed, steers me to my room, *No, you must have a* dry *suit*, and, agreeably, I defer to her wisdom. But how on earth did I get wet?

Suddenly, Julian is here, and we are lost on a sunny residential street in some city or another, and it's very spring-like and sunny out, and I am in a rage, and I am kicking a garbage can and howling, when *out of the blue with no warning*, there is my friend Jo! At the end of the street! What is she doing here? Has she been sent to collect me? (She has.) She looks as if she is moving quickly but the air has obviously become liquid, impeding her progress. She arrives. I fall against her chest, sobbing with relief. Her sweater is pink and very soft. Her earrings brush the top of my head. She is real. I am saved.


# Hypomania
*July 1998*


It was a mixed episode, Lentz tells me when I come down from the rafters around April. Brian's gone, and after pushing it away for all of tour, it hits me in the gut when I get home. I pace the halls at night, doubled over myself with grief. My parents have finally split up, after twenty-five years. My own marriage, well — Julian and I alternate between screaming at each other and ignoring each other completely. Suddenly I'm not just his crazy wife. I'm his wife with one book out and a novel in the works. More than ever, I am everything that is wrong with his life. I am the reason he can't hold a job, I am the reason he's not in school. I'm never home, I just left him and went tooling around the globe. His resentment poisons the air.

I try to make it work. I'm attached to him. And I said I was going to be married, and so, goddammit, I'm going to be. I don't want everyone else to have been *right*. But eventually, in May, Julian slams out of the apartment. When he comes back, I'm in my robe, sitting on the couch in the dark, having a drink. I offer him one. He sits down in his armchair, twirling the ice in his glass. We have a remarkably civil midnight conversation, and a few days later, he moves out.

It's obvious. This whole business of marriage — what was I thinking? I'm not suited for marriage! It's too *slow*, too *settled*, too *sedate* for someone like me! I'm a girl of the world! I've got places to go, things to do, people to see! And why not? Apparently people like my book. It still hasn't really registered with me that the past months spent talking day after day to strangers about something as raw and frightening as a life-threatening eating disorder has left me a little shaken, a little unstable, and desperate to forget the whole thing. So I'm flush with money from its publication and the sale of a novel. I'm the successful single girl, not a care in the world, I'm Mary Tyler Moore, tossing my hat in the air. It's summer, and I'm on a roll.

Here's how you make absolutely sure that you'll keep getting crazier by the day:

- Ignore everything your psychiatrist tells you. Disregard all his warnings about the way you're living your life — in fact, do absolutely everything he tells you not to.
- Don't always take your pills. They're a hassle, and what if they make you dull? You don't need them. And if you're going to take the pills, take them with a glass of wine. It will make the mood swings even more exciting.

- Don't sleep; you've got to make sure your body clock is as fucked up as possible. The less you sleep, the more manic you'll get, until soon you'll go completely over the edge.
- Drink caffeine. Tons of it. Take your morning pills with coffee. It can't hurt.
- Work around the clock — it's important to put yourself under as much stress as possible.
- Eating normally would stabilize your blood sugar, so don't do that; it's better to keep your body in as unstable a state as you possibly can for maximum results.
- And, above all else, drink like a fish.

Me, I drink up all the liquor in the world, all the booze in several men's liquor cabinets, all the wine in my own collection and then all the wine in the collection I buy to replace the first one, all the wine and martinis in the bars in the city. Anything I can get my hands on. There is never enough.

I am absolutely convinced that the booze helps me control my moods. It raises the volume and heightens the colors and fills me with a sense of happiness when I want to come up, and when I need to come down at the end of the night, it blunts my thoughts, my perception of the shrieking world around me, and lets me black out, or sleep, whichever comes first. I have worked out an elaborate system of just how much to drink, at exactly what time, to keep my mood humming along at the perfect high. It doesn't cross my mind that the booze itself is one of the reasons the highs and lows are so extreme.

I wake up in the morning, running through the day in my head — the work, the cleaning, the laundry, the party tonight. I fling the covers off and make the bed with absurd precision, hospital corners, get it right, get ready, pour myself a liter or so of coffee, land in front of my desk, and start tapping away without so much as a thought about what I'm going to write. I go for a few hours, then run off to throw in the laundry, hop up for more coffee, write a million e-mails, call my agent for no particular reason and babble for a while. I get a flash of inspiration and grab one of the dozen or so yellow notepads that litter my office to scribble down my ideas for the next several books, and back to the laundry, in with the whites, then back to the desk — I flip madly through books, looking up obscure facts that are suddenly absolutely crucial to the making of my point, the central point, the one that clinches everything, drop the books in a pile on the floor, scribble notes on yet another notepad, and then I need something I wrote on one of the notepads three days ago, I need it right this second, and I rip through the notepads — but wait, the laundry, and I'm flying downstairs and staggering back into the apartment under the weight of piles of every piece of fabric I can find, clean or dirty, the point is the excellent efficiency of washing and the necessity of absolute cleanliness, dump them on the living room floor, and now it's time for a glass of wine, the very thing, white wine goes perfectly with laundry, who would drink red for laundry? Twenty-six floors above the city, in this apartment that Julian has recently vacated, I stop for an instant to soak in the gold late-morning light streaming through the windows. Then I haul out the ironing board and iron everything, the socks, the sheets, I pull down the curtains and iron them too, and since I'm on a roll, I get down on the floor and iron the carpet, *Oh, Marya, stop being weird,* I chastise myself, and then I fold everything with perfect sharp creases, creases that would do my grandmother proud, wait! I am inspired! And I dash back into my office and whip off another few pages, an excellent day, two chapters, I go out to the kitchen and pour another glass of wine, toss it back, grab my purse, and zip out into the sunny summer afternoon.

The days tumble over one another, each full of obsessive shopping for my perfect apartment, for the perfect dinner parties, perfect evenings out with friends, each day turning my head toward man after man so quickly I can hardly keep their names straight. The nights are all the same, a party or a date. They end with me getting out of bed and putting on my clothes, *You're leaving?* Or they end with me getting out of bed, putting on my robe, and telling them to leave, *Do I have to?* Or they end with me fumbling with the key in the lock and letting myself into my apartment, kicking my shoes off on my weaving way down the hall.

The doctors call it *hypersexuality*. It's one of several typical goal-seeking behaviors that are common in mania, all of which involve rabid energy and a total loss of impulse control — this game I'm playing involves risky one-night stands, a compulsion to seduce, but no real interest in the sex itself. The sex isn't the point. The point is to shut off the maelstrom in my head.

Someone catches my eye: my mind empties out of everything but the need to get him. My heart thumps, and there's a dull, mute pounding in my skull. Sound fades, and I am only aware of my single-minded mission — I must catch him, I must win. It's a rush, a pure, clean high, uncomplicated by thoughts. A few words, a few glances, a brush of the back of the hand, and he's mine. I am no longer anxious, no longer fearful, finally neither low nor high. I find myself in unknown beds or my own, staring at the ceiling, drumming my fingers on their backs. I feel the weight of their bodies, crushing me, pinning me down. They are solid, real. I am an object, useful but hollow. The absence of thought fills me up.

And then the game is over. I've won, and I want them to take their sticky, heavy bodies and go home.

I litter the city with unsuspecting, nice guys, drawn in by the same things every man has ever been drawn in by — the over-the-top everything, the whirlwind that my hypomania creates. They call me "passionate." Only certain men are interested in women like this, and somehow I find them all this summer, and eat them for a snack. It's endlessly entertaining, when it isn't boring as hell.

# Jeremy
*Later That Summer*

It's night. I'm in San Francisco visiting a friend. We're in a bar, for a big change. There's a crowd.

*Nice to meet you,* he says, and extends his hand. He holds mine a little too long.

*Likewise,* I say. I am suspicious. So far he is sharky. All he needs is a gold chain. I dislike his goatee. He looks like the devil.

*You're Marya,* he says. He looks at me intensely, as if he means to communicate some important bit of information that I urgently need to know. The bit of information is that he is a player, and that he wants to play. The bit of information is the bait.

I always bite.

*As far as I know,* I say.

*I've read your work,* he says. (My *work?* I think, raising an eyebrow. He means *Wasted. Work* seems a little grand.)

*Really,* I say, and look away. I glance around the bar, through the haze of bluish smoke. We are very young and very hip. We are arrogant beyond belief. We never stop performing. Someone climbs up on the table and does an impression of someone we don't like. We live to be liked. We will absolutely die if we aren't adored.

*I love it,* he says.

*What?* I lean forward to hear him.

*I love your work,* he shouts.

Ladies and gentlemen, there they are! The magic words!

*Oh,* I say, and wave my hand.

*No, really,* he says. *I've been reading up. You're amazing.*

Folks, can you believe it! Bonus points! He said it! *Amazing!* My head grows to the size of a watermelon, making it difficult to hold up.

Next, we are standing in the living room, separated by a coffee table, screaming at each other, *Fuck you! No, fuck you!* Someone overturns the coffee table. Something breakable is thrown, and, predictably, breaks. He punches the wall, his face the color of a tomato. I collapse on the floor and thrash my arms and legs.

No, wait! Not yet. Sorry about that. I skipped a part.

*Can I call you?* The crowd is thinning out. Only the die-hards and the drunks remain. It's two or three or four A.M. Everyone staggers out onto the street, heading for one-night stands or empty beds.

*Depends,* I say, picking up my purse.

*On what?* he asks, smiling his sharky smile.

*If you can find my phone number,* I say, and smile, and go.

I win this round.

Now, the trick is to get rid of him before he finds out what a fucking freak I am.

Because, of course, I'm mad, and he doesn't know it yet. I haven't gone crazy right there in front of him. The crucial moment hasn't come — the moment when he's standing in the middle of the room, his arms dangling at his sides, staring at me in disbelief, unsure what happened and when it will happen again. And he hasn't said it yet: *You crazy bitch. You crazy fucking bitch.*

But he will. They always do.

His name is Jeremy. He lives in California, getting rich on the tech boom. He is alarmingly beautiful — bronzed skin, light brown hair, liquid brown eyes the size of saucers — the women of his family tssk, *Those lashes are wasted on a man.* He's the original pretty boy, gorgeous and knows it and flaunts it shamelessly, and he's smart enough and funny enough, and he'll do in a pinch. It's the nineties, and I am all of twenty-four. Everyone in San Francisco has too much money and too many credit cards and is drinking too much booze. There's quite the little scene. And so Jeremy and I hit it right off.

In a hypomanic leap, we fly off to New York, whirl through it, have sex continuously and drink up every bar in the city and go to parties and clubs and generally do what you'd expect two very young, very arrogant, pretty little kids to do. We decide, a day or two in, that we're in love. We destroy the hotel room. We make a lot of ridiculous promises and grand statements and a hell of a mess.

A week later, I'm back in San Francisco, moving into an apartment on Nob Hill.

It's taken me exactly two months to leave my husband, find a new playmate, and move across the country to my brand-new life.

IT'S A CARNIVAL, California in these years. The neon lights that blur in the rain and seem to smear across the sky; the open doors of bars spewing out laughing, shouting people and sucking more of them back in; the thundering, pounding bass in the clubs that seems to shake the street outside. And the parties, and the darling little restaurants, and the spectacular lofts, with their to-die-for views of the city and the bay, and the gorgeous clothes, the witty dinner guests, the third man, the hipsters, the scene, the endless, ever-present players playing their incessant little games, the stakes as high as a fortune to be made or lost overnight, or as small as getting the haughtiest woman in the room into bed or just getting the man of the hour's card, *Call me sometime,* and the academics with their scruffy beards and their incestuous fucking and fighting, and the poets and the writers, and the suicidal musicians, and Starbucks and eyeglasses so ugly they're fabulous, and the knighting of nerds, and the ever-shrinking cell phones, and the endless strings of degrees, *Harvard? Berkeley? Yale?,* and the money — good God, the money, rents skyrocketing, people paying their rent in stock options, IPO parties every night, twenty-two-year-olds driving around in identical black BMW convertibles, and the coup de grâce, the stunning success, the hot new kid, the spidery bodies, the buffed-up shoulders straining at too-tight black T-shirts, worn with fabulously ironic pants, and the terribly cool clunky square-toed shoes, and the fat wads of cash, the sterling silver money clips, the limitless credit cards, and the weekend trips up to wine country, in the convertible, with the gang, and the wine tastings, and the wine collecting, and the art scene, and the hot new artist, and his lover, and their debacle, and the spectacle, and the debauch, and the grabbing at more, more of anything, everything, *give it to us, we want it, all of it, where is my server, my dish is cold, drop by for drinks, we'll lunch, call me, she said she'd call me, he'll call me, shoot me an e-mail, I'll shoot you an e-mail, hey, good to meet you,* glad-handing, kissing the trembling air near the eye, *let's go down to the club, crowd in, scoot over, this is so-and-so, we should play squash,* murmur to the waiter, *Bring a round,* slip him a hundred, and now the gang's all here, and we are going to do what we do, which is dance, and drink, and devour one another whole.

It's the tech boom. San Francisco has done a weird wrenching metamorphosis over the past thirty years — that bohemian, tie-dyed, free-love, flower-in-the-barrel-of-a-gun era is finished, now the province of the leftover hippies and the kids who are searching for a cause with their beat-up guitars in hand, and with that era have gone the things that mattered: civil rights and feminism, which are of no concern to us — why should we care? Our rights, our educations, were handed to us on a silver platter. Women are as ruthless as men. And the men? They feel about women the way straight men have always felt about women: they want them hopelessly, they're scared to death of them, they want one to look good on the arm and make them look yet hipper, younger, richer, more successful, more on top of their game. What else is new? There are good men and bad men, as always, and good and bad women as well. The only difference is context, environment: San Francisco in the late nineties is a hothouse. Everything in it grows out of control.

Including this crazed relationship. And certainly including me.

It's a *love affair*, with all the drama and Sturm und Drang that phrase implies. It's growing wild in the heat of the San Francisco autumn, the only time of year when northern California gets sunny and hot, and it wraps itself around us, roping us together so close that it is becoming difficult to breathe. And so we live breathless, and no matter how close we get it isn't close enough. We want to share the little breath we have, pass it back and forth between our mouths. I have become inseparable from the way I feel about him. And maybe it really is love. Love's a kind of madness, isn't it?

At first it's bliss. It's drunken, heady, intoxicating. It swallows the people we were — not particularly wonderful people, but people who did our best, more or less — and spits out the monsters we are becoming.

Our friends despise us. We are an epic. Everything is grand, crashing, brilliant, blinding. It's the Golden Age of Hollywood, and we are a legend in our own minds, and no one outside can fail to see that we are headed for hell, and we won't listen, we say they don't understand, we pour more wine, go to the parties, we sparkle, fly all over the country, we're on an adventure, unstoppable, we've found each other and we race through our days like Mr. Toad in his yellow motorcar, with no idea where the brakes are and to hell with it anyway, we are on fire, drunk with something we call love.

I've long since stopped taking my meds. On my way out of Minneapolis, I swept into Dr. Lentz's office, informing him that I was off to California, that I was madly in love, that I knew absolutely I was doing the right thing, *obviously*, how could he fail to see that? *Marya, this seems a little sudden. It seems more than slightly ill-advised* — what does he know? I left with the last of my meds and no refill prescriptions, and when I ran out, I thought nothing of it, because, at last, I was *completely* sane. At last I'm living the life I was meant to live, the right man, the right town, the right friends. I'm not just surviving, I'm thriving. Never been better. I'm on my way at last. The "mental illness" I supposedly had is gone, never to be heard from again.

"DON'T MOVE," he says from across the room. I'm lying on my side on the bed, basking in the afternoon light. Through the bay window, the sun is a pure, transparent gold. The bay glitters, a saturated, impossible blue. The sheets are white, tangled and whorled and soft with sweat. Everything is still.

"Why?" I say, half opening my eyes. Through the bedroom's French doors, I see him flung in a chair, naked.

"You're perfect," he says. "You look like a cello. The dip from your chest to your waist to your hip."

His cello lies on its side in the corner, untouched. He will not touch it the entire time we are together. I am enamored of his cello. It implies everything about him that I want to believe. I hold my breath, not wanting to break the moment open and spill it all over the floor. This time I will do it right. I will not let us fail.

Time has slowly spun to a stop and hangs in the air. It is an effort to move one's limbs, turn one's head, due to the thick invisible fog of unmoving time. The lazy days bleed into one another like watercolors left out in the rain. And so I lie here on my side, heavily, pressed down by time. Stay here, says time. Don't move. If you move, time will pass, this will disappear. He will go up in smoke, leaving only the faintest shape of himself in the chair.

"How long did you want me to lie here?" I ask.

"Forever," he says, smiling his glittering, terrible smile. "Until I say."

"But I have to get ready." The sun moves across the bay window. I feel it slide across my back. "I can't very well go like this."

"Let's not go. Let's forget the whole thing. Let's get in the car and put the top down and drive up to wine country and eat at a little country inn and drink gallons of red wine. No, wait. Never mind dressing. Let's stay naked all day."

"We've *been* naked all day. We haven't left the house. We've eaten nothing but grapes. Besides, I'm tired of sex," I say, smiling.

"What? How can you be tired of it? I'll never be tired of it. I'll make love to you all day. Every day. Forever."

"Forever?"

"Forever." Suddenly he's all seriousness, all intensity. Is it real? "Marry me," he says impulsively.

I laugh and launch myself off the bed and turn my back. "I'm getting dressed," I call over my shoulder. "I'm going to dinner and out to the club." He follows me down the hall.

In our absence, the violet early evening light pours in the bay window, filling the still room like water poured into a glass. The glass is delicate. The thin, tight surface of the liquid light trembles. But it does not break. Time does not pass. Not yet.

Everything this year is amplified: the colors, the sounds, the sense that I'm caught up in something much larger than I am, something fabulous, something grand. Everything is tactile, the taste of the wine, the feel of the excellent fabric, the heel of the fabulous shoe, the thrum of the road under the wheels of the car. And it's California, where everything is powerfully strange. Everyone wants it to be home. Everyone left where he or she was from with dreams of transformation. Everyone runs away to California once, or at least all the lonely, hungry people do.

The sharp scent of eucalyptus and sea salt stings the nostrils and fills the lungs. I have to breathe deeply to soak it all in. I draw the deep breath again and again, and it is never enough. The breathing makes me dizzy. I stagger around, elated, half mad.

The place is manic. The time is manic. I fit right in.

FOR A FEW MONTHS, everything is perfect, crystalline, the heady bliss of new love rushing through every moment, every day. But then, without warning, the swings start again.

The alarm goes off. I jerk awake, heart pounding. Jeremy lies beside me, peacefully asleep. I fall back into the bed, feel myself sink like a stone, turning slowly through the water toward the bottom, where I rest, staring at the surface a long way above. The cavern that opens up in my chest is here. I fight it, distracting myself with anything, Jeremy, writing, parties, friends, and fountains of wine, but morning comes and it's back, and I lie here, the pressure of emptiness inside my chest crowding my lungs, making it difficult to breathe.

I drag myself out of bed, stand with my head against the cupboards in the kitchen, pouring coffee, trying to shake the cobwebs out of my brain. I go into my office — a glorified closet — and sit down at the desk and stare at the computer screen, dreading the day.

A few hours later, my fingers are racing over the keys, my head spinning with words, I'm elated, laughing out loud, jabbering to myself — this new life is beauty itself, it's heaven, I'm finally happy, in love, blessed, and I race through the hours, unaware of time's passage, ears ringing, alive.

Two o'clock. I feel it coming. My fingers slow, then stop. I stare at what I've written, slump in my chair. Where did it come from? Where did it go? My mind drags itself around in a circle and finally lies down. My chest empties out. I push back from my desk, go into the bedroom, crawl under the covers, and curl up in a ball, praying that Jeremy doesn't come home and catch me like this. I swear to myself that I'll be out of bed by five. But the idea of ever getting out of bed again exhausts me and I close my eyes, wanting to sleep, but sleep doesn't come. I lie there, hating myself, for hours.

My eyes snap open. I must have dozed. I throw the covers off and swing my legs out of the bed, glance at the clock — it's five! It's evening, the day is done, the night is here, it's time for a drink! I leap up, race for the shower, stand there singing, the cold water shivering me out of my fog. I leap out again, run through the house into my closet, what to wear, what to wear? I must look like

I've been up all day, productive, working, just like everybody else, and I race into the kitchen, open a bottle of wine, and start chopping things for the fabulous dinner I'll make for my fabulous boyfriend when he comes in and we begin the fabulous evening, which will never end.

But new love only lasts so long, and then you crash back into the real people you are, and from as high as we were, it's a very long fall, and we hit the ground with a thud.

The fights start. I'm getting crazier, day by day. And Jeremy? He's a small-town boy who landed in the big city, and now he's possessed by an attempt to find an identity. The game of the pretty player is suddenly not enough, seems *fake* to him, and he is consumed with the idea of the *genuine,* earnestly becomes a vegetarian, is indignant and superior about my smoking, idealizes Che Guevara for reasons that are unclear, reads books about the civil rights movement, identifying with the oppressed (he is a vice president at one of the biggest software companies in the country, and makes six figures at twenty-five), teaches himself guitar, goes to hippie jam sessions (the only one there in carefully torn Armani jeans). He can't decide whether he disdains my work — Rupert Murdoch, The Man, owns my publisher, for God's sake! — as an utter failure of moral character, or likes to shine in its light. In private, he criticizes everything I do and everything about me. In public, he shows no objection to the parties we go to, or the glad-handing, cheek-kissing, martini-drinking crowd — he's my biggest fan, brags about me, keeps a hand at the small of my back, likes the attention and the praise just fine.

He's the most amazing man I've ever met, fascinating, beautiful, glamorous, and I will do anything to keep him. I'm obsessed with him. We're in love.

He's a run-of-the-mill, insecure, pretty-boy asshole. We hate each other and want the other one dead. We fuck and fight, and dress up and go to the parties, the perfect couple, witty, laughing on cue. Then we head home, screaming at each other in the car, speeding through the city, me drunk, he horrid, and the door shuts behind us, we kick off our shoes, hop in our corners of the ring, and when the bell goes off, we fly at each other, swinging blind. We have sex constantly, when we're not fighting, and it's always fantastic, and it persuades us, every time, that it's meant to be, that we are made for each other, that if we'd just stop with those silly fights, everything would be perfect again.

And then it's perfect for a few days. He brings me flowers. I wear lacy lingerie. We stare into each other's eyes over dinner at a fancy restaurant, our love renewed.

But no matter how many times we make up, there's the fact of me and my mood swings and my drinking. Even if Jeremy were perfect, even if we weren't trying to destroy each other's lives, my mood swings would still be there. And I'd still be drinking myself to death.

The fact of the matter is that Jeremy likes my drinking. And he likes the fact that I'm crazier than hell. This pattern is now an old one with the guys I get involved with, most recently, before Jeremy, with Julian. For one thing, when it's good, life with me is a constant party. We drink all the time. He fills my glass as fast as I can empty it. I'm excited, exciting, full of ideas and energy, great to be around. And then I go too far — I drink too much, he holds me up, laughing, as I stagger, go into deep funks, and he comforts me and makes it all go away. My drinking and my crazies are my weakness. He exploits this to the hilt. It gives him something on me. When he comes home after work to find me lying in bed, *Oh, honey, are you all right?* And he strokes my hair. *Why don't you have some Klonopin. Here.* Even better, when he's not playing the savior, he's playing the saint: whenever we fight, it's my fault. I was drunk, or I was crazy, or both. He's untouchable. He screams at me until I'm a crumpled mass on the floor. I give in. He's right. I'm a fuckup. *I'm sorry,* I say. *I'll get better,* I say. And suddenly he's all care and kindness, bent over me, picking me up, rocking me in his arms. *There, there.* I cling to him, pathetic, humiliated, grateful that he's still there. I don't deserve him. He's too good.

I put my head down on the table and cry. Because it's happened again. I'm found out. I'm damaged. Fucked up. Broken. A fraud. I knew he would figure out sooner or later that I was impossible to love. And now he has, and I love him, and I'm certain he has tried, really tried, to love me back. But trying to love me is too much for any sane person to bear. I watch their backs, one by one, as they walk away.

RIGHT NOW — here in the middle of an endless breakup, close to deadline on a book that isn't half finished, soaked in booze, partying all the time, taking off on sudden cross-country trips without telling anyone where I've gone — right now is the perfect time for me to go back to college.

I never graduated during those years I was studying in Minneapolis and Washington. I was working too much, and spent too much time crazy. I'm embarrassed by my lack of a degree, and I hear about a tiny little school with a degree in poetics. Perfect. As weird and obscure as possible. And it's all about books.

If there's one thing that mania is good for, it's school.

Racing off to the funky, rundown pink building in the Mission District every morning, I'm happy as can be, clinging to this lifeboat, something that shakes me out of my creeping afternoon torpor, evens out — at least a little bit — my careening moods. I can bury myself in centuries of poetry and philosophy, I can write hundreds of papers, do research, I can pour out poetry, I can argue and debate and critique. Given the fact that I've been in college for about a hundred years, I'm taking all graduate classes, and they hire me to teach a few undergrad classes. Here, outside the terrifying San Francisco *scene,* it doesn't matter if I'm playing the player well enough. There is no *kiss kiss.* I can just be a crazy writer. And I can get caught up in the drunken, roaring, arguing, fucking, scribbling bunch of lunatics who go to this school. Out with the martinis. In with the bottle of whiskey, no glass. In with the day full of lectures, workshops, writing, the evenings spent at dive bars where we get plastered, shouting and laughing and pompously quoting at length, in with the all-night weekend parties, the tumbling conversation, the impromptu poem, the fucking in the back room, whoever's nearby, the empty bottles that litter the place, the promising writers, the next generation of poets passed out on the floor.

I love it. I love the school, the work, the way it's making my poetry better, the piles of reading I carry home every night and spend hours poring over in my closet, the pages stained with ashes and red wine. I work like mad. I spend less and less time with the old shiny scene or even my close friends. I work so hard I think I'll die. My brain physically hurts at the end of the night. It's an incredible high. This is how it should be. Once again, I have a future. The hours writing and in school let me ignore, for a little while, the lifelong feeling of failure. Because, no matter what other people might think when they look at my life, I can't see, have never been able to see, anything like success. It doesn't matter what I do, what I publish, what the critics say, what people tell me. None of it feels like mine. Nothing I've ever done feels real. It's as if books and articles have just sprouted up in my house one morning, someone else's, mistakenly bearing my name. That's one of the reasons I've gone back to college. Finally, maybe I'll believe I can really do something. I want a degree. *Then* I'll feel real.

And finally, here at this weird little school, with these people who fancy themselves mad geniuses, I'm not about to be exposed as a fuckup, a hopeless crazy freak.

*High-functioning* is a qualified term. At school, sure, I'm functioning at a very high level. *Nonfunctional* would better describe the rest of my life. By now, Jeremy has moved out, and left to my own devices, I've completely devolved. I haven't done laundry in a month — scared of the laundry room, for some reason — and the pile of laundry in the closet towers over my head. Cleaning products are scary lately, so can't clean the house. The overdue bills pile up on my desk, unopened. I am afraid of all grocery stores except one, so I skulk through that one to the deli, buy two kinds of pâté and several kinds of cheese — eating anything other than these two things is somehow complicated and intimidating — and then rush out to the parking lot, dive into my car, and drive home as fast as I can. Often enough, though, I get lost in a city that's not even fifty miles square and just not that complicated, but my mind starts racing, repeating street names in a singsong in my head, the stoplights and flashing WALK signs confuse me, one-ways confuse me, and I wind up crossing the Golden Gate Bridge and back several times before I shut the door behind myself and pour myself a drink, shaking, wild with relief. Jeremy comes over every now and then; we fuck, fight, part screaming and are broken up again. I cry, laugh my head off, race around the apartment, organize my books by color and size, reorganize them by genre, try on all the clothes in my closet and throw them on the floor, jet into my closet-office and pour out a furious poem, laugh with triumph, shred it up in despair — I drink heavily throughout — write again, whipping open the books I'm supposed to be reading and flipping through the pages until I find the *one quote,* the *perfect quote,* and, crowing with glee, e-mail it to a friend, who writes back, *Where the hell are you? Where have you been?* But I'm currently occupied by studying the grain of the wood floor on which I am lying, face-down, consumed by a fog of self-hatred. All is darkness and desolation. Drunk as a skunk, my mood swinging down fast, I stumble to bed, crawl in fully dressed, and squeeze my eyes against the parade of bloody images that fills my head until I fall asleep.

I still haven't made the connection between my drinking and the maniacal swings of my mood. I don't see the chaos around me as moods. I see it as a chaotic life that I'm simply too weak to manage well. And, for that matter, I more than welcome the highs, and the fact that the alcohol makes them even higher. And the lows, the screaming fits that morph into deep despair and back up again, the terrifying flights of fantasy, the inability to control my impulses? That's all just me being my usual fuckup self. I think the alcohol is *helping* me manage my life.

Still, I'm a little *stressed*. So when I finally decide to see a therapist, bipolar hardly crosses my mind. I want a therapist who can help me deal with all this stress and tell me how to manage it. Maybe I have *low self-esteem*. Maybe I'm not finished *working through my issues* with my parents. What I want is to become the kind of person who can pay her bills, do her laundry, clean her house, *and* go to school full-time, *and* teach, *and* do research, *and* publish, *and* write a spectacular novel, *and* have a perfect relationship, *and* be the life of the party, and, okay, maybe not drink *quite* so much, *and, and, and*. I want to be superwoman, and the fact that I'm not makes me hate myself and constantly wonder why I'm such a waste. The problem is that my life is chaotic. If there were no chaos in my life, there'd be no chaos in my head.

So I look up a psychiatrist in the phone book, and off I go.

# Therapy

1999

Another waiting room, this one in a ritzy office in a wealthy part of San Francisco — tree-lined streets of little boutiques, bistros, salons, crowded with people in excellent shoes who have nowhere better to be in the middle of the day. This psychiatrist charges a mint and doesn't take insurance. Her office is a study in expensive furniture and fabric; soothing tans and creams prevail. The first visit, she puts me back on a hefty dose of Depakote, the med

Lentz had me on in Minneapolis, and she also gives me a generous prescription for Klonopin, the tranquilizer he gave me to "take the edge off" the anxiety.

"I'm telling you I'm losing my mind. I can't take this," I say, pacing in her sunny office, tapping my nails on the walls, playing with the plants.

"What, precisely, can't you take?" She's very tall, extremely well dressed, and exceptionally poised. Her poise makes me a little insane.

"I can't take these fucking *mood swings!* It never stops! I'm all over the fucking map!" I fling myself onto the couch, then fling myself up again and pace some more, gripping my head in my hands. *"Aaaagh!"* I yell under my breath, keeping my voice down, trying to hold still. She makes me incredibly nervous, sitting there smiling her mild smile. "And I can't take the anxiety. It feels like something is wrapping around my chest and squeezing. I can't breathe. My heart's racing. My thoughts are spinning. I can't keep up with them. It's all right when I'm writing, or when I'm at school. But the minute I'm alone again, the thoughts start up. I can't *see* for all the thoughts. I'm terrified all the time."

"Are you taking your Klonopin?"

"*Yes!* It doesn't help!"

"Maybe you aren't taking enough of it."

Klonopin's a benzodiazepine, and those can be very addictive. I used to love it, when it still worked. It was like mainlining a drink, the mellow calm instantaneous and complete. Now I have to take handfuls for it to even make a dent, and the last thing I want to do is run out. If she says I'm not taking enough, by all means, bring it on.

"How much can I take?" I ask, perking up.

"Take as much as you need," she says, waving her hand. "I'll write you a prescription for more."

"But it doesn't seem to matter how much I take," I groan. "It wears off too fast. As soon as it wears off, the thoughts start up again and I get all panicky." I want something that will knock me flat and keep me there until the world goes away.

"More should help. Just take it whenever you feel the anxiety coming on. And it's important that you don't forget to take it. If you miss a dose, you could go into withdrawal. It acts on the same neuroreceptors as alcohol," she says.

"So I might as well just have a drink," I say, finding this a little odd.

"It won't be as strong," she says. "Take the Klonopin."

"Speaking of drinking." I sigh and fall back on the couch. "I went to an AA meeting the other night."

"Why?"

"My friends talked me into it. They keep telling me I'm an alcoholic." I click my nails against my teeth. "Obviously I'm not an alcoholic," I say, rolling my eyes. "But I'm drinking an awful lot." Not that I want to stop. I have, however, begun to notice the vast difference between the way I drink and the way everyone else drinks. And everyone else in my life drinks quite a lot.

"I don't think you have a problem." She dismisses this with a sniff.

"I got alcohol poisoning again the other night," I say. "I was still drunk when I showed up to give a lecture. And I still wasn't sober when I got to the AA meeting."

"So you had a little too much to drink. It happens. How much did you drink?"

"There were four bottles of wine in the trash the next day. And I'd already been drinking before I started in on the wine."

"Well, you don't *always* drink that way," she says.

"Yes I do."

"Really, how often do you drink?" she says.

"Every day."

"Lots of people have a drink every evening."

"That's true," I say, reassured. "So you don't think I have a problem?"

"I think that's a little melodramatic," she says, raising an eyebrow at me. "Listen, I wouldn't work with you if I thought you had a drinking problem."

"Well, *that's* good," I say. "I knew my friends were just overreacting."

"So what else is going on?" she asks.

"School is great. Everyone is completely brilliant. The classes are brilliant. The professors are brilliant. I'm sleeping with my professor. He's brilliant."

"You're sleeping with him?"

"Jeremy and I broke up. I can sleep with whoever I want."

"Who else are you sleeping with?"

"Oh, a few people here and there. No one in particular."

"These are one-night stands?"

"No," I huff, "I wouldn't call them that." I am dropping into beds left and right. I'm juggling half a dozen sometime-lovers and it's not enough. Periodically, I dismiss the entire cast of characters and start looking anew.

"Well, it sounds like things are going really well," she says, looking at her watch.

"They're not." I suddenly feel very small. I gaze at the expensive cream-colored carpet. "I can't deal with it," I nearly whisper. "It's too much. It's going too fast."

"What is? What do you mean?" She sighs. She has that here-we-go-again tone.

"Everything. I don't know what I mean." I stare out the window. The air conditioner hums. She sits with her long legs crossed, not getting it at all. I don't know how to make her get it. I don't know what I want her to get. For all her obliviousness, the fact is that I'm not telling her everything. I allude to the chaos, mention the drinking, say I'm scared, but I still make light of these things.

"It's just kind of a nightmare," I say. "My life is a nightmare. The affairs are a nightmare. The stress is a nightmare. The book is late. I'm turning into a monster. I don't care about anything. I feel like I'm going to explode. It never lets up. I feel like I'm choking on it." I look helplessly at her. She gazes calmly at me.

"Are you taking your Depakote?" she asks.

"Yes," I say. "I'm not sure it's helping too much." A psychiatrist with any wits at all would be alarmed at my own admission that I was drinking too much, and would make the obvious connection between the fact of the drinking and the fact that my meds weren't working. But apparently she doesn't have any wits. Depakote and alcohol are an especially toxic combination — both are processed by the liver, and in high enough doses, both can seriously damage it. Even alone, Depakote's not a med to be played with, and its levels in the bloodstream are supposed to be carefully monitored. This psychiatrist doesn't check my levels once, despite the fact that she's upping my dose almost every time she sees me.

"I think the Depakote's working. You'd be in much worse shape if it weren't." She looks at her watch and writes me a prescription. She rips it off the pad and hands it to me. "I'll see you next week."

They ask me at parties, *So, what do you do?* I say I'm a writer. *Really? Fascinating! Fabulous shoes!* I pretend to be one of them, but I'm not and never will be. I begin to have anxiety attacks at the very mention of dinner parties.

But here I am at yet another one. The woman across from me mentions that her mother is a psychiatrist. Brightly, she turns to me. *You're on medication, aren't you?*

My wineglass stops on its way to my mouth. I am mortified. Everyone at the table is mortified. Except the chipper woman who asked. I am a freak show. I am not one of them. I am a failure as a wife, already divorced at twenty-five. I will never get married again. I will never learn to play house. I will never be a success.

*Yes,* I say, and my wineglass completes its route to my mouth, and I take a swallow and set it down. I play with the stem of the glass and stare at my place mat. Surely someone will say something soon. Surely we will not sit around here staring at me much longer. Soon someone will say, *Anyway —*

Thank God, someone clears his throat. *Anyway —*

*So what are you taking?* the bright woman chimes in.

I want to die. *Depakote,* I say.

*I've heard it's a good med,* she says. *But aren't you on tranquilizers?* she asks. Will this never end? *I should think you'd need something to calm you down?* She smiles at me.

*Klonopin,* I say, and stand and push my chair in. *Excuse me.* I hurry to the bathroom, my face burning, near tears.

Because I have no other hope of keeping myself from total collapse, I trust my therapist completely. She tells me to take Klonopin, I take Klonopin. She tells me to take massive, toxic doses of Depakote, I take them. She tells me I don't have a drinking problem, so I don't. She's the professional. I swallow my pills each morning and night, with my bedside wine.

I'm working around the clock on the book and school and teaching two classes, drunk or sober, it doesn't matter, and my stress level is through the roof. I've blown through almost all the money I made on *Wasted* and the advances for the novel as well, and I'm not quite sure on what. My friends are giving up on me. I'm not sleeping, I'm having compulsive, risky affairs, hardly eating. Why eat? There are plenty of calories in booze.

Another night, another party, another fabulous red dress: I am in my bathroom putting on red lipstick. I am made up like a little garish doll. I will be the perfect guest.

But I am not well.

My hand shakes. I smear the lipstick. I try to clean it up, only smearing it more. I am gripped with terror. I cannot go. I cannot go to this party. They will see and laugh at me. My lipstick is crooked. My dress is not right. I am not well, and they will know it. They will see it. They will say, *She is not well. Oh my. She definitely is not well.*

I am sitting in the closet in the laundry basket in my dress and fabulous shoes. There is lipstick all over my face. I am sobbing. I hold my head in my hands and pull my legs into the laundry basket. I pull the laundry over me. I am very small and well dressed and my lipstick is done poorly and I cannot leave or I will die.

I am not well.


# Losing It
## *Winter 1999*

I am suddenly in Oregon, having driven there from California in the middle of the night. I am on a crowded sidewalk in LA. I am in a hotel room in New York. I don't know how I got here. Anywhere.

I am in Minneapolis, drunk on my mother's couch while the ball drops at midnight in Times Square on New Year's Eve 1999, and it becomes the year 2000, and everyone cheers. I pull an afghan over me and drink white wine from the bottle. Why bother with a glass?

I am inexplicably standing in front of an undergraduate classroom at my school, teaching Shakespeare. There has been a terrible mistake. I am a failure. I am a fraud.

I am on my seventh martini at lunch.

God knows whose bed this is now.

It seems always to be night. I am always in my car. Things flash past. Lights smear across the sky. The Golden Gate Bridge, always a popular suicide spot, swings its mammoth girth beneath my wheels. I am driving a hundred miles an hour. I dimly remember having dinner with the person in the seat next to me, with whom I may or may not be having an affair. He is screaming and laughing hysterically. I switch lanes with the speed of a racecar driver. I am a racecar driver. I am the Indy 500. I am the car. He screams. I fly.

I am now teaching my class in a bar. It saves time. No need to move between class and happy hour. Happy hour gets longer and longer. Happy hour is all day. In the morning, I get up, swallow my wine and meds, stagger into the kitchen, and pick up the bottle of vodka to steady my body, which shakes so hard I can barely hold the bottle to my mouth with both hands.

At night, the bottle is always dropping to the floor. I swing my head toward it and follow it headfirst. Red wine or vodka or scotch spills all around me. I pick myself up and stagger to bed. Clean it up later. Once I've steadied my hands with the bottle. Which I will then drop.

I am disappearing. Such a hassle; you're sitting there quite peacefully and then all of a sudden you're in Mexico watching a gecko eat the red hibiscus. You're skulking through the Tenderloin, conspiring with the bums. You're lying on the kitchen floor in a cocktail dress; your mother is there; *Darling, do get off the floor, it's not polite, it's really not; no, darling, would you please not climb into the cupboard; darling, are you feeling all right?*

I dress myself neatly and head off to school. I actually make it to lunch before I have a drink.

My chemistry's in chaos. I am sleep deprived, poisoned with meds, pickled with booze. That I have made it all this way without dying or killing myself or someone else is a miracle, or a joke. I am a joke, my life is a joke, I win an award for teaching, I delay the book once again. I hole up in my apartment with my bottles and books. I faithfully take my meds and wonder why on earth they're not working. I know I'm going crazy, and the people left in my life watch me turn yellow from the alcohol, shrivel up like a raisin, clothes hanging on me, hands bony and blue, a chatty head that spins from ecstasy to horror to a mask with empty eyes.

It is only a matter of time.

# Crazy Sean
*June 2000*

He is mad before me.

By this I mean he is mad before he meets me, and this summer, he goes mad before I do.

If only things would stay simple: the sound of the foghorns at night, the wild calla lilies that grow along the fence, the cool sharp fog that wraps around my face and throat. But it isn't that kind of summer. And this time I have a partner in madness.

Madness will push you anywhere it wants. It never tells you where you're going, or why. It tells you it doesn't matter. It persuades you. It dangles something sparkly before you, shimmering like that water patch on the road up ahead. You will drive until you find it, the treasure, the thing you most desire.

You will never find it. Madness may mock you so long you will die of the search. Or it will tire of you, turn its back, oblivious as you go flying. The car is beside you, smoking, belly-up, still spinning its wheels.

But at first, as always, it fools me. At first it is lovely, showy, hallucinatory, neon bright. I am viscerally, violently alive. I don't know when I turn the corner from merely crazy to completely psychotic, but when I do, Sean turns with me. We draw into ourselves, our eyes rolling back in our heads so that soon we can see nothing but the chaos and terror of our own minds.

We meet when I'm teaching summer school in San Francisco. I

pace in front of the class, leaping, punching the air, pouring out everything I know — I am wildly manic and usually drunk by early afternoon, and the board is crowded with my mad scribbles, so tangled up they're indecipherable. Teaching allows my manic stream of thought to focus on the one thing I still care about: words. Sean is one of my students. Our eyes meet and we read each other's lips, knowing each other intimately at once. When we speak, we hear the weird, warped voice of something insane.

Sean, a slight man, very pale, his short-shorn dirty blond hair receding already, is an astonishing writer. He gives me his novel. It's very dark and very beautiful. Sean is slipping into a psychotic depression, and I am flying toward a psychotic mania. Quickly, our relationship is tight, intense, obsessive. We pour out pages and pages of letters to each other, spend hours each day e-mailing when we can't be together, the connection between us sudden and essential and profound. If both of us are not already losing our slim grips on reality, we will be soon.

But we don't know, or care, anything about that. There is nothing strange about us. Medication isn't necessary. We don't talk about mental illness, which has nothing to do with the perfect union of minds that we have found. Our minds have reached a pinnacle of perception, and we see things the way no one else can see them, and the way we see them is the way they really are.

It is decided that we will leave. We will run away. We will go to the desert, where nothing can touch us, where the lives we hate will be forgotten, escaped. We will find ourselves a map. We will find our way.

The point is the driving. It's the cheap motel, the dust, the sweaty, salty, dirty skin, it's the wind in the window, it's the water, it's the map, which is for tracing where we have been, not where we are going. Mornings, we start driving in any direction, to see what there is to see, to see where we end up next. We collect the names of towns like children collect rocks. We mark them on our map, which is spread out on the beaded motel bedspread or on the burning hood of the car, heads together, we are *here,* we say, and *here,* and *here,* we trace our path with a red pen, fingernails stubby and filthy. In the car, we're propelled by some weird force. Our feet are heavy on the pedal. The place back there fades in the rearview and we fly into the arms of something fantastical, more real than real.

We're gone for days, then weeks, a month. No one knows where we are.

THE BORDERLANDS.

We climb out of the car in a nameless town where there is a store, a post office, a white adobe church. The metal cross catches the sun and reflects it so brightly it burns the eyes. The flash of white light repeats itself on the back of my eyelids. We go into the store. The people in it look at us strangely, perhaps because we are gringos and perhaps because we are filthy and look a little nuts. We find a pile of maps. They are maps of the deserts that extend down into northern Mexico. We unroll them on the floor. Which one, which one should we buy?

*We could get this one,* I say, unfolding a map of the Chihuahuan desert. Sean glances at it.

*Too far left,* he says, and bends his head over a map of Arizona's Organ Pipe Cactus National Monument. We've been through Joshua Tree and Death Valley, where we said nothing and stood shoulder to shoulder, looking out at the vast expanse of the slender, twisted, black bodies of trees. We wandered off onto it, like walking through a de Chirico, or a Dali: all emptiness, haunted silence, cracked ground. We wandered till dark. Sean had a GPS with him. That was how we found our car.

Then through the Painted Desert, where I pointed out the window at rock formations and color striations. His head turned, almost in slow motion, as he followed things as they went past. The speedometer read over 90. It was excruciatingly slow.

*This one,* Sean says, triumphant, looking up from his map. I crouch next to him. I nod. *Of course,* I say.

We leave with a topographic map of the Sonoran Desert. It shows no roads, no towns. Only the infinitesimal, perfectly accurate lines that indicate where a hill rises up a hundred feet, where a stream circles the hill, the lines rippling out from a high point and widening down to a low. With this map, we are ready. Now we will know where we are if we get lost. We will be able to say, *C72, lat 623',* yes, obviously, now we can see. It all comes clear. We are explorers. We have the finest map known to man, the one true map, the map for those who grasp the real significance of the single step this way or that.

We get back in the car. The sun is falling. We drive past a sign that says GRINGO PASS.

Ahead of us is the border crossing, marked by what looks like a tollbooth made of shabby clapboard. We slow down and come to a stop. The border patrol watches us. We are frightened. They are police. We discuss our options.

*Straight through,* he says. *That's one.*

I nod. *Or around,* I say. *We could go a little east and see if there's a fence.*

*They shoot you,* he says.

*True,* I say. *Then that won't work.*

There are two buildings in Gringo Pass, at least on this side of the border. It looks like there is one more on the other side. We wonder if that is also Gringo Pass. We can't be sure whether we are in Arizona, or if, by virtue of being at the border, we are in Mexico instead. This confounds us. One of the buildings says, in flickering neon letters, REST ANT & STOR. The neon glows bright white in the purple-blue coming night. On the other side of the road, a large white sign reads, in painted red letters, GRINGO PASS MOTEL. Both buildings are low, flat-roofed. We are sitting there in my truck in the middle of the road. The decision is momentous.

We pull in to the motel's parking lot. There is only one room left. There are no cars in the lot. It is the most expensive room, the proprietor apologizes. "Thirty bucks. Busy night," she says. She is very tiny and old, her face made of worn leather. We stare at her in awe. She slides the plastic key-chained key across the cracked counter. "Housekeeping suite. There's pots and pans. Anything else?"

Sean snaps out of it. He pulls his hat off with a flourish. "Where might a man imbibe?" He looks at me. "Sorry." He turns back to the woman. "A man and a woman? As you can see." He gestures at me with his hat. "We are not lovers," he explains. She shrugs.

"Suit yourself. Booze at the store." She waves a hand at the window. "Cross the road. Decent chili, eggs."

"Chili eggs!" Sean declares, fascinated.

"Chili, comma, eggs," I whisper, elbowing him in the ribs.

He stares at me. "Of course," he says, mortified.

He is losing his shit for the day, I see. I haul him outside and down the walkway to our room.

Inside, we pull all the pots and pans out of the kitchen cupboards, put them back, and go across the road to the REST ANT. We devour bloody steaks. We head into the STOR and buy a couple of bottles of whiskey. We go back to our room and pull our gold-colored, fraying, scratchy chairs out of the room and into the motel parking lot. We settle in with our notebooks to write. We pick up our bottles of whiskey from the ground, slam shots, and cackle. The border guards drive through the parking lot, looking for us. We are relieved that we are invisible. We laugh knowingly at their stupidity. We shout sections of what we are writing. *Listen, listen!* we gasp, laughing, knowing that we understand.

When you are mad, mad like this, you don't know it. Reality is what you see. When what you see shifts, departing from anyone else's reality, it's still reality to you. Sean and I know that what we see is true, and real. We know that we have each finally stumbled on the one other person who understands this, and we know that what we believed before was an impoverished, colorless misapprehension of what actually is. We wonder at the miracle that is us.

Crazy Sean walks ahead of me. We are in the desert. We have no map. I am talking to myself, certain that I have come to find the secret treasure. I stare down a snake. We walk in circles for weeks, or minutes, or years. Time has escaped me. Everything is sand.

Crazy Sean stops and turns. He says to me: *It's over, isn't it.*

He reminds me of Jesus. I nod. *Yes,* I say. *It is. What is?*

He shakes his head and sighs and squints into the sun. *What?* he says. *What is? Lots of things are. De facto,* he explains.

*Ergo sum,* I agree, and eat some gorp I find in my pockets.

We stand on a high white rock, looking up as the sunrise, or sunset, rises up, or falls down, over a flat red mesa.

*Where are we?* he asks me.

I think about this. *Do you mean literally or figuratively?* I reply.

*Biblically,* he says.

*Ah,* I say, and nod.

We lie down on the rock and sleep. When we wake, it's pitch-black but for stars. We have no water.

*We'll die,* says Crazy Sean. He wraps his arms around his knees.

*I expect we will,* I say.

Peacefully, together, we are crazy, and we don't know where we are, and we are out of water, and we have no idea how to get home.

So we get up and start walking. It gets light as we discuss Dante, and Faulkner, and the nature of hell. We walk into the center of the desert, or into the center of the reeling sun, but again the light fades out and there in the night, at the end of the road, we are somehow back at the Gringo Pass Motel. The cook at the REST ANT spins our plates of meat onto our table, wipes his hands on his apron, and turns back to the kitchen without a word. We drag our chairs out into the parking lot again and guzzle whiskey like it's water and we are dying of thirst. We discuss the essential goodness of gold qua gold, as opposed to silver, though we allow that silver has a certain appeal to crows; and the crow, though not the raven, has meaning in and of itself; though the raven does matter, in a different sort of sense.

We speak continuously of death.

Texas. Scorpions.

The fear sets in.

How long have we been gone? It doesn't even occur to us. We scream to be heard over the wind. Colorado. We are paranoid, afraid of the crowded bar. We are afraid in the grocery store, trying desperately to find booze. We are coming in and out. We are a radio station. We are a short wave. We are the news. The fluorescent lights are threatening and burn my eyes. The terrifying checkout girl sneers. We recoil, run out of the store, lock ourselves in a motel room, all orange shag carpet, one of those horrible seventies globe lamps dangling from a chain. The chain concerns us. We discuss which of us should hang ourselves first. There are logistical problems; for example, getting down the dead one would entail undoing the chain from the ceiling, and then putting it back up, and then hanging oneself next; we decide we will skip it, and watch a horror movie on the television. It is a terrible movie. We are petrified. We are screaming. Someone is pounding on the door. We turn the TV up so our screaming can't be heard. In a fit of brilliance, Sean leaps out of the corner where he has been hiding, grabs the light's chain, and yanks it to the floor, where it smashes into a trillion pieces of orange glass lost in the orange shag carpet. That's good, then. Neither of us will hang ourselves tonight. We drink until the night has passed.

The day whirls around in a circle, and we tumble into the night again. It is the next night, or the one after that, or we have been driving for years. The road has narrowed to a red thread down which we are careening. Crazy Sean is telling me he loves me and has to kill me to save me. He's sobbing and trying to take the wheel. We haven't eaten for days. Someone is screaming. It may be me.

Idaho. We tear down the narrow highway. Sean is going to kill me. He says my soul is abandoned. His is black. He can feel it. He can feel the cancer of his soul. He will not shut up, will not stop talking, crying, filling my ears with cacophonous noise. We speed through narrow tunnels of concrete bordering a one-lane road, leaning around the bends, nearly lifting off. I tune him out. Somewhere nearby, someone is crazy. I am sane. I must stay sane or we will not survive. He *will not fucking shut up!* I scream, taking my hands off the wheel, tearing at my hair, beating him about the head, and he huddles away, crying, and I hate him, he is weak, he is not a good soldier, he has failed the battalion, the war is lost because of him, the car swerves, scrapes the concrete wall, I grab the wheel and we drive on.

Utah, red mountains. Washington State. Is it morning yet? Where have we been? We drive through Seattle like sensible people. We are speaking gibberish, hating each other and ourselves. Our language is tangled. We cannot make ourselves understood. I take him to his mother's house and drop him off.

In my rearview mirror, he is tiny, holding his sleeping bag.

# Oregon
*August 2000*

I am driving through the dark, very fast. I glance at my speedometer: 110 mph, but that isn't so very fast after all, when you consider, and compared to other things and speeds, and there is no danger for I am invincible, I am flying, and it is very urgent that *I get there, to the place I am going, I must arrive immediately,* the space between places upsets me, the map in my mind sprawls out in all directions, I crest the top of a hill, or maybe a mountain, it's really quite high, the air is thin and cold, the vast and utter spill of the blue-black sky, like velvet, but spinning, crawling within and around itself, amazes me, the molecules of sky (but are there molecules of sky? Is it truly a *thing in itself?*) seething, and the sparks of stars are electric — I feel the hill must lead down into the deeper dark, for the road spins out before me like a snake's tongue unfurling and I see no side of the road, the road is suspended in the sky like a magical bridge over what must be a long divide, the mountains splitting apart from one another, withdrawing into themselves and leaving this wide swath of bottomless sky, and I turn off the lights and I fall through space, I fly, my wheels leave the road and I am free.

I am feeling my way through the little market in town. I am near the mustard, and I search the shelves for something to keep me alive, for I have to hide away from the world, and I need food in case of *fires, bombs, or acts of God*. The aisles seem to lean over me, threatening to collapse, and the bright white lights in the buzzing dairy case confuse me. I keep to the back of the store, not wanting to go out front, where the clerk might see me and suspect me, or someone might open the jingling door, coming in for their morning coffee and the paper — when I came in it was just barely getting light, the purple sky reeling overhead — and I can't have anyone see me, for they might see how crazy I am, they might know. I need to get out of here before I am seen. I hurry through the market, dropping things into my basket, anything in a can, sardines, soup, peas and carrots, beans, tuna, smoked oysters. I need to stock up, I need to fill the shelves at the beach house with food, like a bunker, keeping me locked away from the world for a while, condensed milk, pickled beets, my hand grabs things off the shelf and drops them in the basket, it doesn't matter what they are.

I stand staring at my hands as I count out my money, the clerk's eyes boring into me, I can *feel* them, he suspects, he can see. I mumble, *Thanks,* and at last it's over. I hurry out to the car with my bags. I make my way to the house, driving like mad on this narrow road, hunched over the wheel, knuckles white, because I am afraid that I will drive off a cliff, just jerk the wheel and go flying over the edge, and I can't do that, I can't, *I don't want to die*. I peel up to the house on this quiet, still-sleeping street, gray wooden fences and lush vines crawling over them, and towering, brilliantly colored flowers glowing in the mist — this is the terrifying outside world that threatens to swallow me whole. The house is familiar today, as if I have been here as a child, but I don't know whose it is. I am alone. I lock myself in and draw the curtains, because it is safer in here where there are locks on the windows and doors.

The cans I bought are impossible to open. The can opener is complex, so I will starve; I will bury myself under the house; yes; I stop crying, much reassured.

I sit at the table with my arms wrapped around myself. I hold myself to the chair so that I do not stand, for if I stand, I might go to the drawer, get the knives, and then who knows what I'd do? I want desperately to be sane. But I can picture myself having just done it, the first stab, and the look on my face, horrified, *But I didn't mean to, I couldn't help it, I take it back —*

I know, sitting here in the house by the ocean, that if I so much as touch a knife, I'll do it again, and this time I might, as they say in the business, succeed. The desire to do something with my hands, to strike, to break, is so powerful it's all I can do to hold them under my arms, crossed tightly across my chest. I keep myself sitting, because I am afraid that if I stand, even if I make it past the drawer where the knives are kept, I might grab my keys and get in my car. And I know, I *know*, that if I do that, I will drive myself off a cliff. At this moment, I understand with all my being why someone would commit suicide: there is no other way to get away from yourself, and I want nothing more than to finally escape the incessant shrieking of my mind, the crawling madness that has infested every part of me, body and brain. Don't ask me why I am focused, particularly, on the knife drawer and the idea of driving off a cliff. They happen to be the means of death my mind fixates on, and they keep me sitting in my chair for I don't know how long. Hours? Days?

Of course, I get up now and then. I get up to get another bottle. Then I put myself back in my chair, as if I am a little kid who refuses to eat her peas and is not allowed to leave her place until she finishes every last bite. I sit at the table with my feet on the chair, peeling the label off a bottle of whiskey, swimming in the drunken, tumultuous sea of my thoughts. I take a swig, set the bottle down, and study it as the liquor burns a path down my throat. It suddenly dawns on me that the drinking may be one of the things that is making me as crazy as I am. It is one of the things that has brought me to this point. I put my head on the table, hand wrapped around the bottle, and close my eyes. I know I can't stop. And I know, finally, that if I do not stop, the madness will get worse, that the alcohol is like pouring gasoline on an already smoldering fire.

I find myself opening the phone book and looking up a twelve-step group. A few minutes later I'm driving like hell toward what seems the only chance I have to save my own life.

*Hi,* someone says. He's enormous, wearing biker leathers and a red bandanna. *I'm Steve, and I'm an alcoholic.*

*Hi, Steve,* the room recites. My vision veers in and out, and my hands shake so hard I can barely hold the Styrofoam cup of bad coffee. The coffee has little waves in it. It spills over the sides.

*Hi, Susan. Hi, Sandra. Hi, Peter. Hi, John.*

They come to me. I look around in confusion.

*What's your name?* someone asks gently.

*Marya,* I say, barely audible, my mouth sticky and dry.

They wait for me to say *And I'm an alcoholic.* A beat. They move on. *Hi, Andrew. Hi, Joan.*

They talk for an hour. I have no idea what they say. My brain skitters over the sound, catching snippets of sentences, a laugh. The circle of faces revolves around me, the room spins, and I grip the arms of my chair to keep myself from tipping over. And then suddenly the meeting breaks up, I'm wandering outside, and it seems that half the group hurries after me, calling my name. They crowd around, looking at me urgently, touching me on the arm. I look up at them, overwhelmed and confused, and try to follow the questions that come at me in a flurry:

*Are you from around here?*

*How long since your last drink?*

*Are you feeling all right? You look a little — pale.*

*Have you eaten lately?*

*Do you need another cup of coffee?*

*Why don't you come back inside and sit down. You don't seem so steady on your feet.*

I am pushed back into the meeting room and guided onto a couch. Someone hands me a cup of coffee. They pull up chairs.

*So,* someone says. *Are you sober?*

I stare at them. *I think so,* I say.

*Have you had a drink today?*

*Just a couple.*

*When was the last time you ate?*

I try to think. *I can't remember,* I say.

Someone produces a banana. *Eat this,* they say. *Come with us,* they say. I am being herded into someone's house. *You need sugar,* they say, and pour me orange juice and a bowl of sugary cereal and I try to figure out what to do with the spoon. They talk to me and I try to understand what they're saying, and my brain is soaked with booze, addled with madness, but they are good people, and they are feeding me, and I am so relieved I start to cry.

They pat me on the shoulder. *Hey,* they say. *'S'all right. You'll be all right.*

*I don't think so,* I say.

Inexplicably, my aunt — my mother's sister, whom I adore — is sitting at the kitchen table with me. I am very startled to find her here. She doesn't explain her presence. Turns out I've been hiding in the family beach house on the Oregon coast. It's hers and my mother's, so I suppose there's no real reason she *wouldn't* be here.

It seems I've called my mother at some point in the last few days. I've been gone for weeks. My parents — now divorced, my mother living in Minneapolis with her new husband, my father with his new wife in Arizona — knew only that I was on a hiking trip with a friend. They've been worried about me for months, listening to me get crazier and crazier during our infrequent phone calls. Whatever I said to my mother when I called from Oregon must have tipped her off that I was not doing so well. (No, not so well.) She called her sister, who lives in Oregon, and asked her to come get me. She also called my sister-in-law, a doctor in a Portland hospital, and made certain that a bed in the psych ward was waiting for me.

But I know none of this. All I know is that I am in the beach house, and my aunt is here, and I am near tears with relief. I try to feign normalcy — give her a hug, tell her I just needed a little getaway, the beach house seemed the very place. I don't tell her that I didn't even know I was *in* the beach house. I smile and tell her I'm writing. I babble and chatter, my speech getting faster by the second. I flit from topic to topic, unable to stop, and she nods, looking at me strangely, worried, and I don't want her to be worried, I don't want her to think I'm crazy.

Out of nowhere I hear myself lighting into HMOs and their evils, their failure to cover mental health services, and I am being extremely articulate, honing my argument, and now I am sobbing, and I say I don't know what I'm going to do, I have no way to get help, and I think it's possible I may need some help, nothing serious, but maybe just something to get me back on my feet, but they won't cover anything and it's all a bureaucracy with no connection to real people with real problems who need help. I watch tears drip from my nose onto the wood grain of the kitchen table and try to get ahold of myself, to start speaking in a nice, detached, intellectual way. This will surely persuade my aunt that I am perfectly fine, outburst aside.

*Oh, sweetie,* she says.

That makes it worse. I crawl up the stairs to the bedroom and climb into bed, sobbing so hard I am pretty sure I am going to break. The feeling of despair is so pure and clean it seems to slice a razor-sharp path through my body. My body gapes open, filling in slowly with the knowledge that there is no hope. I find this peaceful. My aunt is bending over me with the phone. I hold it to my ear. My mother's voice. More soothing noises. I am crying too hard to hold the phone, so I hand it back to my aunt.

Now I am in a car. The towering green-blue pines and rocky cliffs that crowd against the two-lane road go by. Now we are at a hospital. Now we are in a tiny, windowless room. Now I am in a chair. My aunt is here. We are locked in. I do not understand the room. There is a TV screen that shows someone in a uniform pacing back and forth outside. My aunt explains that it is a security guard. To secure what? Me. I am concerned and ask if the figure has a gun. She tries to explain. The uniformed person makes me incredibly agitated. I have a great many questions about this new situation. I cry, wanting to know if they will come to get me, if they will let me out, if they will help me.

I don't know what happens next.

I AM IN A CAGE. I am dreaming, but I am not asleep. It is a *daydream*. But then it is night; I do not know how to explain it to the figures in the room, who surround me. I cannot move; I flail but in *a very contained sort of way* because it would seem my ankles and wrists are restrained. The figures in the room *murmur*, which must mean I'm crazy again, because otherwise they would speak in normal voices. But I am strapped down + they murmur + I cannot lift my head + for it is *full of medicines to calm me* + aha! It is not a cage for there is *no roof!* Which means = it is a bed with bars. And the figures peer over me and study me as if I am a rat. Or perhaps I have just been born and they are admiring my perfect little ears. And then a face comes into focus: a savior! Surely he will tell me where I am, for if he is here and I am here then = he must know where we are *but there is a sudden flower;* it is a sunflower; I shriek, *Sunflower!* It is the color of rust; is that even possible? Is there a flower the color of rust? I realize it is threatening; why has he brought me this flower; it seems to say *I know you.* Rather than saying, for example, *Get well, obviously.* As a daisy would say; however, I dislike daisies, have always disliked them, to the point of *truly hating them,* for no reason that I am aware; van Gogh painted sunflowers! The sunflower is redeemed. So I take it and eat it. Then they take away my sunflower, which I love very much; they say, *We'll just put this in a vase;* which is so uninspired a notion I laugh at them for they must be very boring to one another and themselves; I am not boring; I am, I discover, full of ideas; I mention the green beans; I can lift my head! I announce that I will leave if they don't give me a dress to wear to the occasion; and some *fabulous shoes.*

The next thing I know, I am coming to, and everyone in the world is standing above me. My mother is in here somewhere. I am aware of her presence. My father is or is not here, it's not quite clear. I understand that if he is not here yet, he will be soon, for this is a highly unusual situation, and he will need to come explain it to me.

There are bars on the bed. The people murmur. I am here, and they are here, which means I am somewhere, somewhere safe, and I don't have to drive anymore, and the shrieking has stopped, and my mind floats in a bath of sedatives, sunning itself on its back like a seal.

I am mad. The thought calms me. I don't have to try to be sane anymore. It's over.

I sleep.

WHEN I COME TO again, the sound has been shut off. My head has become a kaleidoscope. It turns and turns, and the shards of color tumble and arrange themselves differently every time. At some point the colored patterns organize themselves into the shapes of people and things, and my head becomes a telescope instead. I watch them on their little planet, unsure how far away they are. They come and go, the view from the telescope emptying out, focusing now on the plastic light on the ceiling above, which is another strata of space, which has a light, which is possibly a star. Then they reappear in the telescope again and I am much relieved. When I move my telescope from side to side, the figures and the colors pan past so fast it makes me dizzy.

I am sedated. I don't understand what's going on. I know only that I am in a hospital and that my family is here. Someone is beside me, my doctor, my mother, my friend, and I murmur a few things, and I hear my sentences begin to tangle into incomprehensible, nonsensical gibberish, and it frustrates me, trying to make myself understood, and I slide back into sleep.

The things that happen are out of order. Nothing follows. My facts are my facts alone.

I TRAVEL from bed to bed. Today I am in a bed without bars. A nice woman with short blond hair is talking to me. I feel as if I am underwater. I establish for myself that she is my doctor. Her voice echoes, garbled, in my head. I concentrate on what she is saying. I try to keep myself afloat. *Do you understand me?* Oh, yes, I nod, wanting to be polite. She is saying something about medication. She uses the word *helping. We are trying to [burble burble]. We want you to know [burble]. Your mother and father are here. Tell me how you. We are. They are. We will. Better soon. As soon as we.*

I hear myself say something. My own voice is very near, so near I am not sure if it makes it from the echo chamber of my skull out into the air. I remember I had many questions that I was saving up for when she came. My questions trip over one another, and I can't keep one sentence separated from the other. The words tangle up. She says, *I'm sorry, I don't understand.* I try to explain myself, but I am sinking, my eyes start to close, I hear myself mumble, getting farther away. *Marya? You're not making any sense.* She stands to go. *I'll come back later,* she says. Frustrated, sinking, I nod.

I am upright. I am wearing my robes. I stare at the table, where a peanut butter sandwich has appeared, though it confuses me and I don't know what to do with it. My hands lie in my lap. My hands are heavy. Someone is watching, and I lift my head. I have visitors. They furrow their brows and look sad. I tell them not to worry, it will be fine. My mouth will not cooperate. I would be embarrassed but I can't concentrate that long.

I SHUFFLE across the room to the little table where they keep crackers and oranges and tea and powdered hot chocolate and lukewarm water. The water is lukewarm so we can't scald ourselves. The movie plays in a loop. From the faraway place in my head, I watch my insane game of one A.M. cribbage with a speechless enormous man who sometimes inexplicably laughs and struggles with a pencil to mark down the score. I do not know how to play cribbage. I have never known how.

My feet in hospital footies are tucked under me. I am a smallish creature, a rabbit or a mouse, swimming in miles of hospital cotton, dazed and riding fluorescent dreams. The colors of the cards blur red-black as I turn my head. I study three dead flowers in a Styrofoam cup: two yellow, one purple. I struggle to remember their names. A man named Beast tried to kill himself last night. I say I am sorry about that. He talks to me slowly and I raise my eyes. He says, *Do you know flowers,* and I say, *Yes.* It takes a moment to force the word but I say, *Yes, I know flowers,* and he says, *Do you know a flower like a firework, an explosion, but purple, or blue,* and I picture the wet bush flush with balls of blue outside the kitchen window, after the rain, when I stared at it for hours, letting the coffee go cold in my cup, clinging to the cup in the face of the astonishing blue while I cried. This was maybe yesterday or maybe last year. It was in the house on the coast or it was in my childhood home or it was somewhere I can't remember now. I pick through the rubble of my brain. My brain is an archaeological site. *Yes,* I say, carefully deciphering the complexities of my cards, *yes, hydrangea.* We stare at each other, amazed.

It is very late now, it is the same night or another night, and the man with the clipboard walks from room to room glancing up at the dry-erase boards outside the doors to check our erasable names to distinguish one drugged figure in the bed marked WINDOW from the one in the bed marked DOOR. He will mark on his yellow sheet: B (BACK), L (LEFT), F (FRONT), R (RIGHT). I am A (AWAKE). This too will go down on the yellow sheet and soon they will come, cooing, to give me an A (ATIVAN), because *wouldn't it be nice to sleep?*

There are two beds in my room. This means I am better now. It means I am oriented. When I came they must have asked me questions to which I did not know the answers — *Do you know what day it is? What year? Who is the president? Do you know where you are?* — but to which I apparently do know the answers now. *Hospital,* I must have said, and that was the right answer so I won, and the crowds cheered. They have moved me from the room where I began, where they murmured, a lifetime before, or last week, where there was only one bed, the emergency psych room. Now there are two beds. Sworls of threadbare blankets wrap around our two figures like cotton galaxies. The thick blue dark gently presses its fingers into our eye sockets, the shallows of our open mouths, the crook of an arm pulled close to the body for heat. A damp and heavy sleep fills the room, a third body, breathing.

These are my facts. There are other facts. I do not learn these facts until much later. The other facts are as follows: I crashed into a depression that lasted for another nine months. The two-year mania in California that led into the psychosis that sent me tearing across the country with Crazy Sean and landed me in the hospital in Oregon for two weeks came to a sudden halt as depression took hold. It was the next stage of the cycle of bipolar: manic depression hits both extremes, one following the other. The higher you fly, per cliché, the farther you fall. After a manic episode, the body and mind are exhausted, completely spent. I hit the wall. I picture myself flattened against it like a cartoon character, two-dimensional, sliding down.

I've spent my fair share of days flung across the bed, racked with a dull, aimless grief, and I've curled up on the floor in a corner of the room, my thoughts black and seething, and I've understood the word *despair*, the word *defeat*. I've felt the loss of the will to breathe, and felt the momentary wish to die. But it was momentary. I was always able to pull myself out. Or, really, mania always returned and sent me flying again.

This is different. I do not have the energy to pull myself free. I do not have the energy to even care that I am trapped. This is beyond caring, beyond a will to die, beyond will. Death is there, but you can barely lift your hand to reach out for it, and you cringe at the faintest suggestion of light. You can wish for death, but it is like wishing for sleep, a sense of exhaustion so profound that your whole body aches. And just as sleep does some exhausted nights, death eludes you. It is right there. You feel it. But it won't come close enough. And if you have the energy to cry, that's why.

*Down, down, down.* It doesn't feel like depression; I am not sad. I am underwater. I am a body. I follow the world through my telescope. I am drugged, and so feel nothing at all, as the doctors scramble to find some combination of meds that will stabilize me. I sleep almost around the clock. The doctor explains to me that I am very sick. She explains to me that I need to stop drinking or I will never get better, it will always be this bad. My parents explain things to me too. They speak slowly. They explain to me, over and over, where I am, but I am profoundly confused. They sit in the hospital all day, every day, propping up my head with their hands, answering my endless, repetitive questions, wondering if I will return to sanity soon, or at all.

# Day Treatment
*Late August 2000*

After two weeks, I am discharged and taken to my aunt's Portland house to recuperate. I go to sleep for a week, passed out on the living room floor. When I'm marginally cognizant again, my mother and I fly back to San Francisco. The plan is that I will enter a day program for people in crisis — people who are severely depressed, manic, paralyzed with anxiety, but presumably not psychotic, and believed to be nonsuicidal. My mother is staying at a hotel near my house, spending virtually every waking moment with me until I get back on my feet. I'm not suicidal because I couldn't possibly make myself care enough that I am alive to summon up the energy to off myself, not that I could even organize such an event if I tried. I cling to my mother like a monkey, her presence the only thing that makes sense.

She drops me off at the hospital for day treatment every morning, and I spend the day in group therapy with the rest of the completely nonfunctional patients. The room feels strange, hollow, populated by motionless silent bodies who sit, unaware of the sunny summer day outside. There is a sense of being nowhere, floating on the hospital floor in the middle of space. The cumulative madness in the room circulates, collecting on our shoulders and weighing them down.

We sit in a circle, trying to talk. The day program tries to give us something to do other than kill ourselves or lie on the couch thinking about how depressed we are and how much we wish we were dead. It is meant as a crisis-management program only, intended to keep us safe and occupied for as long as the episode lasts and until we are able to function on our own again. Most of the patients are depressed. I am not sure why I am here. I don't feel depressed. I feel nothing at all.

At home, my mother sits with me, talks slowly and gently, as if talking to a skittish dog. Her presence is the only thing that I am fully aware of. I am terrified all the time. I ask her the same questions over and over, make her repeat the answers until my fear lessens a little bit, only to fixate on something else to fear. I make her explain everything to me, and I nod, but I don't understand. *Oh yes. I see.* I see nothing but the reeling sun. The world is enormous. I am a tiny speck on earth, and I cling to my mother's ankle, crawling up her leg like a flea.

"But what if I get lost?" I am frantic. We are trying to leave my house.

"You won't get lost. I'm with you."

"But what if you lose me?" I stare into her face with the fervent faith in her rightness usually seen in zealots.

"I won't lose you. You can hang on to my sleeve."

I nod. "All right," I say. I pace, then stop. "What if *you* get lost?"

"Then we're screwed." My mother laughs so hard she nearly falls off her chair. I don't think it's funny at all, and start drawing a map.

Another day of day treatment. They have steered me onto the correct floor and into the correct room, and now I am lying on the floor of the psych ward lounge. The sunlight blares into the room. The institutional curtains are from the seventies, orange with little white squares. They are bleak and so I close my eyes. Periodically, someone tries to rouse me, but it is a Herculean effort to lift my head a few inches, to whisper that I can't stay awake. Dimly, I watch the other depressed people sitting in a circle, on couches and chairs. I am bewildered by the fact that they are upright.

There is a young woman on her knees, rocking, wailing, afraid. Her voice tears at my ears and I think I will die if she does not shut up.

I fade in and out of a sedated sleep. There is a perky young woman. I've met women like that. They take their perky, happy faces out in public, and wear them around, smiling and smiling, and then they go home and shoot themselves in the head. I watch her. She smiles and chatters on. "So my friend Dave called me this morning, and he said, 'What are you doing?' And I said, 'I got out of bed. I ate some cereal. Now I'm lying on the couch.' And he said, 'You rock!'" She laughs. "So I felt good for a minute. But then I hung up the phone and everything emptied out and I wanted to be dead all over again." She laughs.

The therapist says, "Cathy? Would you like to say something?" All heads turn to Cathy. Cathy is enormously pregnant. Her face is entirely still. She stares into space. Her hands are folded on her lap. I understand that she cannot move her mouth to say no, and she cannot shake her head either.

"Aren't you even excited about the baby?" the perky woman asks, horribly. "Doesn't that make you happy?"

The woman is not excited about the baby. It does not make her happy. The baby is just one more thing that requires her to be alive. I want the perky woman to go away and leave Cathy alone. The agitated woman rocks and wails.

Everyone in this room is crazy. I fall asleep again.

At the end of the day, I follow everyone else out of the building. Someone asks me how I'm getting home. I stare at her, drawing a complete blank. Well, do I need a ride? Blank. Where do I live? I recite my address, which I know in case I get lost and have to find a policeman who will guide me home. Just to be on the safe side, I recite my phone number as well. Then I remember — my mother and I agreed that I would brave the bus and get home all by myself. Right-o. This person goes away. I stand on the hospital steps, holding my purse by the strap. I go down the steps, look both ways, and cross the street. This is easy. I take the bus all the time. I see other people standing on a corner. I join their group and we all turn our faces in the direction from which the bus will come. We stare that way for a while.

Then a car drives up and I watch while all of them climb in and drive away.

I look around for the bus stop sign. There is no sign. I am frustrated with myself. What an idiot. I keep walking down the busy street until I come to another cluster of people. "Is this a bus stop?" I ask no one in particular. Everyone turns to look at me, then goes back to watching the road. I stare at a woman who is reading a book until she looks at me. "Is it?" I demand. "Is what?" "Is this a bus stop?" These people are deaf! "Yes," she finally says, giving me a look and going back to her book.

Well, very good. I climb onto the bus with the rest of them and take a window seat. I settle in to enjoy the ride. Everyone is being very quiet, on this bus. I look around. Everyone is being quiet because they're all looking at me. I swish around to face the back of the head of an elderly Asian man. I sit there being unnoticeable. A moment later, I venture a quick glance over my shoulder. Still staring! What is it? I check my fly, rub my nose, straighten my glasses, and then I hear it. They're talking. I train my ears on what they are saying, but I can't make it out. There is a little boy sitting next to me whose feet dangle off the seat. I wonder momentarily where his parents are, then consider whether I will ask him what they're saying. If I ask him, he could consider me odd. He could get up without a word and change seats and stick his little freckled nose in the air. So I say nothing, listening to the rising hum of them, whispering, talking in low voices, getting louder, and *still* I can't make it out. I look around, trying not to be obvious. A very old woman the size and substance of a feather is hanging on to her grocery bag with both arms and glaring at me. I have done nothing to her. Why does she glare? There is a gaggle of horrible teenagers with black fingernails and green eye shadow and teased pink and blue hair. They represent my adolescence and terrify me. They are talking, their heads bent together, gesturing subtly in my direction, just like the girls at school used to do. Just ignore it. Ignore it. They can't hurt you. A businessman holds on to the post and pretends to read his newspaper. He is watching me over the top of it. He thinks I can't see him, but I can. I see them all. I know their tricks.

The din of their voices, all sibilants and hums, rises to a particularly disturbing pitch.

"What are they saying?" I can't take it anymore, it just comes out. I know I'm being weird, but this paranoia will not subside, no matter how I tell myself it's all in my head. I bend down to the little boy's ear, trying to be both inconspicuous and nonthreatening. He looks up at me. I smile a great big smile, feeling a little wild. "Don't worry," I say. "There's no reason to be afraid of me." This widens his brown eyes considerably, and I realize my error in even *mentioning* being afraid, but he is a brave soul and doesn't bolt. "Just tell me what they're saying," I whisper.

"What who are saying?" he whispers loudly. Now everyone is looking at him too, because he has been caught talking to me.

"Shhh!" I hiss. "The watchers." I nod my head over my shoulder. "Them."

He cranes his neck around. "They're not talking," he says in his deafening whisper. He looks back up at me.

"They are!" I say. "You just can't see it. They're sneaky, the watchers. They like to keep you off-guard."

He stares at me, his eyes cartoon-huge. The bus slows and the bus driver calls out the stop.

"I have to get off now," the little boy whispers. He points over my shoulder. "That's my mom."

I look. "She looks very nice. Off you go."

"Are you going to be all right?" he whispers, worried. His mother will wonder why he has lost his voice. He will say it is because he was talking to the crazy lady on the bus.

I nod earnestly at him. "I'll be fine."

He makes a dramatic swipe of his forehead with the back of his hand and says, "Phew!" He hops up, waves, and is gone.

I make it as far as the next stop, listening to them with their evil hiss and hum, and then I bolt off the bus, my hair blowing in its exhaust as it pulls away. I look around. I have no idea where I am. How long was I on the bus? What neighborhood is this? There are houses, and it's relatively clean, so it's not the Mission. There are no tall buildings, so it's not downtown. There's no marina, so it's not the Marina, and there are neither strip clubs nor Italian restaurants, so it's not North Beach. There's no fog, so it's not the Sunset. I turn in slow circles. But it's also not the Richmond, where I live.

That leaves the Presidio. Even when I'm sane I don't know where the Presidio is, and I don't know how to get back by car, let alone by bus. I start walking. I walk up and down the beautiful streets overlooking the bay, the Golden Gate Bridge enormous across the sky. I start to run. I run and run. I hop on one bus and find the watchers and jump off, and I hop another one, and they're there, too, and I ride around the city for hours, getting on and off buses, too frightened to speak to ask for directions — what, ask the watchers? They watch me run, slow down to a walk, run again. They turn to one another in my wake and start talking about me. I pass little outdoor cafés and boutiques and sushi restaurants and cheese shops and bars and bodegas and nightclubs and through empty industrial areas and through the park, more than once. I get lost in the park on my best days. This is not one of my best days. I walk in circles, hop on one last bus, get off when the watchers get too loud and, miraculously, am standing in front of Mr. Chao's vegetable stand. I stumble toward him, nearly upsetting the melons, and he says, "Whoa, whoa!" He smiles at me. "Cabbage?"

The next day, my mother drops me off at the hospital again, and again I spend the day sliding in and out of a stoned, drooling sleep, sitting up, tipping over again. The wailing/rocking woman has been hospitalized. The chipper woman wears a yellow dress. Cathy is sitting with her back to the room, staring out the window. No one sees me. I crawl under a chair.

MY MOTHER has to be somewhere else for the evening, and I am feeling a little odd. Alone in the house, I pull myself to my closet and stand there, wavering on my feet, looking for a dress. I'm supposed to go to a benefit tonight. A friend of mine called to ask what time I was going to arrive. *Arrive? Arrive where? How can I possibly go out? How can I possibly get out of bed? And why on earth should I do so?* I pretend I have some idea what she's talking about. Having managed to get the details out of her — where, what time — I hang up and rack my brain. I finally sort out that the benefit is for an organization on whose board I sat. Ah, yes. A holdover from my other life. My past life, where people made the grave mistake of allowing me to do things like teach and sit on, you know, *boards*. I organize myself into a dress, first putting it on backward and then inside out, concentrating very hard in an effort to find matching shoes, making sure that not only do they match my dress but that they match each other as well.

Fumbling with my keys, I start the car and drive to the party, whispering the directions over and over under my breath, terrified that I will get lost somewhere in the city and be unable to find my way home. I have been to this place a million times, but now I have no idea where it is. I lean forward over the steering wheel, squinting out at the road. I drive about five miles an hour, cars blaring their horns and whipping around me. My vision is strange, wavy, the other cars weaving too close. I flinch away from them, jerking the wheel. I make it to the party and walk in, trying to pretend that I am steady on my feet and not swerving into walls. The gathering, talking, laughing, glittering people all around me, and I retreat to a corner where I can hang on to the wall.

Immediately I understand that coming here was a very bad idea. I am clearly unwell. My head is full of cotton, and my mouth doesn't want to move. I am dizzy, my perception of space is off. The sound is turned up to a shrill, piercing screech. The terrifying people eddy around me, their faces looming large in the telescope, filling the lens. Their voices reverberate in my skull. My face freezes in a smile, and periodically I nod, knowing that that is what I am supposed to do. When they laugh, I laugh. Their mouths are huge and yawning, and I see their glistening teeth. Eventually they go away, swallowed by the seething crowd, and I shrink backward, trying to blend in with the wall. In desperation, I take a glass of the champagne that is being passed around. My hands are shaking so hard that I need to use them both to get the plastic glass to my mouth.

In an instant, I am much improved. Suddenly brave, I follow the server with the tray of champagne like a dog and take another glass. That's better! All I needed was a little drink to lighten up. I talk to everyone, I throw my head back laughing — the friend who called says mildly, *I thought you'd stopped drinking?* — and I assure her that it's just once in a while, on special occasions like this. I guzzle champagne, emptying plastic glass after plastic glass, setting them back on the passing trays. I am having a perfectly marvelous time.

The next thing I know, it's night, and I am walking out of a liquor store with two bottles of scotch in a brown paper bag. I get in my car and drive home.

Somehow, I am not exactly sure how, Crazy Sean is living in my house. This is one of those things that to this day I can't explain. He seems to have teleported himself from the side of the road in Seattle where I left him to my house in San Francisco. Crazy Sean joins me on the porch. We sit there drinking. Well, I for one lie on the ground, but never mind. I drink the better part of two bottles in about an hour.

All of a sudden, I am being raced through the emergency room in a cocktail dress and all my jewelry. The lights flash past.

Without warning, my mother is there. This confuses me. Does my mother live here? How did she get here? I thought she went home.

I'm back in the psych ward. The booze out of my system, I sink back underwater, the depression closing in around my body. I hold my breath, floating down. My limbs are too heavy to swim back up. Everything is blunted. My heart thuds against the inside of my ribs. It annoys me. It continues to move when I want to be utterly still. I wish it would stop.

While I am in the psych ward, my family agrees that I clearly can't stay in California by myself. I am completely nonfunctional. I don't dress. I don't eat. The not eating has nothing to do with my eating disorder, which has been in remission for years, and everything to do with the fact that the depression has sucked away the energy to do anything at all. It's obvious that I'll start drinking again if I'm left alone. It is decided that I will move to Minnesota to live with my mother and stepfather for as long as is necessary. We pack up one suitcase and abandon everything else. I understand only that I will not be in California anymore.

I am sitting on an airplane. My mother is propping my head up with her hand.

## Attic, Basement
*Fall 2000*

I am in my mother's guest room. I am lying in bed. I am utterly still. The light is blinding. I pull the pillow over my face. I am dimly aware that in the course of about two months, I have gone from a job teaching college, a lovely house near Golden Gate Park, and half a dozen maxed-out credit cards to lying in a bed in my mother's attic, from which I have not emerged in a hundred years. I am filthy, heavy. I weigh down the bed. There is no reason to move. They've taken all my credit cards and closed all my accounts. They've quit my job for me and dropped me out of school. My car and all my things are right where we left them, in California, now the burden of my furious friends. Periodically my mother appears with food, or tea, or other unnecessary things. I watch her mouth move.

Awake at night, I sit on the floor watching TV with my mouth hanging open. In hell, *Jerry Springer* reruns play all night. *Jerr-ry! Jerr-ry! Jerr-ry!* Days go by. Then weeks. Months. It seems that I will never leave the room. Maybe I won't. Maybe I'll stay here forever. I can't bring myself to care.

My mother drives me to Dr. Lentz's office every few days. I hadn't seen him in two years. I have nothing better to do, and going there differentiates one day from the next. Still in my pajamas, I go down the stairs, clinging to the railing, and get in the car with my mother. I lean my forehead on the window and watch the bleak city go by. The world is ugly and surreal and a very long way away.

In his office, I sit curled up in his chair with my head on my knees. He tries lithium, Depakote, Tegretol, Topamax, and nothing is working. It makes me slow. It makes me shake. But it doesn't help. *Are you suicidal? Are you taking your meds?* I shake my head no. I nod my head yes. I whisper, *Make it go away.* He says he will. He says he's trying. He says something will work soon. *I'm sorry,* he says. *Hang in there.* I stand up and shuffle out of the office and get in the car and the bleak winter streets go by in reverse and I go home and climb back into bed and stare at the wall, lurching in and out of sleep.

"Sit up," my mother says, pulling on my shoulder until I am partially upright. She hands me a plate of soft scrambled eggs. She makes me foods I liked as a little kid, in an attempt to get me to eat. I mouth the eggs as if I am very old and have no teeth.

She rolls up the blinds. I shade my eyes with my hand, my plate balanced on my chest, my hand shaking so hard the fork taps erratically on the plate. She sits down in the rocker that she rocked me in when I was born. This depresses me. The attic room has windows on three sides. Outside, the leaves are turning red and gold and brown. It is autumn, which depresses me. Time is rolling by without me. I am trapped in my body, in this sunny little room, in this single bed, in these sweaty sheets.

"Were you sleeping?" she asks.

I give up on the eggs and set them on the bed stand. "I don't know."

"I was thinking," she says, "that maybe we could bundle up and go for a little walk. Just a few blocks, if you felt like it. Get a little air. Wouldn't that be nice?"

I stare at her, alarmed.

"All right," she says brightly, changing tacks. "What about you try to come out of your room?"

My eyes widen.

"Just for a little while. I'll come with you. We won't go far, just downstairs. You don't have to do anything. You don't have to talk. Maybe you could look at a book while I work. Could you just give it a try?"

I put my head back against the wall and tears leak down the sides of my nose. I note the tears and do not care. "So complicated," I whisper. "Completely overwhelming."

"All right, honey. It's okay. We'll try again tomorrow. So right now, maybe you could sit up all the way. Maybe you could read."

I shake my head. "Hands are shaking. Can't hold the book. I think it's the meds."

She looks sadly at me. "The day isn't being good to you."

I shake my head. "I'm sorry I'm such a freak," I say.

"You're sick. You're not a freak."

"You must hate me. I should go away. I should get out of here so you guys can go back to your regular life." That is more than I have said in days. I am obsessed with the idea that they secretly hate me and are only tolerating me because they have to. "You don't have to take care of me, you know. You could tell me to leave." My head spins with this thought, and I imagine how many steps it would take to get even as far as a door.

"I know that," she says. "This is just a good place to rest."

"Resting," I say. I'm not sick. I'm resting. I like the sound of it.

"Resting," she agrees.

I recede into my head, look out the window at the trees. She sits with me quietly for a while, then gets up and leaves, running her hand over the top of my head on her way out.

FALL ROLLS into winter. The trees give up the last of their leaves, and I watch snow fall past my window, collecting in perfect drifts on the black branches. If you put a camera in my room, you could watch the seasons pass in time-lapse. You could see me too, lying in bed, lying on the floor, sitting on the edge of the bed, always staring into space.

One night, out of nowhere, the image of a glass comes to me, sharp and precise: a glass of scotch, two cubes of ice. The thought is clearer than anything that has passed through my mind in months. The image is so sharp I can see it, taste the booze, feel the burn going down. The doctors' warnings don't even enter my mind — *the meds won't work, your liver's shot, you're going to die if you keep this up* — to hell with it. Suddenly I am on my feet.

My mother and her husband are asleep. I tiptoe through the house and creep down the basement stairs, wincing as they creak. I feel my way to the light switch, flip it, and survey the scene. I will find the booze if it kills me. I know it's down here. I will sniff it out.

I pick my way through boxes, stacks of ancient magazines, towers of old, worn books with cloth covers and gilt-imprinted words. I step over a sewing machine covered with dust, and over a steamer trunk. I open a door and find a small room containing a bin of coal, a cord of wood, and piles of old clothes. I climb behind the washer and dryer, look under the sink, go rifling through the racks of clothes. An hour ago, I didn't even know I needed a drink. Now it is my entire purpose in life, and I can't find it, and I am about to scream.

Maybe I find the energy to focus on something because of the need for alcohol. But maybe, irony of ironies, the fact that I am out of bed means that I am actually getting a little better. That won't last if I get a drink. As soon as the alcohol is in my system, what little effect the meds may be having will be nullified. The alcohol will, in fact, lift the depression — and skyrocket me into mania. It's happened a million times before. And right now, lower than I've ever been, that's what I want. More than anything, I want out of this hell. When that craving for a drink sets in, you don't think about the consequences. You don't think about the fact that there are many levels of hell, and the alcohol will merely take you to another one. It's instinctual. It's not a rational decision. It's a need. It has to be met. The need is all you know.

By this point in my life, I'm both a raging alcoholic *and* a person with uncontrolled bipolar. The two have become discrete issues that will have to be treated in and of themselves. Treating the bipolar won't cure the alcoholism, and treating the alcoholism won't cure the bipolar. But until I stop drinking for good, any attempts at treating the bipolar will fail.

I've never consciously noticed that I use alcohol to control my moods and have since I was a kid — and so I don't realize that its properties as a mood stabilizer have long since disappeared. Like any alcoholic, I ignore the fact that the booze stopped working the way I want it to work a long time ago, and can only remember the fact that, once upon a time, it did. And maybe it will right now.

So I keep digging through my mother's basement in the middle of the night, desperate for a drink.

I spelunk my way back to the stairs and look around the room, hoping I'll see something I didn't see before. And I do. There under the stairs is an old record player, a busted-in speaker spilling split wires, and a pile of boxes. I make a dive for them and start yanking them open, their soggy, bent cardboard ripping in my hands. I shove aside boxes full of letters, moldy hats, wool scarves, old kitchen utensils, and there it is. I see the box. I crawl toward it, breathless, crushing boxes as I go. I open it up and find a collection of bottles. Relief floods through me and I nearly dance with joy. I get greedy and start opening boxes all around it, and there's more, the hard stuff, some of the bottles already open, half gone. There are ancient bottles with fancy necks, round bottles, tall slender ones, all of them covered in dust so thick my fingers are sticky with it, brandy, aquavit, bourbon, port, cordials, vodka, gin, whiskey, and, praise Jesus, scotch.

I am a little kid on Christmas Day. I am a bride kissing my groom while everyone cheers. I am a soldier who just got laid. I am triumphant. The occasion clearly calls for a drink.

The depression lifts overnight. It's hard to believe, but that's exactly what happens. One day I am nearly catatonic, and the next I go rocketing into a mixed episode. Still, it's better, to me, than depression — at least I am in motion, albeit feeling like a fraying nerve. Everything is moving at a shrieking pitch, and my thoughts turn black and bloody. This hell is garish, sharp, and it cuts at my brain. I dream about blood. Death is everywhere, I breathe it, I smell it in the room. I want it, but the thoughts are spinning so fast I can't grasp it, I go flying past, riding some demon merry-go-round where all the horses smile their evil, mocking smiles.

There are many things that might trigger one of my episodes. But alcohol will.

I turn into a monster, screaming at my mother, getting more and more agitated every evening, ramping up into rabid, nasty mania by night. I go crashing out the door, headed for God knows where. In the morning, she finds me lying in bed with my face to the wall. She opens the blinds. *You have to have light*, she says. No. *Please close them. Please.* Depression settles in for the day. By evening I am nuts again, and go out into the night, and come back again to lie in bed, hiding from the sun. I can't think straight. I turn into Jekyll and Hyde.

I sit in the basement every night after I come stumbling home from wherever I've been, huddle under the stairs with my boxes of booze, drinking as much as I can possibly contain before I lurch back up to bed and pass out. I try to be careful. I can't run out. But of course I run out. For the first time in months, I have a reason to get dressed. I find my way to the bar, the neon signs and glittering bottles I know.

I have no more credit cards, no more cash. But at the bar, there are always men. And where there are men, there is money. I am humiliated, disgusted with myself, but I have no other way to get booze. It's easy to find a man who will keep me supplied, take me home, give me a place to sleep it off so I can go home to my mother's house not reeking of alcohol. She suspects that I'm drinking. I lie — just going to a coffee shop to read, or just having tea with friends! *At least I'm getting out! At least I'm getting well!* She backs off. I come home after she's gone to bed, stumble up the stairs, creeping past her bedroom door.

I can't keep their names straight. And then I find the perfect sucker. He's nondescript, without personality, ideas, or goals. He is a thing that occupies a barstool. He thinks it's cute when I drink him and his friends and everyone else under the table. Unfathomably, improbably, stupidly, he falls for me. I have lost all sense of human decency. It's no excuse that I'm sick.

I don't ask myself why I'm doing this. My vision has narrowed. I have become an animal, focused on survival. I stare straight ahead and press forward, terrified, clutching the bottle in my hands, living one day to the next, never slowing down long enough to see what I'm doing to myself or anyone else.

Then the real party begins. I'm back to the lipstick and heels, the spinning faces, the lights. But this party is different from the old fancy scene. This party takes place in filthy dive bars, where the stink of stale grease and spilled beer fills the air, where the thick smoke spins slowly under the Budweiser light over the pool table, where someone like me couldn't possibly be, but where someone like me absolutely belongs. I try not to think about how far I've fallen. I am broke, desperate, foul-mouthed, shitfaced, stumbling, slurring, clinging to a man I don't even know so he will keep me in booze. Drunk, at night, I'm manic as hell. I'm gregarious, excited, full of laughter and grandiose plans. Anyone who knew me before would back away as I sprawl on the floor. I'm trashy. I'm trash.

The mixed episode rages on, and I rage on, crashing through my mother's house, curling up in bed, flying out the door at night, hurtling back to the bar, getting more and more manic as the night wears on, then waking up disoriented, confused, squinting at the awful sun. I dress myself in last night's clothes and walk home, wishing to God I'd get hit by a car.

One night, I go into yet another rage at my mother, stuff my things in paper bags, and storm out the door and into my bar guy's car. Now I am living with him in his father's basement. He's in his thirties and still sleeping in his childhood bed. His floor is covered wall to wall with trash, clothes, magazines, dirty dishes, endless quantities of crap. I lie in bed at night drinking whiskey from the bottle, chattering on like a macaw until I pass out. We're perfect for each other. Apparently I have agreed to marry him. I have trouble remembering his name. I will work on this.

We move from his father's house into the upstairs of an old house that should be condemned, and there begin what he calls my John and Yoko months. He thinks it's funny. I take up residence in the bed, next to the bedside table crowded with bottles of wine and whiskey and pills. I lie there watching Thin Man movies. I drift in and out of blackouts, or sleep, it's hard to tell which. When the clock strikes five, I haul my drunk, depressed ass out of bed and get ready for the evening. The evening is the bar. I am drunk twenty-four hours a day. My tolerance is so high it takes me eleven drinks to get a buzz on. I find the perfect high around sixteen. Of course, I always overshoot the mark. By the end of the night, who knows how much I've had. I'm stumbling through the parking lot, elated. He's holding me up as I slip on my heels like a pig on ice. It's winter. It's freezing. I lie in bed, sweating alcohol, my skin clammy and gray. He feeds me fried peanut butter and banana sandwiches. I eat them every couple of days, like an anaconda. I don't look away from the television. I wash the sandwiches down with whiskey. At night, at the bar, I come alive. By morning, I am dead again.

Ridiculously, one night, I find myself in detox with the bums.

The cops escort me there during a particularly elaborate meltdown on a busy street and drop me unceremoniously at the door. I pitch a fit. I am wearing a very nice dress. Do they know who I am? I rage like a drunk rages. They ignore me the way you ignore a drunk. In the morning, they let me out. A few days later, I'm back in.

# Valentine's Day

2001

I snap out of a blackout to find that I have just put my foot through the windshield of the bar guy's car. I have no idea why. I've had seventeen double martinis — I know this because I count them so I won't drink too much. I fly out of the car and down the icy street in my dress and heels. He's chasing me. I'm pulling out of his grip, screaming. I run up the stairs to the apartment and call a friend, who is surely delighted to hear from me at midnight on Valentine's Day. I lie on the kitchen floor in my dress, pouring a bottle of wine down my throat. My friend tells the bar guy to take me to the psych ward.

Dr. Lentz: *How are you feeling this morning?*

It's bright. I'm still in my dress. The sunlight pierces me and I am filled with despair. I'm still drunk. I tell him I feel like Cat. *You know, from* Breakfast at Tiffany's? I slur, lifting my head off the pillow to look at him and letting it fall back. *She doesn't name him because she doesn't want to get attached to him? So he has no name? He's just Cat? Get it?*

*I get the reference.*

I am greatly relieved. He always understands.

*Do you know what your blood alcohol level was when you came in last night?*

No.

*It was point three-five.*

*Is that a lot?*

*That's higher than hell.*

Even my psychiatrist is disgusted with me. By my count, that makes everyone, including me.

And now I am sitting in a dirty snowbank on Central Avenue. I've fallen into it. I'm holding a near-empty quart of vodka. I'm crying, mostly because the liquor store's not open yet. It's seven A.M.

I give up and stick my head in the snow.

Maybe it sobers me up. Anyway, I find a cell phone on my person. I call my father, crying.

*Marya, put the bottle down,* he says firmly.

I am stunned. Truly, stunned. I have never heard such an amazing idea in my life.

Carefully, I dig a little hole in the snow for the bottle, and I put it down.

I'm lying with my face against the door of a cop car. My cousin is a cop. My father has called her to come pick me up. She's not impressed.

I'm lying in the ER. My aunt and uncle — I've gotten the whole family involved now — appear when I open my eyes.

*It's the shits, ain't it?* Aunt Andy says.

I nod. *It is,* I manage to spit out of my cottony mouth.

She nods. *I know.*

I'm on a psych ward, screaming for more Klonopin. Klonopin

acts on the same neuroreceptors as alcohol, and when you're taking enough of it and go off suddenly, you can get pretty sick. It doesn't occur to me that the same thing will happen once I come off the alcohol itself. *Don't you understand that I'll go through withdrawal?*

*No offense,* says the nice nurse, *you're already in withdrawal.*

I am in a room, which is spinning. I stand up and try to find the door, but I crash into the walls and give up and stumble into bed again.

I'm sitting in a folding chair, looking around a crowded room. Someone is standing on a platform, yelling, *Hi! My name is Connie, and I'm a drunk!*

*Hi, Connie!* everyone yells.

Motherfucking Christ. I'm in rehab. They've finally got me. It's over.

In a way, it is — at least this part, the years when alcohol both disguised and worsened the bipolar. As I've said, sobering up won't cure me. Getting sober, in fact, exposes the bipolar in all its awful glory. But getting the alcohol out of the picture at least gives me a chance at managing my mental illness. When I get the alcohol out of my system, Dr. Lentz finds a combination of medications that brings the world into focus. Even I can tell that the madness is receding.

I walk out of rehab two months later. Over the next several weeks, I slip and have another drink more than once. But one day I wake up sober. June 9, 2001. The sun isn't too bright. The crushing bear of depression is gone. The mania has broken. I lie in bed, watching the branches covered with new leaves sway back and forth across my window. I can breathe.

# Coming to Life

*Summer 2001*

I am sitting on the porch swing of the little rented house in Minneapolis where I am living with my fiancé, the bar guy, a seriously unfortunate situation that is soon to end. I'm swinging a little, watching the cars go by. I am holding myself carefully, like an egg. I am fragile, barely there. I imagine I am transparent, that you can see right through me to the screen behind, and the oak tree beyond that, and the little green house beyond that. I take extreme caution when breathing. I hold very still so that I will not upset the tenuous balance of my mind, tip it on its side, send my thoughts sliding all over again.

Time barely moves. The world quivers around me. I step carefully through it, not touching anything. The dust on the porch must not be disturbed.

This is the world. I am trying not to take up very much space or make any noise, because there is a kind of silence that bewilders and fascinates me, and I am afraid of my voice. I am afraid of myself, the self that was mad. The madness sleeps under the house, its scaly tail over its nose. I walk carefully in the house, placing my feet one in front of the other, making sure the floor doesn't creak.

I've become concerned with solid things. I like the oak tree and the little house, the kitchen, with its hefty pots and pans. I like the food I buy at the store every day, and I like the store, its heavy sliding glass doors, its rows and rows of produce, its aisles of boxes and cartons and cans. I take things off the shelves. I look at the writing on them, and I look at the price. I put them in my basket. They will stock my cupboards, giving proof that I live there, that I am in a place, that I am capable of living my life.

I sleep at night. In the morning, I do my tasks. First, shower. Next, get dressed. Dressing is essential. So are sensible shoes. Next, go to the kitchen. Real people pour themselves bowls of cereal and read the paper. So far, I don't read the paper, because it overwhelms me, implying as it does a larger world, a world beyond my little street. I wash the dish and put it in the rack to dry.

Next, I wander around the house, touching the furniture and walls. I have become so brave that I get the mail. When there are bills, I write the checks, feeling wild and a little dizzy. This way the lights will stay on, and the water, and the phone. I understand that if I complete my tasks, nothing will go wrong. The world is an orderly system of cause and effect. This is a wonder and an enormous relief.

The real things matter. They are the bones on which one hangs a life. I've never understood this before. Back then, I couldn't be bothered with dishes or meals or bills. When the madness had me in its teeth and thrashed me back and forth, I didn't even know what the real things were, or how to do them, or what they were for. Now I know: they keep the madness at bay. It sleeps quietly under the house, only occasionally grumbling in its sleep.

I only think about the here and now. When the memory of madness slides in by mistake, I empty my head of everything until it passes. Sometimes, a fly buzzes by. Sometimes, I see a neighbor. When he waves, I am stunned at having been seen. It takes me a minute, but I wave back. Then I go inside. That's enough of the world for today.

I cook an elaborate dinner, delighted with the organization of recipes, their one-step-at-a-time. The bewildering man comes home and pours himself a drink. He will drink all evening, because that is all he does. I am terrified of the drinking, of the bottle itself.

When he isn't there, I sit with my hands folded in my lap, holding completely still. If I hold still, I will not get up and get the bottle and start drinking, because if I start drinking I will not stop. And the madness will come roaring up through the floor.

I understand this because the people at treatment explained it, and Dr. Lentz explained it further. It, too, is cause and effect: *if* I have a drink, *then* I will keep drinking. I know this to be true. I have plenty of evidence. And furthermore, *if* I am drinking, *then* my meds won't work. *Marya, if you want to make this work, you just can't drink. You need your medication to be effective. You need to get your life under control. If you keep drinking, neither of those things can happen. I can't help you if you won't help yourself.*

My meds are helping. I have evidence of this as well. I have a house, toothpaste, food, a porch, and a porch swing. It is finally quiet, almost silent, in my mind. Dr. Lentz has explained that the madness is there, and will always be there. But it will keep sleeping, as long as I don't wake it up. I live in quiet terror, and try to put it from my mind.

I've called an uneasy truce: I've acknowledged that I have bipolar. I think I have accepted it. But really, what I've accepted is the medication. I tell myself that if I don't drink anymore, the illness will clear up, but as long as I'm at it, I might as well take the pills all the time, just to cover all my bases.

I have a strikingly simplistic understanding of what having bipolar means. I go by the just-like-diabetes theory — a mental illness is just like diabetes; it's something you have to take medication for, and *that's okay.* I never use the word *bipolar* outside of Dr. Lentz's office or the confines of my parents' homes. I'm not eager to mention a *mental illness,* either. It implies all the things I don't want to believe — that I'm hopeless, completely dysfunctional, totally divorced from reality, possibly dangerous. I know that's what a lot of people think when they hear the words *mentally ill.* Depression, that's one thing — lots of people have depression, and they're not crazy. Bipolar, schizophrenia — *that's* crazy. *That's* mental illness — the psychos, the nut cases, the incurably insane, the muttering bag ladies and bums, the freaks. So I take my meds, and don't accept the name for what I have.

I refuse to believe that I'm beyond help — and that's how I see mental illness. In truth, I'm not beyond help. But there also isn't a cure. And I don't want to believe that. I want to believe that if I do it right, if I do what they say, if I take the medication and don't drink, the madness will never bother me again. It will get tired of waiting around for an opportunity. It will go away.

When I wake up in the night drenched in sweat, dreaming of the old place, the reeling sun and neon lights, the leering people, the parties, the cop cars, the disappearing friends, and I fear that I've gone mad again, I get out of bed and move through the house like a thief, touching things, tapping the walls, until I am certain that I am here, that it's now, that I'm safe.

It's the end of the summer, and the world has come into focus. The blurred edges of things have sharpened. I take on solidity. I go down to the crawlspace under the house. Madness has vacated the premises. I know, now, that I am well. Lentz is wrong. The madness will never come again. I know it as surely as I know I am real.

## Jeff

*Fall 2001*

Every evening, I go to my twelve-step meeting and mumble my name as we go around in a circle. While I sit in my little group, I rack my brain for something to say, but nothing comes. I think I will shatter if I speak. There will be pieces of me everywhere. I sit with my arms wrapped around my knees. I do this for three months. Then, one day, I say something, and everyone stares at me in shock, as if they hadn't been sure I could actually talk.

Fall comes. I brace myself for the blues, but the days pass and they don't come. The meds are working. I'm sober. I'm going to be fine.

One evening, I watch a man from my meeting lie on the ground, staring up at the red and yellow leaves on the trees.

"I'm in a world of hurt," he says to the sky.

I fall in love with him with a thud. Not because he's in a world of hurt, but because he's lifted his face from the ground and caught me looking at him, and smiled. Because his face is kind. I look away, and look back. He's still looking at me. He sits up. "But I'm all right," he says "This will pass."

I'm in no shape to be in love. It's a terrible idea. I'm already engaged, for God's sake, and less than six months sober — the usual suggestion is that you stay out of relationships for a year. But for some reason, in whatever haphazard fashion, it works.

I break off the absurd engagement to the bar guy and move into an apartment by myself. It's not lost on me that the one-room studio is half the size of my one-time living room back in California. Gone are my silk curtains and my velvet couch and four-poster bed. Gone are the fancy job and the limitless credit cards. My room contains a mattress, a desk, and a chair. I eat with my plate on my knees, sitting on the edge of the bed. I write, the novel now starting to take shape as I finally have the discipline and clarity to work on it every day and the focus to write well. And I start seeing this man.

His name is Jeff. His wife just left him and his mother just died. He's been diagnosed with depression, and his meds aren't working yet. He's a complete disaster area. I walk around his house in wonder. There is a dining room table, but no chairs. Dust covers every surface, an inch thick. There is no food in the refrigerator. Every room in his house is painted a different, hideous color, the doing of his ex-wife, who apparently liked to paint. The basement is packed full of dozens of boxes of useless things, jars and shot glasses with obscure logos and coffee cups and crock pots and ugly vases, the shelves on which the boxes sit sagging and covered with mold. It's the house of someone who hasn't been out of bed for months. In fits of energy, he has bought himself two midlife-crisis cars, three deluxe mattresses, and a set of copper pots and pans. He's trying to buy enough things to stave off the stifling depression he's under. It isn't working.

I stand in the doorway to his bedroom. He's in his suit, all the way under the covers, including his head. His dress shoes peek out. It's three o'clock in the afternoon.

"Hi," I say. The room is painted insane asylum green.

"Hi," comes a muffled voice.

"How was your day?"

"Not good," he says.

"Sorry to hear it." I lean against the door frame and jingle my keys. "Do you want to come out of there?"

"I'm being a walnut," he says. He sticks his nose out of the covers. "You could come get in."

"No thanks. I think you should get up and at least change your clothes. If you're going to be depressed, you shouldn't be wearing a suit. You should be in your pajamas."

This gets a muffled half laugh.

"Do you want me to go away?" I ask.

"No!"

"Then I'm going to make something to eat. And then you're getting out of bed and eating it. And then you can get back in bed if you want, but I'm going home."

"Don't go home!"

"If you don't get out of bed when I make dinner, I'm going home." I turn around and pick my way through the rubble and go into the kitchen and unpack the groceries I've brought.

A minute later he's standing in the doorway, his hair standing on end and his tie askew. He's taken off the shoes. "I'm out of bed," he says.

"Good. Chop carrots," I say.

"Now will you stay?" He sounds so small I want to fold him up and put him in a little box and keep him in my pocket.

"Sure," I say, and hand him a cutting board and a knife. Bewildered, he looks at them. "Carrots," I repeat.

"Oh," he says. "Right."

I have never been the sane one before. It is so nice I don't mind that he's in his own kind of madness. I know mad. I can handle mad. It's just a matter of feeding the mad thing, and getting it out of bed, and opening the curtains and letting in the light, and you do it over and over until the madness fades into the background and the person emerges again.

And since I seem so sane compared with how I've been all my life, I begin to believe I am. I do tell him I have bipolar, and jokingly say that he might want to think twice about getting involved with me. In fact, I give him a list of a hundred and one reasons not to date me, and *bipolar* is at the top of the list. I feel like I'm poisonous. So I give him my disclaimer, and hope for the best. But I also tell him it's all in the past.

He takes a leave of absence from work, and we fly to Florida for a month. We've been dating only a few months, and everyone thinks we're completely nuts. Lentz worries that it's yet another of my impulsive acts, a debacle waiting to happen. But it isn't.

In Florida, Jeff lies on the couch most of the time. I cook and write until he staggers up and needs to be fed. When he starts feeling better, we start going for drives. Soon, he's laughing, and I begin to find out who he is.

He's the kind of man who wouldn't have come near me with a ten-foot pole even a year ago. He has no time for flashy scenes. He wears green wool sweaters and sensible brown boots. There is no other word for him than *kind*. He's exactly who he says he is. He fascinates me. I watch him while he sleeps, wanting to take him apart and see how he's made. He snores like a freight train. He is tangible, solid. He holds down the bed. With him here, the roof isn't always flying off. With him here, needing my presence, I understand for the first time what it means to be good to someone. It's the first time I have ever been unselfish in my life. He needs something I have, so I give it to him.

Falling in love happens so suddenly that it seems, all at once, that you have always been in love. We tumble into a life together just like that. We go from starry-eyed to angry to companionable in the space of a few weeks. In February, we go back to Minneapolis. His depression has lifted. In April, we buy an old Victorian near one of the city lakes. One Sunday, we're sitting at breakfast and decide to get married. So we do.

## The Good Life
*Summer 2002*

It's been a year since I got sober, more than a year since the madness. I have taken on shape and weight. I am visible. When I walk, my feet make a sound. I am twenty-eight years old and married. The man I have married is real, and he laughs easily and often, and he is so big that at night he makes a dent in the center of the bed and I roll into it and get squashed under him. I no longer float up and hover by the ceiling. I will stay. I whisper to myself, *Stay, stay, stay.*

I open my eyes. I look through the window at the whitewashed, pale blue sky of early morning. The kind of light, like dusk, where you can hardly see another person. It is only a dark figure, its face obscured, shadowy and ethereal. The figure ties his tie. He thinks I am asleep. I watch him, an inky blot against the pale, thin dawn light. It's like spying. I am secret, here in my bed, the dogs curled and warm at my belly, snoozing. They have no interest in morning. Jeff turns, and I close my eyes. I breathe slowly, pretending to sleep. He bends over me and kisses my cheek lightly, so he won't wake me. He opens the bedroom door and closes it carefully. It clicks shut. Then silence pours into the empty room, like water filling a vase. The vase holds roses, their heads bent, dying a little. They, too, are only a dark stain on the light. The silence pours in like the tide filling in a tide pool. It pours in like blood, seeping thick and heavy —

Oh, for God's sake, knock it off.

But it's lovely, says the madness, protesting —

No. This morning is perfect. The white light, coming up now, is perfect. This morning I am well. Wait — I double-check. I feel around me in the bed. The dogs, under the covers, stir, then settle in again. One of them snores a quilt-muffled snore. I smile. The leaves outside the window are thick and green, and the dark, delicate branches touch and tap, like fingers, against the glass, against the light. The early light is so lovely I almost hold my breath. This morning is perfect. I am sane.


I KICK BACK in the chair in Dr. Lentz's office, telling him how wonderful everything is.

"My life is perfect," I say. "It's incredible. Everything's different now. The writing's going well, Jeff is good, my friends are good, my family's great. I feel incredible. I'm totally alive. I'm crazy busy. We have people over all the time. The summer is wonderful. I'm happier than I've ever been."

"You're not doing too much?" he asks.

"Of course not." I sigh, rolling my eyes. "Everything is perfect. Just right."

He smiles, shaking his head. "I have to say, it sounds pretty good."

"It is. It absolutely is," I say. I lean forward in my seat. "It's nothing like it used to be. That's ancient history. I've turned over a new leaf. I'm a totally different person." I laugh, delighted. "I'm not crazy anymore."

He scribbles something on his little pad. "I think, honestly, that your bipolar is in remission."

"You mean I'm well."

He smiles. "I mean you're in remission."

Same thing.

I throw my purse over my shoulder and stride out the door into the perfect, sunny summer day.

JEFF SWINGS ME around when he comes home. I am wearing an apron, laughing, and Jeff is kissing me. We are in a movie, a movie of normal people. It's a boring movie. No one will want to watch it but us, but we watch it, amazed.

"Peanut!" he cries, setting me down. "How was your day?"

I dance around the kitchen with my spatula and tell him. My day was perfect. I did everything right. I wrote a new chapter. I did laundry and folded it and put it away. I got the mail and paid the bills. I went to the store and came home and carried the groceries up all by myself. I had coffee with a friend, and the Johnsons are coming for dinner, we're having pasta, and salad, and I made bread and I bought five kinds of cheese, and olives, and for dessert a blueberry lemon tart. The crust is from scratch. The pasta is homemade. I made three kinds of sauce so people can choose.

I forget what it's like to be mad, a blissful sort of amnesia. This is the nature of bipolar: when the episodes end, it's back to the regular world, and the regular world looks like heaven, and you relish your sanity. How could this be just remission? Lentz is wrong. My mood has leveled out. My family is breathing a little easier. Jeff seems to be the rock that will keep me grounded for good. He treats me like a queen, a miracle, and for the first time I am loved not for the constant excitement, the insane *passion* that always drew men in and then, of course, pushed them away, not for how I look or what I do, but for who I am, quirks and strangeness and flaws and all. In the circle of his love, I can finally relax, breathe easy, love him back with everything I've got. And for the first time, I have something to give.

I relish the small tasks and the chores and the hours I spend writing in my office. I sometimes just walk around the house, a little disoriented, trying to grasp the fact that I live here, that all the pretty things are mine. I close my eyes and open them and everything is still there. The days tumble over each other, sunlit and gorgeous, drenched in things that are real. I find myself making plans — for the evening, for the fall, for the coming year, for my life. I've never been able to do that before — the madness always intervened.

Sometimes, I get the uneasy feeling that I'm fooling everyone. In the middle of a gathering of friends, at a party, at a show, on a walk with Jeff, I'll remember the past. It leaves me a little shaken, bewildered by how I've gotten from there to here. I feel it in the pit of my stomach, the shame of it, the feeling that I am getting away with something, living a life I don't deserve. It's someone else's life. I've snuck in and am squatting in it. I'm wearing someone else's wedding ring, occupying someone else's house, and everyone loves the woman I'm pretending to be, not me. Who would love me? I hate the person I was. She disgusts me, her and her mess and her madness, her garish excess, her disorderly excuse for a life. She was a monster. She was sick. Suddenly I can feel her in me, like bile in my throat. I can't let her out. The spell will break, and she will take over again. I want to forget her. I want her dead.

Then the feeling passes. I believe in this new world with a religious fervor. It is my savior. If I am very good, they'll let me stay, and soon, if I work hard enough, I will belong.

I decide I should get a job. I have all this boundless energy, energy to spare. Finishing a novel isn't enough. I'll work full-time, keep writing, and still have time left over to live my overflowing life.

# The Magazine
*November 2002*

I'm at a celebration for the opening of a new section of Minneapolis's city magazine. I had my first job in journalism here years ago and, hired again, have thrown myself into the creation of an arts and entertainment section. I thought it up, pitched it, designed it, hired the freelancers, wrote the features, and edited the thing. The people at the magazine have gone nuts. There are notepads with my name on them, radio ads about my section, the publisher keeps taking me out to lunch — my job is to grab a younger readership for stories on the Minneapolis arts scene, revamp the magazine's image, and make the publishers money in the process. Horrified by the notepads and ads, I'm trying not to think about what I'm suddenly supposed to be. I just brace myself and go galloping into my job.

There are people everywhere, laughing and drinking white wine. People I've never met come up to congratulate me. I'm a little overwhelmed, so I keep smiling, figuring it can't hurt. My editor pushes me forward to say something. I have no idea what comes out of my mouth. I have no idea how I wound up here. I say something that is apparently coherent, and now people are clapping. It dawns on me that they think I am a real person. And now that I think of it, I *look* like a real person. I see myself through their eyes: I am dressed in real-person clothes. I have a real-person job. I drove here in a car that I own. I drove here from a house that I own, which also contains my husband; not only do I have a husband, I realize, but I have a *second* husband. Julian's a lifetime away, our divorce came and went with little fuss. The wild years are over. I'm sober, I'm not crazy anymore, and here I am, a new person with a real life at last.

I look around myself in alarm. There are the photographers. There are the ladies who lunch. There are the wealthy patrons of the arts, the hip gallery people, the mayor, the music people in black. There has been a grave mistake. Someone let me in.

So I'd better have fun while it lasts.

I'm a whirlwind of activity. I make phone calls, assign stories, juggle meetings, edit, interview, and write and write. I'm going to succeed if it kills me. Any success I've had before this doesn't count. This is different. I'm going to show them all.

I sit in the morning meetings, brainstorming stories, trying to believe I am one of them, trying to pass. Their voices are level; I try to keep my voice level. They do not get worked up; I won't get worked up either. They are respectable people. Very Minnesotan, very mild, very nice. I glue myself to the chair, do not wiggle or hop. I amuse them with my interruptions and ideas and cackling laugh. But they see me, they like what I'm doing, so I belong. I am officially a person at last.

"I'll take it," I say, scribbling in my notebook. I look up at my editor, who's standing in front of the dry-erase board in the meeting room. "I'll take the story."

"But you took the last one."

"I'll take this one too. I have plenty of time."

"You're editing a section by yourself."

"It's a light month." I swallow my coffee and poke at my bagel with my pen. "I really want to do it." I jiggle my knee under the table, wishing this meeting would move along.

The editor laughs. "All right," he says. The other editors look at me a little strangely. There seems to be a concerted effort at this magazine to move as slowly as possible. I am a little bit resented for my incessant work. People keep telling me to slow down.

"You wanted to see me?" I say, standing in my editor's doorway. I love this guy. He gave me my first job here when I was nineteen.

"How are you?" he asks.

Niceties! Nonsense! "Fine," I say. "What's up?" I go in and sit down.

"I'm a little concerned that you're working too much."

I blink. "I'm not. I'm working as much as I need to to get all my work done."

He nods, smiling. "Maybe you shouldn't be doing quite so much work?"

Ridiculous! "I'm just making the section as good as it can be."

"And it looks great," he says, nodding and nodding. "It looks really great. I just don't want you to burn out."

I laugh out loud. "Of course I'm not going to burn out! Don't worry about me. I always work this much. It's just how I operate. I like to get things done, and I don't like to waste time. Hey," I say. "I'm just trying to give you my best." I smile my most winning smile.

He shakes his head and laughs. "Okay," he says. "Whatever you say. Just don't be afraid to ask for some help, all right?"

"All right," I say, hopping up. All right, all right, all right! "Thanks!" I say, and leap out the door.

"They're driving me crazy!" I shout when Jeff comes home from work. I spin around in my office chair while he drops his briefcase and kisses my head. "It's always, *slow down, slow down, slow down,* doesn't anybody want to get anything *done?* Don't they get bored? Sitting there in their cubicles, churning out the same old articles they've been churning out for years?" I jump out of my chair and charge down the stairs, calling, "Dinner!"

I start at the magazine working thirty hours a week. That creeps up to forty, then fifty, sixty. By August 2003 it's eighty, and I'm whipping up and down the aisles between the cubicles at the office. I'm out late every night at openings and shows. I wake up at the crack of dawn to work on my novel, which is finally nearing completion, then race into work, where I move in fast-forward, delighted by the efficiency of my various systems, clicking along; answer the phone, assign the story, edit the piece, make the call, set up the interview — stopping briefly when someone comes over to talk to me, talking to them a million miles an hour — dash out of the office for the lunch, dash back in for the meeting, sit down at my desk, e-mail the writer, file the press releases, scribble the notes, get a little burst of energy and gallop down the hall, gallop back, crash into my chair, and slowly the office is emptying out, and I'm typing, and people are stopping by to say good night, and I'm typing, and I am humming under my breath, whole symphonies, all the parts, and I keep typing, and suddenly it's totally quiet.

I peek over the top of my cubicle and survey the cubicle farm. All the little ants have gone home. I notice that it's dark outside. I look at my watch: nine o'clock! Jeff! I grab my coat and go running out of the office. I tear through the streets, his car is there, he's home! The little yellow lights in the window are delightful! I take the stairs two at a time, burst in the door, run through the house, and fling myself at Jeff, "I'm sorry I'm late! Lost track of time! Did you eat? I haven't eaten. What do we have? How was your day?" I'm throwing things in bowls and stirring wildly and boiling water and I have about fourteen hands, and he tells me how his day was, "You're kidding! Oh, no! What a jackass! Good job! That's great!" and I break out my symphonic song, and throw whatever I was stirring into a pan, and he laughs at me, and I laugh, and we laugh and eat dinner and have sex and then he falls asleep, and I lie there.

My head is humming. I worry that it is humming so loudly it will vibrate the bed.

It doesn't feel like mania. No no, it's *happiness,* it's *energy.* I'm doing everything right.

EVEN THOUGH I've gone crazy every summer for most of my life, this year it's not crazy — I'm just having a fabulous time. There's a theater festival in town. Two weeks of hardly any sleep, parties, people everywhere, my days spent writing wildly in the office, churning out stories on both the festival and the rest of the art scene, and then there are the interviews, and the meetings, and I'm still racing along on the novel.

I'm on fast-forward, alive with the old addiction to thrills. My speech speeds up, I'm flinging my hands around, my heart is pounding like mad. There is drama and gossip at the festival, and I need no sleep and no food, and I ignore Jeff, vacating the house completely, doing precisely nothing like running a home life. No night is too late and nothing is too much and nothing is enough.

At the end of the festival, there are two hundred people in our house, fabulous food, endless booze — thank God Jeff and I don't drink — music blasting, people spilling out into the yard, every floor of the house packed with wildly gesturing, heavily inebriated actors, all of them seemingly moving as fast as I am. People crowd into my office, sitting in piles on the chairs and the floor, shouting and gesturing. I'm euphoric. The conversation gets louder and louder, we laugh until we fall out of our chairs. I'm at my most charismatic, my grand schemes seem perfectly reasonable. Mania is contagious, pulling people into its whirlwind orbit. I'm the pied piper. There's nothing wrong with *me*. Absolutely *everyone* is crazy. I'm riding the swell of excitement with everyone else.

The party breaks up around four o'clock in the morning, and at six I hop out of bed and keep moving. Work has never been better. I've never written faster, never worked so hard. It's fucking *great*.

Madness? This isn't madness. This is more fun than I've had in years. Why would I want to come down? This is just how it is now, this is how it's always *supposed* to be — I've hit my stride, and I just didn't realize how painfully *slow* I'd been going before. Everything before, pshaw. That was nothing. Ladies and gentlemen, you've never seen anything like it. Watch *this*.

*Fall 2003*

I'm taking my meds without really thinking about them, and I show up for my appointments with Dr. Lentz, sighing with irritation that I still have to bother with this nonsense. I report — and believe — that everything is going well, better than well, so he has no reason to think that anything's wrong. I brush off his incessant questions about whether I'm doing too much. What is it with these people? Lentz, my parents, Jeff, my friends — all of them making a fuss, telling me I'm doing too much, nattering on about the job, the book, the parties, the shows. How could I be doing too much when I'm doing everything *right*? The meds are obviously working brilliantly, as anyone can see with even a cursory glance at how great my life is. It baffles me that Lentz has any doubts, and I tell him he's just stuck in the past. Everything's different now. He has nothing to worry about, and neither do I.

For a few more blissful weeks of fall, the mania carries me along on the crest of this fabulous wave. By this point I'm a royal pain in the ass, and Jeff is taking the brunt of it. The only thing wrong in my life is Jeff and his constant harping on me for never being home, never doing my share, never paying attention to him. He whines and whines and it drives me absolutely nuts. I'm not doing jack shit around the house. Never mind the dishes. Cleaning be damned. I have no time for such banalities. Jeff is a boring old grump, with his interminable slowness, his inexplicable crankiness. Marriage isn't going to hold me back, *settle me down*. Indignant, I explain to him, loudly, that he's a misogynistic ass. To hell with his resentment of me and his martyrdom.

I come crashing in at three in the morning, wired to the gills on caffeine and the excitement of the night, and slide with exaggerated slickness into bed, fuming at Jeff's sulkily turned back. Irate, I flounce off to the guest room, where I lie with my eyes flickering across the ceiling, plotting my excellent, righteous dismissal of my marriage, of marriage in general, my takeover of the magazine, my centrality to all things good and exciting in town. Perhaps I should move to New York once I've conquered Minneapolis. I'll write for *The New Yorker*. No, I'll become editor of the *New York Times*. California — now *that* was the time of my life. I wasted it, wasted it foolishly, what a sorrowful loss. But no matter. I see my sorry ways and will rectify them now.

And then, almost overnight, a spider web of cracks starts to spread across my brain. I dismiss all the grandiose plans — what crap! What am I thinking, fooling myself into the belief that I'm capable of anything at all? My moods go careening up and down without warning. I'm manic, I'm blue, I'm dashing around in a panic, I'm curled up in bed in the empty, washed-out light of afternoon — and then I'm bolting back up, manic again. But the mania is painful, sharp-edged — I'm agitated, constantly anxious, gripped by random, sudden fears, and I whip around aimlessly, compulsively making lists, worried that I will forget something, that I'll lose something, that I'll fail at something important, that I won't get something done. I'm irritable as hell, and I snap at anyone who has the nerve to suggest that I'm not doing so well — their stupid comments about my moodiness, their idiotic worries that I'm working too much, their constant harping on the fact that I'm not being reasonable about anything at all. I'm perfectly reasonable. It's just that I'm stressed. It's just that people expect too much of me. I can't handle it. I rage at myself for my incompetence, my laziness. I am a failure and a fraud. They're going to find me out. I laugh sharply, talk too fast, and then suddenly fall silent. The voice of the person talking to me fades away. From far off — *Are you all right?* I snap to, shake my head to clear the fog, put a smile on my face, *Of course! I'm fine!*

It's afternoon, and once again the blues wash over me. The office is making me crazy. I can't stand the noise. I have to get out of here. I grab my purse and practically run. Once home, I throw off my suit and crawl into bed. Everything is quiet now. I pull the covers over my head. My head is pounding, filled with static. There is something wrong with my head. I will myself asleep.

I start calling in sick to work. Home, I whirl around aimlessly. I write dozens of pages every day, and every day I delete them. I pace, I panic, I worry I will get fired. *No, no, you won't get fired,* my editor says. When I go into work, I stay there late into the night. When I don't, I dive into and out of bed, and pace, and talk to myself, *I'm not going crazy. It's going to be fine.*

I lie in bed and stare at the wall, bleak, knowing I am going mad.

*Stop it. Get up. You're not going mad.*

I wake up at four o'clock in the morning every day to find the gnarled old terror in my chest, familiar and despised. I clench my eyes shut, then lurch up and stagger toward my office, start hacking away at the book, get lost in the work, the light slowly rising outside, from black to indigo to violet to a pale, thin winter blue, and the piercing sun comes up, and I look at the clock — fuck! I'm late! And I go hauling into work. My mood swings wildly from fury to desolation, and I'm stumbling around with exhaustion by the afternoon. I pour more coffee down my throat, sick to my stomach all the time, shaking so hard I can barely hold my pen, *What's wrong with you? You're making a fool of yourself, everyone's looking, everyone can see.* The paranoia is back. Everyone hates me, is making fun of me, is disgusted by me, wants me fired, wants me dead. I keep my head down and work, snapping often in meetings, shouting, demanding to be heard — and then, humiliated, I run out of the meeting in tears, back to my desk, *Pull it together, freak! Fuckup! Can't take it, can't deal, failure, they're looking, don't you see? This is simple, do it right, stop screwing everything up, you embarrassed yourself in there, you're going to get fired* — and I either stay at work until midnight or bolt from the office at two P.M. To say I'm erratic is an understatement.

I can't get the chaos of my mind to stop. I'm confused, and don't want to tell anyone. I can't remember conversations, can't keep tasks straight. Someone at work asks me to do something, and I wind up in a bathroom stall, crying, panicked, because I can't remember what it was. My desk is a sea of Post-Its, each of them with indecipherable notations that are supposed to tell me what to do. I'm afraid of the office, afraid of downtown, afraid of driving, of speeding, of getting stopped and searched, afraid of things being out of place, afraid of the laundry, the dishes, the mail, sharp objects, spirits, sleep, nightmares, afraid of being looked at, afraid Jeff and my friends hate me — I plead with them to admit it, to just get it out of their systems, so I know the truth and can end this incessant uncertainty that's driving me mad.

We throw a Thanksgiving party for fifty people, another one of my blowouts with endless people streaming in and out. The next day, with no sleep, Jeff and I fly out of town at four A.M., to *relax, get away, get me back on my feet*. We get home and I've only gotten worse. Christmas is parties, all-night wrapping, the watchers are everywhere, following me around the mall, I'm hemorrhaging money, I've completely stopped sleeping.

By now, my friends and family are panicked. Jeff, who's never seen me go crazy before, is trying frantically to assuage my fears, keep me calm, get me to sleep. There are times when he has to pick me up from the office in the middle of the day, or night, because I can't figure out how to get home, or am afraid of leaving the building — I am fixated on the unspecified danger of parking lots. Other days, I call him from home, terrified of everything, the sun, the stairs, all the rooms in the house, especially the kitchen. I beg him to get rid of all the sharp things, scissors and razors and knives. I'm afraid they will come at me and slice up my eyeballs. I fail to mention that I'm also afraid of cutting myself up.

And then it happens. On New Year's Eve, Jeff comes home from work. I'm sitting on the bed. He sits down with me. I tip over into his lap. Everything is fine, now that he is here.

And then Jeff looks down and sees dried blood all over my hands. He yanks my shirt off. I've sliced up my arms. I'm as shocked as he is. I don't remember doing it. I haven't done it in ten years, not since I wound up with forty-two stitches in my arm and no real understanding of whether I'd attempted suicide or not. I am totally confused.

Jeff puts me in the car and drives me to the hospital.

Emergency room. Flashing lights. The cop outside the room. Hours and hours spent waiting. Finally the psychiatrist comes. Jeff watches while they drag me, kicking and screaming, away.

# Part III

## The Missing Years

These years are mostly lost to me. Madness strips you of memory
and leaves you scrabbling around on the floor of your brain for
the snatches and snippets of what happened, what was said, and
when. I spend these two years caught in the revolving door of
madness, going in and out of the hospital seven times, traveling
from my bed at home to a bed on a locked ward, the weird world
of the ward becoming more familiar to me than the one outside.
This is the best I can do to piece the scattered memories together,
to give some semblance of continuous time, to fill the hole in my
life that madness made, and will not repair.

## Hospitalization #1
*January 2004*

*Hi,* someone says. He is very gentle. I am in the hospital. It is night.
I register that fact and write it down on a small slip of paper: *LO-
CATION Abbott Northwestern Hospital, TIME Night.* I stuff it

in my pocket with the other crumpled pieces of paper that I keep so I can read them when I get lost.

*Hi,* he says again. He towers over me. We are in the lounge, a small triangular room enclosed by unbreakable glass. There are games. The games are always missing pieces. There is no way to play Scrabble. You have to make up your own language, which actually works just as well; none of you makes sense to anyone else, but you do understand one another at some deep level, as if you are all in on some conspiracy or joke. The games underscore the deep futility of all things.

*Hi,* he says yet again. I look up at him out of the corner of my eye. It is very black outside and we can see the skyline of the city, where I know I have been, though that was years ago, which might have been a few days before. I am sitting in a pile of magazines, playing solitaire with half a deck and keeping an eye on a man who is no longer towering but has a face resembling a large moon, glowing.

*What's your name?* he asks.

This one I know. Very firmly, I say, *Marya. My name is Marya.*

I am extremely satisfied with this name. No one ever knows how to pronounce it except for the other patients on psych wards.

*Marya,* he says in wonder. *That's a pretty name.* He holds out his hand. *I'm the prophet Jeremiah,* he says, and we shake hands very seriously.

He looks away thoughtfully, gazing into the broad expanse of night. He turns his face to me.

*Have we met already?* he asks. He holds out his hand. *My name is the prophet Jeremiah. I mean, I am the prophet Jeremiah.* He pauses, laughing softly. *That's why my name is Jeremiah.*

I nod, understanding that he is mad, and I am grateful that I know my name, which is *Marya.* I am in the *Hospital,* where all the nurses know me, and I am safe, for this particular moment in time. It is *Night.*

*

THERE ARE FOUR rooms in this world, and I don't know how they are connected — my room, the main room, the padded room, and the room with the Plexiglas walls. There is also a hallway, but I don't know where it leads or how it is related to the rooms. I have flashes of places: there is the view of the ceiling when I am lying on a bed with white sheets and a crinkly sound (the plastic-covered mattress). I can feel the bedsprings in my back. I worry they'll eventually start coming upward in a screwing motion, twisting into my back and right through me, screwing me to the bed. And then there is the main room, where I sit all day and all night. Beyond that is the room with Plexiglas walls, which upsets me a little; if I were in that room, I could be seen, so I stay out here where I am invisible. Except at night. At night, the Plexiglas is bright and safe, the light at the end of the tunnel, and the fluorescent lights move into your skull with their comforting crackling buzz. Sometimes I stand outside it and press my face against it, looking in. Sometimes I go in and press my face against it, looking out.

I am at my best at night. I have strange, fleeting meetings with the other people on the ward. I play a complex game of solitaire and do not look at the people behind the desk. I get in the habit of making myself a cup of orange tea. I sit with my back to the desk. I put my feet on the heater, my Styrofoam cup between my hands, and look out into the dark, which is made of velvet so soft and heavy you could gather it up in your hands if you weren't locked in. When I get up and go to the window, I see the ground some number of stories below, and it is blanketed with snow, which looks blue in the moonlight. The trees are bare. This is how I know it is winter.

HERE ON THE WARD, the pacers pass through the main room on their way up and down the halls. Some of them mumble to themselves, or shout and fling their arms, only to be shushed by the staff. Others are quiet, heads down, thinking whatever thoughts they think. The twitchers sit for a second, then bounce up, turn circles, sit back down again, twitching, in contrast to the ones who are motionless, hunched over their laps, staring dully at their feet or the floor. Then there are the people like me, wrapped in blankets or robes or hospital gowns over their pajamas. Some of us have loved ones in our lives who will bring us things like slippers, or clothes; some of us get dressed, but others stay in pajamas all day. Occasionally you'll have your screaming, your frenzy, your drooling torpor, your bizarre, loud commentary, sometimes delusional, sometimes threatening, and then you'll have your padded room. From that padded room, you hear muffled screaming, or muffled roars, and the dull thump of the person inside pounding on the heavy metal door.

I am sitting here on my heater, peaceful, bothering no one. I am listening to the hum in the room and in my head. My mind is slow and sticky. Sometimes a thought tries to go through it, but its feet get stuck as if in mud. I don't remember if I came in manic or depressed. I have always felt this way. I have been in here forever. There was no life before this life, here where the twitchers and the pacers and the still ones wash over me like a stream, and I am a small stone, worn smooth.

From out of nowhere a woman comes flying at me. She wants my seat. She wants to be by the window. She is shouting, waving her arms. She is leaning toward me, and her face seems to veer close and then far away. It is not attached to her body. Her body is near, threatening. She is angry with me, furious, she hates me, she will kill me if I don't move, I am looking at her funny, I am watching her, she says, she *knows* what I'm thinking. She hits me. It takes me a minute to register this fact. I watch her hand move toward my face, batting me with her fist the way a cat bats a ball with its paw. The feeling of being hit comes to me, delayed. I find I have lifted my hand to my face as if to be certain that it's there, that it has been hit. Magically, instantly, the staff is hauling her away. Where did they come from? They drag her by the arms, she is still leaning toward me, her face contorted and red. Her shouts fade away and I sit looking at my hand.

"How was your day?" my mother asks, patting my knee, later that evening. We are on a couch. I have my feet up under me.

"A girl hit me."

"What?" my mother asks, sitting up. "Who hit you?" She looks wildly around the room.

"Her," I say, pointing. I don't see what the fuss is. So she hit me. So what? It seems like nothing spectacular or unusual to me. The woman I point to is now curled up in a chair, her arms over her face.

"When did she hit you? Why did she hit you? What did the staff do about it? Are you all right?"

"I'm fine. Obviously." My mind slogs along, trying to keep up with my mother's words and her anxiety, which exhausts me. My eyes are heavy, it's a struggle to hold them open, though I am not what you would call tired, in the traditional sense. I simply am. It doesn't matter to me whether it is night or day. All I know is that in the day, we shuffle from group to group, and sometimes meals come on trays that are stacked on metal carts that are wheeled onto the unit by men in blue scrubs, and sometimes I eat the meals and sometimes I stare at them and don't, and sometimes I go back to group and sometimes I wander down the hall and lie on my bed. The bed sags in the middle but I have come to love it anyway. I get under the covers and curl up in my little sphere of warmth, the sheets pulled up over my nose. I listen to myself breathe. In the evening, visitors come. My mother comes and stays a little while, until I get confused and the effort to track what she is saying gets too exhausting and then she knows without my telling her to go away. When she leaves, she always tells me she will be back. I always forget, and call her the next day to be sure. Sometimes it is my father who comes, sometimes my friends, and on weekends my friends Megan and Ruth or my mother or father or aunt or uncle stay all day. There is somehow always someone there. When they come, I am relieved at first, and they think I am doing better, because I am good at pretending, and I pretend to follow the conversation, and I laugh at the jokes, which set off a tiny spark of recognition in my brain — for a moment a thought connects with another thought, and I feel a surge of hope, and sit up, lean forward, now I will follow, now I've got it. But then, after a minute or two, my mind goes wandering off and the conversation around me surges ahead. I lose my place, they slip off into their world and I into mine.

THE FIRST FEW times I am in the hospital, Jeff is unsure of what's going on. Later on, when I've been in and out several times, the staff will get to know him, and they'll tell him how I am, what's happening, what's going to happen next. But not at first, so he's confused. He says, "But you were all right, a few days ago. You were better than this."

"I don't know what happened," I say slowly, my mouth struggling to form the words.

"Did they change your meds?"

"Maybe. I'm not sure."

"Did you talk to the doctor?"

"I think so."

"What did she say?"

I think as hard as I possibly can. "I don't remember," I say.

"But they won't tell me."

"No," I say. "Sorry." I brighten up. "You can make an appointment to come in and talk to her with me."

"All right," he says. "I'll do that."

I am relieved. If he talks to the doctor and she tells him what is going on, then he can tell me.

# Hospitalization #2
*April 2004*

My room looks like this: there are two single beds. One of them is mine. I make it perfectly every morning, and it stays perfect until I crawl back in, defeated, in the early afternoon. I make it so tight that the thin white blanket, which has black print on the edge that says *Property of Regents Hospital,* even though we are here in *Abbot Northwestern Hospital,* holds taut across the sag in the center of the bed. The corners are folded and tucked under the mattress. These are called *hospital corners.* My grandmother taught me to make the bed this way, and she said it needed to be so tight you could bounce a nickel off it, and when I made it that way, she let me have the nickel, and I secreted it away in a sock.

The other bed is unmade, a soft tangle of thin blankets and sheets. Sometimes there is a person in the tangle. She is softened, like the blankets, and lies there in a pile of limp limbs. Her arm is over her face. Her hair spills over the pillow, thick oily hunks of it. She hasn't showered in days.

There are two industrial metal chairs, straight-backed, with black plastic covers on the seats. For some reason, the chairs are not usually pulled up to the cheap, wobbly desks, but are backed against the white plaster wall. The desks are made of plywood and covered with woodgrain-patterned plastic sheets, and why they are in here is beyond me. They become merely a place to put things — your hospital-issue toothbrush and toothpaste, deodorant, discarded used bandages if you have cut yourself or slit your wrists. I myself line these things up very precisely, the toothbrush and toothpaste and the many pens and pencils I collect, in case, and the books and magazines I cannot read, and the folder full of multicolored worksheets they give you in the groups, the worksheets with the emotion faces, rows and rows of line drawings of faces, each with an emotion word written beneath. At the top of the page it says *What Am I Feeling Today?*, and shows the faces illustrating the options. The clock ticks loudly while the group leader waits for each of you to come up with a word, any word, and always the same words are chosen: I feel *agitated, anxious, angry, sad, elated!, confused,* the last of these with a little wavy line drawn for the mouth and crossed eyes.

Also in the folder are the *Dialectical Behavioral Therapy* worksheets. These show two overlapping circles, one of which is labeled *Rational Mind,* one labeled *Emotion Mind,* the overlapping center (it looks like the MasterCard logo) reading *Wise Mind,* which is the mind you are supposed to use, as if you have any control over your mind whatsoever. Then there are the sheets with bullet points outlining the symptoms of depression, from your lecture on that topic. This is given by the irritable woman who dresses in the most unflattering clothes possible and has terrible, tightly curled hair. She doesn't like me because she is sick of seeing me and sick of my saying, *Isn't this all fairly self-explanatory?* And she smiles the tight smile and looks put out and says, *We all need education about our illness.* As if she is included in this *we,* as if she will not go down to the cafeteria at lunch with her friends and complain about the obnoxious woman who keeps showing up on the psych ward questioning the *value of her work,* and as if she will not at the end of the day leave the locked world and go home. Working with crazy people is exhausting. Mental health workers burn out quickly, and some of them keep working and start hating the patients, who know that they do.

And there are the *Self-Esteem* worksheets, and the *Alternative Activities* worksheets from occupational therapy, where people bend over the paint-stained table and struggle with their med-unsteadied hands to thread the dull needles with which they will make yet more leather coin purses, or paint sheet after sheet of thin paper watery black, or scribble enormous, angry explosions with red and orange pencils and crayons, the force of their scribbling tearing the pages. When time is up the occupational therapist will ask us to rate on a scale of one to ten the degree to which this *alternative activity* helped distract us from our *current situation,* and to rate how we feel now as compared to how we felt when we came in the room.

Abandoning our pictures and coin purses behind us, we walk empty-handed back to the main room, where some of us will collapse in front of the television, watching the pretty flashing colors, comprehending little and caring less. Others will resume our twitching or pacing or sitting dead still. I myself will stand in the middle of the lounge trying to figure out where I want to go, and will eventually shuffle down the hall to my room and get back in my bed, still wearing my slippers. I will gaze across the narrow space between my pillow and the pillow of the woman in the other bed. She will open her eyes for an instant, her face squished against the pillow, and say, Is it morning yet? And I'll say, No, it's afternoon, and she'll close her eyes, tears leaking from the corners, and turn over on her other side and face the wall, and I will turn over and face the opposite wall, and this is what the room looks like: two cheap desks, on which sit two green folders holding the worksheets, two metal chairs, one window that lets in only enough light to expose the narrow stretch of tile between the two single beds, leaving them in shadow, along with the two indistinct lumps that lie on them, the rise of hip and shoulder under the thin white blankets, faces obscured by lank, heavy hair.

THE DAY BEGINS with decaf. I tunnel through the confusion that closes in on me when I wake up and go down the hall to the main room, where our breakfast trays sit on the metal cart, getting cold. I take the plastic cup of decaf and the plastic silverware — plastic so we cannot stab ourselves with forks or dull knives — from my tray and wander over to the heater under the window and climb up. The cup of decaf is my ritual. It's how I mark the time. There is coffee at breakfast, lunch, and dinner. The coffee is slightly above room temperature, smells sour, tastes like water flavored brown.

Coffee is the high point of my day. I wait for my visitors to come, for they will bring my beloved decaf Americano, my treat.

After breakfast, we file down the hallway, those of us who have got some of our wits together, a motley crew wearing sweatpants, pieces of pajamas, stocking caps, torn T-shirts, shorts, heavy coats, or wrapped up in blankets that trail behind us, making us look like little girls dressing up in our mothers' nightgowns and pearls. I wear the fuzzy purple pajamas Jeff has brought me from home. The staff person unlocks the door and we are in the no man's land of freedom, between units, and then the staff person unlocks another door, and we go through and that door locks behind us, and then we are on Unit 48, where the older psych patients are kept and where we have group.

The only group for which we don't get handfuls of worksheets is group therapy. We go to group therapy after check-in and sit in a circle of chairs. Though when I am well I am an extremely talkative person, when I am sick, I lose the power of speech, the desire to speak, any sense of what I would say if I opened my mouth. And so I listen intently to the ones who do talk, feeling as though I am trapped inside my skull, a mute, disconnected from the others, from the world. Group therapy is mostly taken up by the chatter of the manic, the sobs of the depressed, the agitated associative ramblings of the schizophrenics, and the mumbling of the men who have just come down from psychosis, who mutter at their shoes and when they're asked to speak up, *So we can hear you, so we can help you,* either look away and fall silent or explode into tirades of insults and foul language that startle the criers and set them off weeping again. These tirades rattle me, here in my skull, and I wrap my blankets tighter around me, pull my feet up onto the chair. I fit perfectly in this chair. Here, I am safe from the creeping, sucking neediness of the talkers, the chattering swells and falls of the manic monologues, the sharp laughter, crowing cries, outraged roars, and the contagious, dizzying flights of associations and electric wild insights and fears.

Then there is lunch. This is usually where I get off, crawl down the hall to my room, and lie in a heap, staring at the plaster wall. Eventually I turn over to watch the clock, and I stare at it for hours, waiting for it to be six, for my visitors to come.

Time moves erratically here. Sometimes a day passes without my noticing that time has begun or stopped, and sometimes I look at the clock and then look at the clock hours later and only a moment has passed. From three, when groups end, until six, when Jeff comes, time moves in infinitesimal increments, the minute hand ticking forward only once every few days. But then he comes. In summer, he strides in, confident, elegant in his creased white pants and bright polo, looking a little like Gatsby, but older and, well, balding. In winter, he comes blustering through the door, bulky in his jacket, his face blown cold by the wind outside. He wraps me up in his arms and squishes my face between his shoulder and his cheek. I cling to him like a monkey, my feet dangling off the ground. He puts me down. Jeff is kind of like a puppy, all energy, bouncing around, carrying bags of food and clothes and magazines, which will give me something to look at, bright pictures and sprays of words, when he goes. Every time I go to the hospital, he brings me a pair of new pajamas as a present. I love the new pajamas. He finds the ones with the softest, fuzziest fabric, and they are either purple or red, purple in summer and red in winter, and they are my favorite thing about the hospital, and I put them on immediately and rarely take them off for the first couple of weeks. They remind me of Jeff when he isn't there. When I get home, he washes them and I put them right back on.

When Jeff comes, he brings dinner and an entire grocery bag of fruit. When I am in the hospital, I crave fruit desperately, and that is usually all I eat all day, until he comes in the evening with dinner, and then I furrow my brow and try to organize my fork in the direction of my mouth. He tells me about his day. He leans forward, holding my hand in both his hands. We face each other on the couch and I curl up very close to him. He is the center of the universe. Every few minutes a fear comes over me that he will leave soon, and I clutch his hand and ask him if he's leaving, and he always says, Not yet, not yet.

## Hospitalization #3
*July 2004*

I sit down next to a very tall young man. He is handsome and young and his hair is gold, not yellow or blond but gold. I ask him if I can cut it and keep some. He looks upward at his bangs.

"Okay," he says agreeably. "Where are the scissors?"

I go to the desk and ask for the scissors. They say I can't have them. I say why not. They say, not safe. I say yes they are. There is nothing wrong with scissors. They aren't sharp enough to cut your throat. They remark that saying things like that is why I can't have the scissors. I shuffle back to the young man and flop into my chair.

"They won't let us have any."

"Why on earth not?"

"Because I have been known to cut myself."

"Did you use scissors?"

"No. Exactly."

"Exactly," he repeats. "The help here isn't what it used to be."

I nod.

"Maybe you could just yank it out," he suggests.

"No," I say, sighing. "Then it would be uneven."

"True," he says. He looks down at his notebook. It is warped, as if he dropped it in water. The pages are completely covered in tight black scribbles and little pictures and hieroglyphs here and there. He turns the notebook around and starts writing in the white space, which is so small I can barely see it. "I'm writing down the system," he says.

"Show me," I say.

He looks at me, deciding if I can be trusted. "It's secret, you know," he says.

"Oh." I sit there, trying to read it upside down, but realize it's written backward. "That's cool," I say. "Backward."

He looks down. "Yes," he says. "I'm very talented."

"You are," I agree.

He ducks his head, shyly. "Oh, okay," he says, scooting his chair over and showing me the notebook. We peer at the page, which is completely unreadable. He points out lines and pictures as we go.

"So what this is is the explanation. You see here, where I've written down the beginning of the system — the man is explaining it a little bit at a time, and between times I work out the equations, which are an advanced physics-calculus-history of the system, which is mathematical, which is the answer, to the questions I have — we *all* have, rather — about the ways in which the plan is worked out."

"What man?"

He taps his skull with his pen. "The man in here."

"Oh," I say, nodding. I take a guess. "Is he short, sort of egg-shaped, with sometimes a blue shoe, but sometimes not?"

He bangs the table, thrilled. "Yes!" he cries. From the desk there is a voice saying to keep it down as it is night and other people are sleeping. *"Yes!"* he whispers. "That's him! Do you have him too?"

"No, I'm no good at math. I can't even learn languages. Maybe he's God."

He leans over his notebook, agog. "Do you really think so? Wow. Maybe he is."

"Well," I say, smoothing my hands out over the air. "Actually, the system itself is God. It's an elegant mathematics, that are God, and he is the angel who comes to give you good tidings of great joy."

He shakes his head slowly, amazed. "How do you know so much?"

"Oh," I say, waving it off. "Actually, I don't know much. For example, I've never heard him explain the system. I just studied philosophy in college. So he is the argument for God, at least from the perspective of Kierkegaard, who I pretty much agree with, because, well, I've seen the little man, and I get flashes of how the system *looks*, but not how it works. Because obviously, he's telling you, because you understand math."

He stands up and shakes my hand thoroughly. "Thank you. Thank you so much."

"Hey, no problem," I say. "I'm just glad I could help."

"Oh, you have," he says, still shaking my hand. He bows low, grabs his notebook to his chest, and says, "My meds just kicked in, so I have to go listen to the man."

"Sure, go," I say. "Myself, I sleep during the day."

"We'll talk more about this later," he says, straightening up and setting off down the hall, which leads God knows where.

The next day, or another, the young man with gold hair, whose name might be Peter, but I have forgotten since the last time he told me, goes loping by, talking at a great speed and gesturing grandly, following on the heels of one of the staff members, who is ignoring him, though not in a mean way. Jeff and I watch the loping young man as we munch on our snack.

"Who's that?" Jeff asks.

"I think his name might be Peter. Don't quote me on that."

"What does he have?"

"Bipolar. He's psychotic right now." Peter, or whatever, spins on his heel and follows the staff back in the other direction. He waves his notebook over his head. "He has a mathematical man in his head," I mention to Jeff.

The staff person passes us, Peter close on her heels.

"I knew it!" he cries, jabbing his stub of a pencil into the air. "This is all part of the plan, isn't it?" He looks absolutely delighted. He spins around and notices us, and sits down next to Jeff on the couch. He shakes Jeff's hand vigorously, then turns to me.

"I knew it," he repeats, satisfied, picking up a tattered magazine, crossing his legs, flipping through the pages, throwing it back on the table, uncrossing his legs, throwing his arms over the back of the couch, and looking around as if taking in a sunny day in Havana. He shakes his head. "This whole thing," he says, gesturing at the psych ward, the patients and visitors and staff. "They're telling me it's not part of the plan. But I *see the plan*." He looks at Jeff and smiles very wide. He leans toward him. "*You* see the plan, don't you?" he demands.

"Of course. It's plain as day," Jeff says, and offers him the bag of chips.

The next time we see Peter, he's possessed, and a horde of hospital security has come to hold him down. His parents watch from the corner. Security hauls him off to the padded room. His parents look around, then slowly sit back down on the couch.

## Hospitalization #4
*October 2004*

The visitors sit at tables, or in circles of chairs, with their person. The visitors watch their person, not knowing what to say. They talk to their person about anything they can think of except what's going on. The people who have visitors have not yet lost everything. Some of the visitors stare at us, rudely, stupidly, as if we don't see them staring, and in truth some of us don't. But some of us do, and we catch their eyes, and they look away quickly, embarrassed, afraid of us, wanting to stare at us some more.

Most of the people with visitors are near enough to sane that they can recognize them, can say, at least, hello, even if they then retreat into their private worlds. The visitors look away from their person, sometimes glancing uneasily at them. They often sit with their arms folded tight across their chests, as if to defend themselves from the madness around them. When their person talks, they look up eagerly, hoping the person will suddenly seem sane, as if he might suddenly break out of his torpor or confusion or delusion or manic agitation and begin talking sense to the visitors, who want nothing more than for this person to stop being how he is.

The visitors dread coming when this is new to them, sometimes even when it's something they've been doing for years. The new ones don't understand what's going on. Some of them resent their person for what they see as willfulness, or weakness. They can barely disguise the anger or disgust that flickers across their faces. Their voices, when they speak, are accusing, or sarcastic. Some of them have for months been telling their person to snap out of it, to cheer up, to get herself together, to stop feeling sorry for herself; they're the ones who are visiting a depressed person, not anyone psychotic. The visitors of a manic person watch their patient with wide eyes, moving quickly to try and follow the hyperkinetic movements and rapid stream of speech and leaps of logic. Many of these visitors, usually family members, speak in low voices, trying to soothe their person, bring him or her back to reality. But there aren't as many visitors for the manic people. Nor are there many who visit the schizophrenics.

Those who visit often, who for years have driven the same route to the same hospital to be let onto the same floor to scan the same room to find the same person, look tired. They sit closer to their person than the others, and their conversation, what there is of it, is a little easier. During the silences, they glance up and absently watch the other patients, not judging them like some visitors, but feeling for them, and feeling for the patients' visitors as well. All the visitors are shut out, and they can only wait for the meds to work, for the episode to pass, for their person to be returned to them, shaky, unsteady, needing their help to reenter the vast, confusing world. At the end of visiting hours, they will get up, go back through the locked door, worried as always, and very, very tired.

ONE DAY, when I am still manic, I am more than alert, I am alive with the whizzing and spinning of my mind. My boss and another editor from the magazine where I worked a thousand years ago come to visit me.

All day, I have been waiting. I have a joke to tell them. I am having a hard time keeping it to myself. I grin and squirm. I think I will die if I can't tell it soon. I thought it up, and it is a most fabulous joke, a joke such as I have never heard, let alone come up with myself. So I have been hopping around all day, going to my stupid little groups, and I've read all the colored worksheets, and made all the little coin purses in art group, and done all the little brainless breathing exercises the group leaders tell me to do.

This is how I thought up the joke: my boss sent me flowers. But get this — they came in a vase! And the vase was made of *glass!* They inadvertently sent me glass! So the staff had to take it away and put the flowers (tulips and daffodils) in a plastic bucket. Which, in my opinion, *completely* ruined the effect. But never mind that. I have a joke. I watch the clock, bouncing in my seat, dying for visiting hours to come. I *cannot* wait.

So my boss and the editor arrive, and I unleash my joke.

". . . so it's *incredibly ironic!*" I crow at the end, my arms wrapped around my legs, rocking back and forth with glee. They smile nervously at me, the way people do when they don't get the joke and are hoping there's a punch line coming. I look at them in their idiot confusion and roll my eyes and lean forward to emphasize my point. "I can't have *glass!*"

Again with the nervous smiles.

Amazed by their stupidity, I throw up my arms. "So I could *kill myself!*" I shout, and begin laughing so hard at my excellent joke that I have to hold my stomach.

Now they laugh, and nod, aghast. "Oh!" they say, nodding. "Yes!"

When Jeff comes to visit that night, I tell him the joke all over again. He finds it hilarious. We laugh our heads off, getting it *totally*.

"I don't think they liked my joke," I say sadly.

"That's weird," he says, handing me my decaf Americano. "It's a *great* joke. I'm sure they just didn't get it."

"They're stupid, then. It's totally *obvious*."

"Totally," he says. "Do you want to sit in the chair?"

I look up at the chair. "Okay," I say, feeling pretty agreeable. Standing up from the floor, I notice that I am wearing my pajamas. My hands fly up to my hair. "Oh my God," I say, eyes wide. "I'm in my pajamas!"

"You are indeed," he says, unpacking a snack. "So what? It's not like you're going anywhere."

"I must have been wearing my pajamas when they came! I am *totally embarrassed!* What are they going to think of me?" I groan and flop down in the chair.

"I'm sure they didn't even notice," he says mildly, and hands me a paper plate.


# Hospitalization #5
*January 2005*

"I brought you Mrs. Crow," announces Ruth, sliding onto the couch and squeezing my knee. Ruth is a twitchy, wiggly, skinny-legged person, very beautiful, always in motion, with enormous eyes and spidery eyelashes she frequently bats, to excellent effect. Mrs. Crow, a stuffed crow wearing a skirt and a rainbow ribbon for a belt, is the talisman. Whoever is in trouble, me or Ruth, gets to have Mrs. Crow until she is well.

Nothing fazes Ruth, or Megan, or really any of my friends. They have their own quirks and eccentricities, and, in several cases, their own diagnoses. To them, my madness is just a part of me, something that happens, and they come to see me, and I am useless company, and I sit there, profoundly grateful that they are there but unable to tell them so.

Christi, Ruth's partner, pulls up a chair facing us. Christi is schizophrenic and visits Unit 47 fairly regularly herself. "How's it going?" she asks me, throwing an arm over the back of the chair. She wears a fine hat. I want it.

"Not so good," I answer. "I'm totally confused."

"That'll pass," she says.

"Will it?"

"Always does."

I raise an eyebrow. "Okay," I say. "If you say so."

"So," Ruth says, tucking Mrs. Crow in next to me and handing me my decaf Americano, making sure I have it in both hands before she lets it go, "who's in here?"

I look around the room. "That guy, over there, he's bipolar." They look over at him. "He had a wife and a kid but he doesn't know what he did with them. He hasn't seen them in a while."

"That sucks," Ruth says.

"He says he used to be the CEO of the government." I pause, uncertain. "Does the government have a CEO?"

"I don't think so," says Ruth. "He doesn't really look like a CEO." He wears a pair of loose, dirty gray pants held up with a length of rope, a white eyelet nightgown, and a pair of tennis shoes full of holes. His toes stick out.

"Course, you never know," Christi says. "Maybe he was a CEO before all this."

"Could be," I say. "Exactly. Like that lady over there." I nod toward her, and they look. The woman, who wears a red suit, is sitting at a table, bent toward the paper on which she is scribbling intently. When she gets to the bottom of each page, she lifts it with a flourish and sets it down on one of several piles she has stacked neatly around the table. She lays the page down, straightens its corners, then does it again. She does it several times.

"That's a patient?" Ruth asks.

"Why else would she be in here working?" Christi asks, cracking up. "It's not like this is a library and she came here because it's nice and quiet." As if to punctuate this, a roar comes from behind us, and we turn to see a man standing up in front of several visitors, his arms lifted to the ceiling. "Lord!" he cries. "Will you tell these idiots that I have *seen* what I have *seen,* and that I must *get out of here so I can spread the word?*"

"That's the prophet," I say. "He's been after me all day."

"Is he schizophrenic?" Christi asks.

"Not sure. Could be bipolar," I answer. "Delusions of grandeur."

"Have you ever had those?" Christi asks.

Ruth laughs. I glare at her. "I get mild ones," I say. "But I've never thought I was queen or anything."

"Are you sure about that?" Ruth asks. "Don't you remember that time you thought you could be a Supreme Court justice?"

"But not queen," I say.

"No," she agrees. "Not queen."

Ruth has seen me in all manner of states. She's seen me manic as hell, depressed, confused, sedated, incomprehensible, and everything in between. But she sits there calmly, agreeable, perfectly willing to follow the circuitous meander of my thoughts, or hold my head up when it's lolling, or sit on the floor with me when I'm under a table. I adore her.

"And that guy," I say, pointing to a young man buried in an enormous coat, the hood up, his hands in his pockets, off in a corner by himself. "He hasn't said anything since he got here. I don't know what his deal is. But her, she won't shut up." The woman I'm referring to is perched at the edge of a chair across the table from a catatonic man who's wearing several layers of hospital robes. "She's trying to convince everyone that her suicide attempt was just her following the orders of the Great Spirits, who needed her."

"For what?" Ruth asks.

"I don't know. I guess just to help out. She's got a thing about Native American spirituality. She keeps saying she's a Sioux princess."

"I don't think the Sioux have princesses anymore," Christi says.

"Well, she's pretty out of it. Anyway, everybody else is just regular manic or depressed. My roommate hasn't come out of her room since she got here. She's starting to smell."

"You've got to wonder what these people are like when they're out," Ruth says.

Christi and I look at her. She looks back at us.

"Oh," she says. "Like you."

Suddenly my hand stops working and I drop my Americano in my lap. We all stare at it for a minute.

"I'll get paper towels," says Christi, standing up.

"Thanks," I say, trying to sort of back away from the coffee, which has spilled all over my front, my feet, and the couch. I look up at Ruth, bewildered.

"Maybe change the pajamas," she suggests, standing and reaching for my hand. She pulls me off the couch and takes me down the hall to my room. She digs around in the paper bags that hold my clothes and takes out a pair of red ones.

"But I like these," I say.

"But they're all wet," she says, pulling my shirt off over my head.

"But they're my lucky pajamas," I say, standing there.

"These ones are lucky too," she says. "Pants off." She hands me the new pajama pants. I put them on and sit down on the bed and reach for the socks, but get disorganized trying to get them on my feet — something about doing it one at a time isn't working for me — so Ruth does it.

"The socks aren't long enough," I say, upset. "They have to go up to my knees or they aren't right."

She digs around and finds another pair of socks and puts them on me, one foot at a time. Christi appears at the door.

"Time for bed," says Ruth, pulling down the covers and standing there like my mother. I crawl across the bed and get in. She pulls the sheet up to my chin, because she knows I like to be contained. She leans down and kisses my head. Christi does the same.

"When are you coming back?" I ask.

"Wednesday," Ruth says.

I feel very small and warm in my dry pajamas. "Thanks for coming," I say.

"Don't be silly," she says. "Of course we came. Go to sleep."

I nod, and am asleep before they reach the door.


# Hospitalization #6
*April 2005*

The first time I was in the hospital, I'd been very clear. I made Jeff swear he would never allow them to do it to me. He swore. I made him swear again: I said, Promise me. Don't ever, ever let them give me electroshock. He promised.

So I signed my rights over to Jeff. I signed the piece of paper that said I would allow Jeff to make the decisions for me should I be too crazy to speak, should *the patient be unable or unwilling to state her own decisions . . . in a state of psychosis or other debili-*

*tating condition;* should I be, for example, insisting on leaving the hospital, I would allow Jeff to tell them to keep me there *for her own safety and the safety of others;* should I be in such a state that I would *be unable to care for herself,* and was, for example, unable to dress myself, wash myself, or speak anything other than gibberish, I signed *her rights and the responsibility of her decisions regarding her* freedom over to Jeffrey Curtis Miller [*SPOUSE*], allowing him to tell them to lock me up and, if he so chose, throw away the key. I signed away my life to my husband, who swore, who promised, he would never allow them to give me electroshock.

Dr. Grau is sitting at the edge of my bed, speaking slowly. Dr. Grau is very small and moves with precise, efficient movements. She dresses quite smartly and her black hair is cut in an excellent short, snappy style, and it gleams. She speaks with a heavy Brazilian accent. *I know it hurts,* she says. *Oh, I'm so sorry you feel this way.* I'm lying in the hospital bed on my side, staring at the other bed in the room, my body racked with such a mind-bending ache that I feel it's possible that I will never draw a painless breath again. Suddenly the pain intensifies, and tears seep out of my eyes. I fail to care, really, that I'm crying. *I'm so sorry. Can you talk to me?* she says. It's the kind of crying that isn't born of sadness so much as sheer physical pain. It is not a real physical pain, but it feels like it is, and the pain takes hold of my rib cage with its hands and clenches and squeezes the pliable bones to such an extent that one realizes one will never escape, one will die of the pain before they can save me from the cruelty of my own mind.

So when she asks me if I'm willing to try electroshock therapy, it isn't Jeff who says yes. It's me. It hurts that much. I won't remember saying yes. I'll remember Jeff sitting in a chair by the side of the bed, asking me if I'm sure. He says, You made me promise I would never let them do it. You made me promise. Are you really sure?

Now I am being wheeled from the psych ward down the hall.

Wheeled not because I can't walk — my legs technically work — but because I cannot, by force of my own will, direct them to move in the usual fashion, one foot in front of the other, forget it, I can't. What hall is this? One moment I am one place, and the next I am somewhere else. In madness, there is no such thing as location, no place where I understand that I am. There is a waiting room. It's not that I recognize it — I surmise it, as I frantically review shards of memory, turning them over in my hand as if they are seashells I find on the beach. And here, I guess, is the room where I lie on the bed and they administer the electroconvulsive therapy, also known as ECT.

The room is white and cold and blindingly bright. Perhaps it is not a bed? Perhaps it is a gurney. Perhaps it is a cold steel table such as they have in a vet's office. I am lying here, and I blink into the lights above my head. I try to count the dots in the squares of particleboard that cover the ceiling. I lose my place. Numbers dance around my skull like the plastic magnetic letters and numbers that people with children have on their refrigerator door. I lie here thinking of the Count on *Sesame Street*: *One two three four five six seven eight, counting! Counting! One two sixteen forty-three, counting, counting!* The nice man stands at my side. *I'm Dr. X. I'm an anesthesiologist.* I think of an Anne Sexton poem: "You, Doctor Martin, walk / from breakfast to madness . . ."

*How are you feeling today?* I am feeling fine. I remember these words and recite them. These are the things you say when asked how you are. After all, it would be odd to say: I'm not feeling. Or, more to the point: I'm not. I have ceased to be. *Where am I?* Here is the nice man. Is he still talking? His mouth moves in some kind of pantomime of speech. He wears a white coat. There is also a nurse. *Where is Dr. Grau?* I must have asked this out loud. *I'm right here, honey.* Dr. Grau looms over me from my left. She lays her hand on my shoulder. *Right here.* Aha: She is *right here.* Then this will be all right. *Where am I? If I am here, why am I here? If*

*(X) Dr. Grau is here + (Y) I am here, then (Z) it is all right.* Where is here again? Can someone explain? The room is white, violently bright: therefore, hospital. I am on a gurney: ergo, emergency room? No, this room is shinier, cleaner, and there is no sound of shouting or crying. But here is Dr. X, the *nice man* who says he is — that's right! — the *anesthesiologist,* which means he has *anesthesia* in his possession. Needles! *I love needles! I love anesthesia!* It feels like dying. *Dying is an art / like everything else.* Sylvia Plath. I'm just *full* of suicidal poets, aren't I? Dr. Grau is near my face. I turn my eyes up to her. She is God. She is putting something cold and slimy on my temples. What is it? Glue. It's getting in my hair. It hardly matters. Who knows when I last washed my hair. I put my hand up to touch it. My fingers come away from it, a thread like snot. A nurse or some other indistinct figure is wrapping a tight band around my right arm, which has *excellent* veins. The vise around my arm is knotted and snaps against my skin. I remark on my excellent veins, *Yes, they're very nice,* noting also that the veins in my left arm *suck,* but not noting that because of this, a lifetime ago, it was very difficult to shoot myself up, being, as I am, right-handed. *You're going to feel a little pinch.* I smile, anticipating it: there it is. I feel the needle slide into my excellent vein. *It might burn a little bit.* It burns. I feel the anesthesia seep up my arm. I picture it: it is *yellow.* No, *gold.* It is a drug. I love a drug. It is malevolent. It is perfect. It is poison. It races up my arm toward my shoulder. *I'm here. Right here.* I turn my head to the left: Dr. Grau. She will take care of me. What are they doing to me? Why? Where the hell is Jeff? I open my mouth to call to him, but then the feeling hits and *I am rocking on the surface of the water. The water barely moves beneath me. It's smooth as sheets under the palms of my hands. The sun is a perfect white sphere; is it a fluorescent light? No. I catch and hold my breath; I beg my mind: stay here — right here — for just a minute more —*

But I grow too heavy and I slide beneath the surface of the water. Its smooth surface does not break but merely bends below me and I disappear. It swallows me and the surface of the water shimmers as if I had never been there at all.

This is the part I don't see. I can only imagine it. They send an electric current through my brain, inducing a seizure. The seizure is tiny. Only my toes curl. Still, I cannot shake the image of myself flopping around like a beached fish. After it stops, they suction the black foaming fluid that seethes from my lungs, the tar from years of smoking surging up out of my mouth because of the seizure.

I wake up in the recovery room. Slowly, I bubble up from the water, consciousness seeping into my brain. I squint in the bright light. I don't know where I am, or where I've been. A nurse appears over my face. She's very cheerful, and I like her immediately. *Do you know where you are?* I look around myself: hospital curtains separating my bed from the next one. *Hospital,* I say. *Good! You're oriented. Do you remember what just happened?* I rack my brain. She asks the year. I shake my head. *What is your name?*

A beat. Then: *Marya. Isn't it?*

*It is!* The nurse moves away. *You just rest, now.*

Electroshock, as safe as it is, is still used as a last resort, after medication has failed to break a severe episode of mania or depression. Doctors don't do it lightly. But often it works. They don't know why it works, but it does. It is sometimes used as maintenance treatment for patients with particularly hard-to-treat cases, and it can make life possible for them again. It has saved my life more than once, a simple electric current breaking through the walls of madness, bringing me back from wherever my mind has stranded me now.

But what happened? Why do I have this incredible headache? Why do my limbs feel as if they've been filled with wet sand? I try to remember something, anything, and can't. What did I do yesterday? What will I do tomorrow? Can I go home? Aha! — I remember something. Jeff. Where is Jeff? Where is home? What day is it? Does it matter? I close my eyes. Perhaps I will stay here forever. It seems as good a place as any.

They wheel me down the hall. From the place where memory, however fractured, resides, I remember these words. Suddenly alive, I recite Lowell to the person who is pushing me along:

> "Come on, sir." "Easy, sir."
> "Dr. Brown will be here in ten minutes, sir."
> Instead, a metal chair unfolds into a stretcher.
> I lie secured there, but for my skipping mind.
> They keep bustling.
> "Where you are going, Professor,
> you won't need your Dante."

MONTHS GO BY, and I tumble through them, going home for a few weeks, a month or two, surfacing from my bed now, only to go back under. Then the drive in silence downtown, and the emergency room, the shuffle to Unit 47, and the staff assuring me it will be okay soon.

I believe them the first time. By the second time, I have my doubts. By the third, I know they are lying. By now, I have simply ceased to care. I sit down on the couch to wait for the cycle to come round again. And it does. And again. One year turns into the next, and I slide back and forth between a modicum of sanity and a state of madness, between the hospital and my house, between the world you know and a world of my own. I get used to the worried, sad, hopeless look on my parents' faces. They begin making plans for the day when I will need permanent psychiatric care. Jeff slips into his own world, resenting me for leaving him this way.

AT HOME, my world is reduced to the hallway between my office and my bedroom. I shamble back and forth, sitting at my desk writing as if possessed, then to bed, where Jeff finds me every day when he comes home. He makes me something to eat and I sit on the mattress eating it. I know this is getting to be too much.

"Are you up for this?" I ask in a moment of clarity. "This." I gesture around me in bed, my days-old pajamas, the pile of dishes on the nightstand, the bottles of pills.

"Of course I am," he says. His voice is tired. He changes out of his work clothes and gets into bed beside me. We spend our evenings watching *Law and Order,* not talking. Of course he's not up for this. No one should have to be up for this. He signed on for a marriage, not for taking care of an invalid wife.

# Hospitalization #7

*July 2005*

Jeff squeezes and kneads my hand. "Your hands are cold," he says, scowling at them, as if scowling at them will warm them up. He rubs them between his mammoth paws. I always forget how big Jeff is until I am here, where I become tiny, smaller than usual, somehow reduced to half my size. I feel fragile, as if someone passing by me might blow me over in his wake.

"I talked in group today," I say, wanting to have something to contribute.

"You did? That's great!" Jeff crows. "What did you say?"

"I don't remember."

"But you talked! That's wonderful! That's better than yesterday! You must be feeling better today!"

"I think I am," I say hopefully. "I think I went to all the groups."

"You're on a roll! You're kicking ass! Good job!"

"But otherwise I just sat around," I say.

"Did you read any of the books I brought?"

"No." I stare at our hands. "I've gotten very stupid."

"You're not stupid."

"Yes I am. I can't read anything. I can't even read stupid magazines."

"They're all out of date anyway." Jeff dismisses this with a wave of his hand.

"But the point is I've gotten stupid."

"You're not stupid. You're just not feeling quite yourself."

This cracks me up. I hold my stomach, rocking back and forth, laughing my head off. "Not quite myself! No, not quite!"

Jeff smiles uncertainly, not sure why this is funny. I'm not sure either. I gasp and let out a sigh. I gaze at Jeff. I adore him. He is the most wonderful person alive. I am suddenly struck by the fact that he is unlike anyone else in the world. How many people could love me like this? How many people would visit every day at six o'clock, without fail? And bring me dinner, and a grocery bag of fruit? Who could? Who would? Why would they? Why does Jeff?

I say to him, "Why are you doing this?"

He leans forward, his face animated. "Doing what?"

"Coming here." I am struggling to form the thoughts it requires for me to ask him the question. The evening is getting later, I'm tired, and he'll leave soon, and there I'll be, left on the couch, a huge gaping space where Jeff was but no longer is.

"Why am I coming here? Because you're here. Obviously."

"But you're leaving soon." That's not what I meant to say. He glances at the clock.

"Not yet," he says, rubbing my hands. "Not just yet."

I wrestle my thoughts to the ground. "But you won't always come back."

He furrows his brow. "Of course I will. I'll be back tomorrow."

"But maybe someday."

He gets a look on his face. "No," he says. "I'll always come."

"Not if this keeps happening." It's dark out now. Soon he will stand up and pull on his coat, dressed, impressive, sane, and he will stride his giant strides to the locked door and wait patiently while the staff jingles the keys, and when they swing the door open, he will look back across the room at me, smile his very best encouraging smile, wave, and turn away. The door will swing shut behind him with a clang. The clang will reverberate through my skull. It will keep clanging, over and over, and each time I will jump, even though it actually only clanged once. And then I will sit here, frozen on the couch, my hands, now limp in my lap, getting cold.

"If what keeps happening?" he asks. I don't know why he asks, because he knows.

"If I keep going crazy."

"You're not crazy." He shakes his head firmly.

I sit there looking at him. "Jeff, I'm crazy."

"You're not feeling well."

"Jeff," I say, not sure he's really getting the point, "I'm crazy."

"You're sick. Right now. Just for a little while." He shakes his head back and forth like a little boy denying that he broke the vase. No, no. Not crazy.

"But what if it isn't just for a little while?" I ask him. My head is starting to tip on the top of my spine, heavy with the dead weight of my brain. But I persist. This is important. I need to know. I need to be sure of him. Without him, the days will stretch out, bleed into one another, no one will come at six and tell me how long I have been in here, assure me that I will get out soon, that tomorrow will be better. No one will lie to me, and their lies are all I have to go on, all the reason I have to crawl out of my hospital bed in the morning, drape myself in hospital robes, put on my hospital footies, and pad down the hall, moving through the eddying stream of noise, bumping into the walls, to sit at the table in the main room of the ward and drink my hospital decaf to demark that another day has begun.

"It *is* just for a little while. You're getting better. You're a little better every day." He leans close and kisses me on the nose. "You'll get out soon. I promise."

I think about this, trying to connect it to the next part of my thought.

"But then it will happen again."

"No it won't."

I stare at him. "Yes it will."

He shakes his head.

"Jeff, it will."

His face falls for a second and his voice cracks. "But you did so well for so long."

I start to cry. I want to be doing well again, for him. I want to go back to the part of the story where I made dinner for fifty and wore makeup and earrings every day and we leaned back in our chairs on the porch in the evening, watching the sunset, our heads tipped back, drinking the summer air.

"I'm sorry," I say. "I didn't think this would happen again."

"It's all right," he says.

"You're going to give up on me."

He takes my face in one of his hands. "I'm not. I'm not, not ever."

I nod miserably. "You are. I don't blame you. There's no reason you should have to deal with this. This is a nightmare. I hate that this is happening. But," I say, starting to cry again, "I can't help it and I don't know if it's ever going to stop."

"But it will."

"But what if it doesn't?"

"It *will*."

There are circles under his eyes. He's working long days, then getting dinner, bringing it to me, sitting with me, my exhausting craziness, for hours, then going home, doing all the things I used to do, the laundry, the dishes, the cat boxes, walking the dogs, cleaning the house, and then he's collapsing, exhausted, in bed. I picture him lying there, a huge lump on one side of the bed, the other side empty, and he's not sleeping well, and he's getting up in the morning and worrying about me, and worrying about the future, and trying not to think about it, and facing the strange looks and uncomfortable silence at work, with colleagues who know his wife is crazy, and packing me bags of clothes and books and our wedding quilt, and hauling all these things to me, and wondering, every time he leaves, if I will ever be better again.

"And you'll get tired of being alone," I insist.

"I'm never really alone." I hear him reciting these things. I ask these things every day. "You're always with me." He glances at the clock.

I sit for a moment, trying with all my might to stay here, to stay with him for these last few minutes. Why does time speed up when he comes? There is never enough time. I finally work up the sentence in my mouth: "What if it's always like this? With me going into the hospital, and then getting out, and then going crazy again, and going back in?"

I can see his eyes going empty, I can hear the rote lines. Do either of us really know why he still comes?

"Think of the good times," he says. "When you're out."

I nod, my face slippery from tears. My cheeks are heavy again, my mind spitting and fritzing, its wires burned out for the night. I am out of questions. But I know that someday there will be a six o'clock that comes and goes, and Jeff won't burst through the door. Or if he does, his step will get heavy, and he won't look at me, and he will hate me for what I have become.

Nine o'clock. Over the loudspeaker, the voice of the staff: *Visiting hours are now over. Thank you for coming. Good night.*

"I have to go," he says gently, leaning forward so his forehead touches mine. I nod. My mind is starting to fill with static. I hate my questions. I slump in the corner of the couch. He gets up slowly, not letting go of my hands. Finally he sets them softly in my lap. My eyes travel slowly up to his face. He lingers a long time, looking back and forth from me to the door. He leans down and kisses my head and leaves.

## Release

*August 2005*

Jeff and I walk out the hospital's front door and down the street to the car. The space around me feels strange; it seems like there should be walls somewhere nearby, holding me in. But there are only trees, the sidewalk, the passersby, the expansive sky. Jeff loads my things into the car, the paper bags of clothes and books, my pillow and my quilt. I get in the car, get tangled in the seat belt. Jeff untangles me and clicks it closed. We drive off. I look out the window at the streets and the old houses we pass.

"Where are we going?" I ask.

"Home," he says. "They just let you out."

"They did?"

"Yes. We're going to go home and unpack your things and then you can get settled. You can get in bed if you want. Or you can go in your office and maybe do a little work."

"Oh my God," I say, overwhelmed.

"But you don't have to. Nothing to worry about. You could just make a nest on the couch and read a book. Or look at a book, whatever you want."

"I can read again."

"I know. Isn't that awesome?"

"Yes," I say. "I'm not stupid anymore." We pass the towering gray brick block of the old Sears building, and then the Yukon Bar, a Kentucky Fried Chicken. "Where are we?"

"Lake Street."

"Really? It looks different."

"It's the same. Things will look familiar when we get closer to home."

As we move southwest through the city, I start recognizing things. "Are we close?"

"Yep. See?"

"I can't drive. I would get lost."

"You can't drive because you're completely dosed up on meds."

"Right." That morning, Jeff and I got a list of the meds I'm on: Seroquel, Geodon, trazodone, Zoloft, Ambien.

"I think these meds are messing me up," I say.

Jeff nods. "We'll try them for a little while. If you're still feeling like this in a week, we'll call Lentz and get you on something else."

"I can't afford to be sedated. I need to work."

"You will."

"When?"

"Soon."

I look out the window. He doesn't have any idea when. My mind, my life are completely at the mercy of whatever I'm prescribed on discharge day. They let you out well before you fully know how those meds are going to affect you; once you're no longer considered a danger to yourself, they let you go, and you return to the care of your outpatient doctor.

Jeff parks and unbuckles my seat belt. He goes around the car and lifts me out, holding me around the waist. I am unsteady on my feet and start to tip. He props me against the side of the car and takes my things out of the back. "Ready?" he asks. "Hang on to my belt."

I follow him up the steps and into the house. I stand there looking around.

"Home!" he announces, setting down my things, picking me up, and kissing me. "At last!"

I scan the room. "You cleaned," I say, smiling. "That was sweet."

"A person should come home to a clean house," he says, leading me to the stairs. There is the mantel with the wedding pictures on it. Here is the cat, rubbing up against my legs, and the dogs leaping and barking like mad. We go upstairs. He shows me my spotless office.

"Flowers!" I say. I turn to kiss him, stumble, and crash into the wall. My vision is swimming, and it feels as if I am pulling to the left, my head out of alignment. Jeff catches me and turns me to see the flowers. They are my favorite, roses, a smoky coffee pink.

He leads me to the bedroom and helps me into bed, then goes downstairs and brings up my things. He sits on the edge of the bed. It's hard to hold my head up, and I rest my chin on my chest.

"Sorry I'm like this," I mumble. I'm falling asleep. "I meant to be better."

"You are better," he assures me. "The side effects will wear off in a couple of days."

I sit up to hug him and tip straight into his chest. He puts me upright again, leaning me back against the pillows.

"I should get up and do some work," I slur, throwing the covers off and trying to stand. My socks slip on the hardwood floor and I slide down, dragging the blankets with me.

"Maybe tomorrow. How about you just get settled in today."

He picks me up and I get back into bed.

"Maybe," I say. "I have a deadline. Can't miss the deadline." I pause, lifting my head with effort to look at him. He wavers in front of my face like a smoke mirage. "I don't like these meds."

"Just give them a couple of days." He stands up.

"Where are you going?" I ask, panicked.

"Just going to get you something to eat."

"But you'll come back up?"

"Right away."

"And you'll stay here?"

"All day."

"What about tomorrow?"

"The rotation's all set. Aunt Andy will be here at seven A.M."

My head crashes left and I lie on my side. "Okay," I say.

While he's gone, I stare at the window. The ivy that covers it is lush and jewel green. Summer, I think. This perks me up. I sit up with effort, scrabble around in the bedside drawer, and find a pen and paper. Pressing the paper to my knees, I write, very carefully, *Summer.* I look at the clock: 2:34 P.M. But what day? "Jeff?" I yell. "What?" comes his voice up the stairs. "What day is it?" I yell. "Thursday!" he yells back. Very good. *Thursday.* I tap the pen against my knees. I'm missing something. I search my brain. Finally, I climb out of bed and go down the hall, resting my head on the wall to my left. I get to the top of the stairs. Confounded, I get down on my hands and knees, turn, and crawl backward halfway down. Jeff appears holding a tray.

"What are you doing?" he asks, setting it down and coming over and pushing me back up the stairs.

"I had a question."

"What is it?" he asks.

"I have season, time, and day. What else?"

He leads me back down the hall. "Date," he says.

"Date!" I cry, delighted. "What is it?"

"August eighteenth, 2005."

I write it down, fold the paper into four squares, and tuck it into my pillowcase. This way, when I get confused, I can check it, just to be sure.

After a week or so of my lying in bed, the cobwebs in my brain start to clear and I venture back into the wreckage of my office, a whirlwind of papers and books. For the seventh time in two years, I put things in their places, stack the papers, re-shelve the books. I look at my desk calendar, still open to the date I went in. The pages are almost unreadable, crammed with black scribbles, the notes I'd taken on the cesspool of my mind, the dozens of appointments I'd made in my frenzy to cram my days full of the endless things I wanted to do, believed I could do — *get PhD, write new book, go to London, start advocacy group.* It's not that I *couldn't* do these things — people with bipolar disorder do things like this all the time. But each item on my list was cooked up in a fit of mania, when anything was possible. In any case, I don't even necessarily want to do these things, now that I've come down. I turn the page to the correct date, smooth my hand over it, and think for a minute. I look in the drawer: razor blades, rusty with blood. I throw them out, along with the Kleenex I'd used to sop up the mess.

Somehow I have finished a book, written several articles, and started a new writing project between hospitalizations — I have no memory of doing any of these things, and I look at the reviews, edited manuscripts, and notes in utter confusion. Since then, letters and hundreds of e-mails have gone unanswered, editors haven't been called back, my more distant friends think I've disappeared or died.

Jeff comes in.

"Whatcha doing?" he asks.

I look up at him. "Starting over," I say.

"All right," he replies, and jogs back downstairs.

A FEW WEEKS later, Megan flops into the armchair in my office. "Hey, chief," she says. She sets a bag of lunch on the desk. "You're up and about."

Megan is a small woman with round glasses and very tidy, sensible, shiny chin-length black hair. She has two main facial expressions: no expression and cracking up. Jeff calls her Marcie and me Peppermint Patty. She looks like she is playing poker all the time: totally still. Occasionally she glowers, when I have done something particularly insane. And then she cracks up, holding her stomach and sort of silently bobbing up and down as if she's on a pogo stick. She's an astonishing painter. We are both very weird. She is essential to all things good in my life.

I am half dressed, sitting at my desk, tapping in short bursts on the computer. I made it as far as pants and couldn't quite get a handle on shirt, but here I am in my chair, chain-smoking and drinking a cold cup of coffee.

"Sort of," I say. "I got as far as the office."

"That's farther than the bed."

"True," I say. "My next project is going downstairs."

"When are you doing that?"

"Not yet. It's sort of overwhelming."

"Maybe later. What are you working on?"

"Nothing. I'm just writing for the sake of writing. I woke up this morning and was going totally batshit, so here I am, writing." I turn away from the computer, pick up my coffee cup, and peer into it.

"That's an apple core there in your coffee cup," Megan remarks.

"I was drinking around it."

"Right." She unloads lunch in front of me, tomato soup and a chunk of bread. "I figured soup was pretty straightforward."

"It is. I can do soup." It's sandwiches that overwhelm me. Too many parts.

"So how's the old mood today?" Megan asks, eating her soup.

"I can't tell. I'm not speeded up and I'm not depressed. I guess I'm middling. Is that where I'm supposed to be?"

"Sort of. You have no expression, though."

"I don't?"

She shakes her head.

"Rats." I pull apart my bread and dip it carefully in my soup. "I'm supposed to have an expression."

"Even a couple of them."

"So my mood might still be a little off."

"Maybe a little flat. But you've got to admit, that's better than nothing. I mean, you're out of bed. You're sort of dressed. You're writing."

"I'm writing garbage."

"Doesn't matter. The point is you're writing. So, see, you might be almost in a mood."

I fall asleep.

"Say, chief," Megan shouts. "You're asleep."

I jerk my head up off the desk. "No I'm not," I say. "Just had a moment." I shake my head to wake myself up. It's still heavy, and tipping to the left. I prop it up with my hand. She's saying something. I'm falling asleep. My eyelids feel like they've got weights on them and are being dragged down. Megan reaches over and takes the soup so I don't knock it over.

"What do you say you go to bed?" she shouts.

I nod, staggering to my feet. "Can you stick around?" I slur. "It only takes a little while to pass."

"No problem," she says, guiding me down the hall and dumping me unceremoniously on the bed. "I'll go get some coffee."

"Thanks," I say, greatly relieved. "That'll be good." I fall asleep again.

I wake up twenty minutes later, totally alert. I go back into the office and find Megan reading a book. She looks up. "Better?" she asks.

I nod. "I fucking hate these meds. This happens every day." I sit down at my desk and stare at the computer screen. Nonsense, pages and pages of single-spaced nonsense. I select it all and hit the Delete key.

"You'll get the hang of writing again," Megan says.

"I hope so," I say. "It's the only thing I know how to do. I can't exactly hold a regular job."

"No," she agrees. "But who cares?"

She's got a point. There are millions and millions of people with mental problems. They work regular jobs, irregular jobs, they work at home, they don't work, they're married or single, they have kids or don't, they do laundry and fall in love and have opinions and grieve their losses and, if they're lucky, take their meds.

That's what I'm learning. I am a person with a mental illness. So it takes some extra effort. So sometimes it's debilitating. But now that I'm learning to manage it, it's becoming not my entire life but simply a part of how I live, something the people around me live with as well, something I can accept. I have to. That's the only way this works.

ONE DAY, I find a note on my calendar, made sometime between hospitalizations: I'm supposed to meet with a Web designer today to talk about my website. I am completely unprepared for this. My meds are still making me a little batty, there are a lot of side effects, and anyway I'm not totally able to track a conversation for any length of time. But I'm determined: I am going to be normal. I am going to this meeting if it kills me.

So I go to the closet and put on the long-unused regular-person clothes, including shoes — after months in slippers, they feel very weird on my feet, and I wobble — and I get in my car, which feels enormous and is awfully complicated, and drive very badly to the Edina Grill to meet this guy for lunch. We sit down, start talking, my brain clears up a little, although I know I will forget everything that is said the minute I leave the restaurant, and my impression of a normal person is exceptional, all the way until our food arrives.

Then it happens. The sleeping thing hits. My eyelids sag and my head starts dragging to my left. I tip over in the booth and slide under the fucking table.

I'm mortified. This guy sticks his head down and peers at me, alarmed. *Are you all right?* Of course I am! *Um, do you maybe need a ride home?* It's all I can do to nod my head and crawl from under the table. I'm dimly aware that the whole restaurant is staring, obviously, and the website guy has to push me out the door and down the street and sort of arrange me in his car. He pulls up to the house. *Can I help you up the steps?* And I'm waving my hand, slurring my words, *Oh, no! I'm perfectly fine!* I stagger out of the car and walk up the steps like I'm drunk, and I make it into the house and crawl up to bed, and I lie there totally horrified.

Okay. We are not quite ready for the real world yet. Noted. Will try again later. I pull the blankets over my head and hide.

SUMMER IS JUST beginning to give way to fall, and there are still lush lawns and thick ivy growing over the fence, the trees heavily green in the breezy September air. Home for a month now, I can finally be out of bed for long stretches at a time before my brain shuts down — a few hours in the morning, a few in the late afternoon, and most of the evening. Leaning on walls, the kitchen counter, the door, my family and friends, I begin to do the things that have gone undone.

There are fewer visits from my babysitters, who have been keeping me company so I don't get lost in my moods. Soon, the babysitters won't come at all. I'll be left to my own devices and thoughts, thoughts that seem to be generated by my own mind rather than by some demon alter ego. I get dressed some days, brave the downstairs, and sometimes even go outside. Finally, I begin to write, a little bit most days. When I can write all day, and write decently, and remember what I've written, and wake up in the morning and do it again, I know I'm well.

Some people with bipolar have only one major episode, or have several and then go into remission and live years without them ever coming back. My bipolar, ultra-rapid-cycle type I, is tough to treat, and the doctors have warned me that it will probably put me in the hospital again. But they can't say how often, or when it will happen next. So I have two choices: live in constant fear that the next episode is just around the corner, waiting to attack; or live as if by doing the right things to keep myself well, the episodes will never come again.

And what if they don't? I can't picture it. I can't imagine life without the thrills, the flights and the crashes, the constant chaos that has ruled me, fascinated me, tormented me, since I was a child. I can't imagine reining in my mind, and my day-to-day pace. If I do, what will fill my days, what will inspire me, occupy my thoughts, drive my life, push me to go on?

But I'm tired.

The doctors offer me a paradox: tame the madness through surrender. Accept that it will be chained to me, pulling, always trying to get loose, for the rest of my life — but also know that if I respect the strength of the madness, I can live in some kind of peace. Only then will it, instead of me, tire out, and sleep.


MUCH IS LOST to these two years of hospitalization. I remember very little, because madness erases memory, and so does electroshock. People tell funny stories about events, parties, trips, that I smile at, confused, because I don't have any memory of what they're talking about. I don't remember finishing my novel, and I barely remember going on tour. Apparently my thirtieth-birthday party was a roaring blast, but I argue with Jeff about whether I had a thirtieth-birthday party at all. I see the hurt cross his face when I look at him blankly after he reminds me of something we did together: special dinners, entire trips — he says they were wonderful — or times with family and friends, holidays, simple moments in our life. (However, he periodically makes things *up* and insists that they happened — *Of course they did! You can't remember that?* — and then he laughs so hard he cries when I panic, hopping up and down and saying, *What? What? I did? I did not! I really did?* We're on a plane and a movie I've wanted to see comes on — *Hey, look!* I cry, punching Jeff in the arm, *that movie I wanted to see!* And he glances up and shakes his head and sighs. *But you already* saw *that!* he says. *Did not! Did not! But you did* — and to this day I have no idea if he's just fucking with my head for fun, or if I really did these things, went to these places, said these words. He finds it endlessly entertaining. Jerk.)

For a few days after I get electroshock, every time, I forget how to get from my bedroom to the kitchen, and where I keep my computer, what book I'm working on, where the pile of pages on my desk came from, where my mother lives — two blocks from me — or how to get there. After electroshock, mostly you lose your short-term memory — what you did an hour ago, what you're doing right now. But the memory erased by madness is the memory one relies on to make sense of one's life. I have precise memories of conversations, crystal-clear recall of books I've read, and a blow-by-blow memory of everything that happened in one year, then nothing for the next two. I piece my life together from stories other people tell me, from journals and photos, from sitting with my head in my hands, searching for anything until I can get a dim picture of a face, a vague memory of something I know has happened but that I have to reconstruct from the wreckage of my mind.

Memory is not all that's lost to madness. There are other kinds of damage, to the people in your life, to your sense of who you are and what you can do, to your future and the choices you'll have. But there are some things gained. The years that have followed my decision to manage my mental illness have been challenging, sometimes painful, sometimes lovely. The life I live, even the person I am, is nearly unrecognizable compared to the life I had when madness was in control. There are things in common, obviously — my mental illness hasn't gone anywhere, and it still, to some extent, shapes my every day. But the constant effort to learn to live with it, and live well, has changed the way I see it, the way I handle it, and it's probably changed me.

After the years in the hospital, I began to learn how to live the kind of life I want. These days, that life is becoming ever more real. But it took a while.

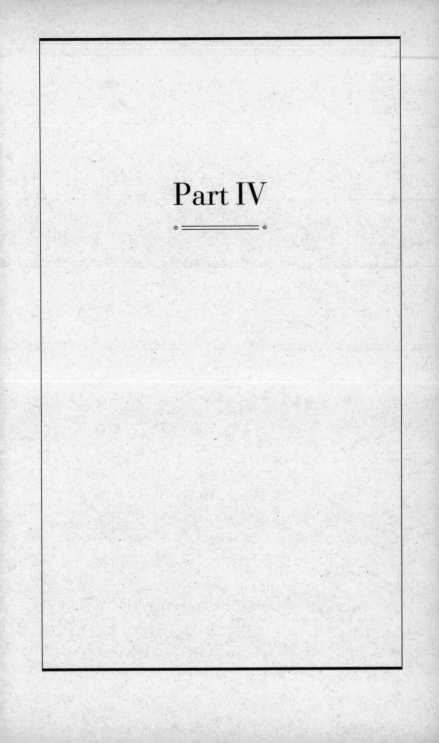

# Part IV

## Fall 2006

Jeff sits in his office. I sit in mine. The fraying rope of our marriage stretches down the hall. Each of us stares out the window, looking in different directions, gazing at nothing, the early autumn evening slipping down. The leaves are just beginning to turn; the ivy that crawls up the side of our house is always first to go, and its tangled red and magenta covers the windows of our bedroom, where we sleep with our backs to each other, balancing at opposite edges of the bed. We lie there breathing, trying to pretend we're asleep, listening to the other one for sounds of life. We slip out of bed, moving carefully, trying not to wake the other one up, and creep back down the hall to our offices, where we sit motionless for hours, waiting for light.

I am getting better every day. I have reentered the world, come running back into my life full of hope. I am ready to be myself again, a wife, a daughter, a friend, someone who is strong enough to let other people lean on her rather than always leaning on them. I want to listen. I want to give. I want warmth and heat and light. I am profoundly grateful. I am overflowing with love for Jeff, amazed at the kindness he has shown me over these past two years. And so I come running into the house, looking for him. I call and call his name.

But he's gone.

He stares into the middle distance when we are together. I talk; he is silent. He turns his face away. He pulls out of my arms and turns his back. His voice carries no life, no emotion; he answers me in short syllables, expending as few words as possible, cutting our interactions short, disappearing upstairs. I try to do it right again. I try to get back to the person I was before I went away. I make the dinners. I do the laundry. I clean the house.

But he's gone.

For two years, his life was a cycle of nonstop caretaking — hundreds of meals prepared for me and brought to the hospital night after night, months of returning to an empty house after those visits, lonely, emotionally drained, exhausted from a long day at work and yet another long night propping me up, comforting me. Then home to face all the tasks of running a house: bills, laundry, cleaning, meals, dozens and dozens of phone calls and messages coordinating visits from friends and family, and, when I was home, setting up the rotation of people coming to the house to be with me.

I was gone too long. He let me go. All that remains is this overwhelming, nearly tactile cloud of resentment. Too much was required of him, and he has nothing left.

He doesn't know how to relate to me. He has grown used to my being sick. He gave up on getting me back and got used to playing savior. Now he is tired of the role; but at the same time, he has forgotten everything else.

In some ways it is simpler to be married to someone who is all need and no give. It's an enormous drain. But there is the benefit too: you become the hero, the center of someone else's existence. You are the saint. You have, in this sense, a great deal of power. You tell this person what to do, and she does it. You feed her. You hold her. You are her mother, her father, her husband, her priest.

And you are never required to relate to her on an adult level. There is never anything wrong with you; any problem is caused by her, her illness, her meds not working, her malfunctioning mind. You don't have to grow. You can settle into your role, running the show, always right.

You relish your role and resent it enormously at the same time. And when your role is upset — when the patient climbs out of bed and walks on her own, makes her own food, drives her own car, has coffee with friends, starts working, does all the things you used to do for her — you see that she now does everything wrong. She screws up the coffeemaker. She shrinks your favorite sweater. She makes the bed funny. She talks too much. And — who does she think she is? — she doesn't always agree with you. She doesn't see that you are always right. She *criticizes* you. You had a system, and she's creating disorder with her sudden presence. She doesn't need you anymore. This isn't acceptable. This won't work.

And so it doesn't work.

We fight. The spilled coffee, the shrunken sweater, the oddly made bed, the wrong word, *don't criticize me, don't blame me, you resent me, you're doing it wrong, I can't stand this;* we fight and fight. Nothing is too small for us. Anything will do, any tiny trigger sets off a shouting match of blame and accusation. We wind up in my office in the dark, crying, sorry, trying to understand how it started. We never can.

He withdraws. He won't talk. We try therapy; he sits there on the couch, clenching his jaw, able to discuss only the things I'm doing wrong, how I'm disrupting his life. He doesn't speak about what he gave up for me. He doesn't mention that he doesn't know who I am, how to talk to me, what to do with me, what a marriage is supposed to be like. And I don't know how to do this any better than he does.

It gets too awful. I can't stand the throbbing rage, the thrum of resentment that is always there, the fights. I spend the nights sitting at my desk, trying to think how I could do it alone. I have become horribly dependent on him, and I hate myself this way. And so I try to imagine what it would be like living in my own place, paying my own bills, running my own life. I feel like a child. I am furious with myself for becoming what I am.

I can't stand it here. So I leave.

I SET OUT to remake my life. I'm starting from scratch. I've never been sane without Jeff. I've got something to prove. I want to show everyone — and I want to know myself — that I can live a sane life alone.

I'm terrified. But I'm also still a little crazy — crazy enough that I go on a spree, buy a condo, get all new pots and pans, go tromping up the stairs with the dozens of boxes of books, carefully unpack the china, paint my new rooms, hang the pictures, furnish the entire place in a day.

I look around. Everything is mine. Everything is exactly where it should be. I am ready to begin.

It starts simply enough: I'm working a lot. I sit at my desk for long days, doing the research and writing this book. I write fast, then faster. I begin to talk to myself. I begin to talk all the time. I am elated at being on my own, *getting everything right,* working, doing the laundry, paying the bills as soon as they come, buying the groceries, going to the gym — everything is perfect, until I have to go to bed. When I go to bed, I lie there curled up in a ball, pillow over my head, trying to block out the thoughts of Jeff. Now, with a little distance, all the things about him that I loved become painfully clear, and I miss the person he was before I got sick. I vacillate between overpowering guilt that I forced him to become this stranger, and rage at the fact that he fell into the role so easily. I hate myself for having been sick so long. When I see him, he's a wreck. He vacillates between giddy joy at seeing me, and horrible, angry tirades, slamming out of my house.

I'm trying to be perfect, and the smallest failure — say I don't wash a dish — becomes cause for rage at myself for being such a fucking waste of space. I work too much, sleep too little, shop compulsively, and I'm dizzy with grief. I swing from elation at my new life to despair at what I've lost and hatred of who I was. So I race away from all of that, convince myself everything is wonderful, block the world with obsessions, manic activity, long days of work, and shopping. I fixate on things. And one of the things I fixate on is food.

I suppose it had to happen sometime. Recovery from an eating disorder is usually provisional — most of us who do recover still have it lurking somewhere in the back of our minds. It lives there quietly for years. But if the pressure is enough, it comes out. We fall back on it. It is as old and familiar as a longtime lover. We aren't afraid of it. It stills our thoughts. We know it. When we are at points in our lives where we know little else, the eating disorder is our long-lost oldest friend.

HERE'S THE HELL of it: madness doesn't announce itself. There isn't time to prepare for its coming. It shows up without calling and sits in your kitchen ashing in your plant. You ask how long it plans to stay; it shrugs its shoulders, gets up, and starts digging through the fridge.

But even that implies some sort of lag time between the arrival of madness and the actual experience of it. In the early years, it's like a switch flips on, and though only a moment before you were totally sane, suddenly you have gone mad. But as you learn to manage madness, you begin to notice sooner that it's on its way. I lick my finger and hold it up to test the direction of the wind: madness is in the air. I can smell it like I can smell snow. It's in the vicinity, though I don't know where or how long it will be until it comes. The trick is to shut the gate, throw sheets over the roses, go inside, lock all the windows and doors, and go down to the basement and sit on a chair to wait.

Sometimes these preparations are enough. The locks on the windows and doors are tight. You've taken the medication faithfully. You've exercised to induce a sense of dopamine calm. You've put every lamp in the house in your office and flipped on the light box — it mimics sunlight for people who get depressed in winter — and the room is lit up as if with floodlights, and you're so hot you're working in your bra. You've stayed off the coffee, you've taken the supplements, you've worked starting at the same time and for the same length every day. You've interacted with human beings at least a few times this week. You've gotten yourself to the point where you can sleep in the normal time frame, from night until morning, and your mornings are not a horrible struggle to stay out of bed, and you make the bed so you aren't tempted to get back in it. You check off the entries on the list that runs your life.

But sometimes the system fails. Maybe it's a chemical shift in the brain that the medications don't block. Maybe it's a stressor in your life that you didn't expect. Maybe there is no reason, and you're just going mad for the hell of it, but you try not to think about that because that would imply that no matter what you do, no matter how tightly you batten the hatches, madness can get in.

You wake up one morning and there it is, sitting in an old plaid bathrobe in your kitchen, unpleasant and unshaved. You look at it, heart sinking. Madness is a rotten guest. You can tell it to leave till you're blue in the face. You follow it around the house, explaining that it's come at a bad time, and could it come another day. Eventually you give up and go back to bed, shutting the door.

But of course it barges in and demands to be entertained. Before you know it, it has strewn its stuff all over the house, and there are sticky plates in its bed, and it refuses to change its sheets. Madness lounges all day in front of the TV, watching *Oprah* and munching on a bag of chips, drinking milk from the carton, getting crumbs between the cushions of the couch.

Soon, your life revolves around it. You do everything you can to keep it comfortable, because you don't want to upset it. You tiptoe around the house and wait for it to leave. In most cases, you wake up one morning and it's gone. There's minimal damage. You pick up its mess and get on with your day.

But sometimes it settles in to stay. Immediately, it is all demands. It starts bossing you around, interrupting your conversations, refusing to let you out of the house. The phone stops ringing. Soon it's just you and madness. You circle each other like boxers, throwing punches to the jaw. But sometimes it takes round after round, and you lie on the living room floor, unable to get up. It refuses to let you sleep. You run out of food. It draws all the blinds and stands peering through the slats. It convinces you you're in danger. It says that people are coming, and they will hurt you if you let them in.

Soon madness has worn you down. It's easier to do what it says than argue. In this way, it takes over your mind. You no longer know where it ends and you begin. You believe anything it says. You do what it tells you, no matter how extreme or absurd. If it says you're worthless, you agree. You plead for it to stop. You promise to behave. You are on your knees before it, and it laughs.

I AM ALLOWED to obsess only after work, and for no more than three hours a day, like some people have a martini and read the paper when they come home. I make myself this allowance because it gives time a border. If I don't do this, I wind up sitting in one place thinking the same seventeen thoughts for hours, sometimes days. Usually I can fix my mind on something I consider sort of worthwhile; for example, I know a great deal about the surrealist period, chaos theory, poker, chess, and rabbits, and now can expound for days, if anyone asks, on the finer points of the history of foot-binding and the San Francisco strippers' union — a pretty neat party trick, if you ask me.

Today I'm obsessing about the better castles of the world, to which I will be traveling in, oh, the next two days or so, or that's what I've decided, having realized that I *desperately* need to go on a trip, a profound realization that comes to me every couple of months and consumes me completely, the end result being that, owing to my extensive research, I could become a travel agent specializing in the hotels, restaurants, and cultures of England; Dubai; any American or European spa; the southwestern deserts; a variety of African big-game hunting lodges; Indonesia and much of the South Pacific; and Florence, Greece, and Provence. The only downside to my obsession with trips is that I occasionally actually *take* them, which sometimes leads to the unfortunate situation of no one having any idea where I am. Anyway, today I get up from my desk to get yet another cup of coffee, but on my way back down the hall, I notice that the dining room table is covered with the remains of last night's dinner party, ashtrays, empty wine-glasses, a vase of red-orange tulips, the color of which is so acute, so pure, so vital and alive that in a wave of despair I suddenly real-ize that everything is futile after all. I become disillusioned with obsessing and realize that I have been obsessing for far more than the allotted three hours, in fact have been obsessing for days, and all my education is wasted on me. I have no purpose in life. I remember that by now I was supposed to have a PhD. Cheered, I sit down and note *Get PhD!* on my calendar for March 23. I clear my schedule for the following year, as I will be a fellow at Yale; and then I crack up, realizing that indeed I *have* been a fellow at Yale, last year, between hospitalizations; which fact is totally absurd in light of my current state of mind, which is clearly *mad;* and which, I now note with a sigh, is not dignified in the least.

I leap up from my chair, suddenly on fire, and dash down the hall, delighted, and I laugh very loudly and shout at the cat, ob-scurely, *Well, motherfuckers, it is indeed a wild ride!* And I am off to dinner with my husband, with whom I do not live, for I am *crazy and no one can live with me, not even me,* and I wonder as I gallop into the night who the hell lets me out of the house.

I peel into the restaurant and fling myself into a booth. I stare at him wide eyed, my chin level with the table.

"I'm a little manic," I gasp.

"I see that," he says.

"It's pretty interesting in here," I say, grinning wildly.

"Yes, I'm sure it is," he says. The waiter arrives. I almost shout, *Watch this!* but restrain myself momentarily, my shout billowing up in my chest. I put my hand over my mouth to contain my incredible wit, not wishing to alarm.

"Can I get you anything besides water?" the waiter asks.

*"No, we'll just have water tonight!"* I shout at the top of my lungs, leaning forward and slapping the table, and then the incredible laugh explodes from my mouth and I tip over in the booth, roaring and holding my sides.

I right myself. I catch a look of horror on Jeff's face and see that the waiter did not get the joke. Gleefully, I put the menu over my head and slump down in the booth, racked with giggles.

"Water is fine," Jeff says, attempting to save the waiter from his own stupidity. The waiter goes away. I continue to cackle, tears streaming down my cheeks. I laugh and laugh while Jeff watches me.

"That was a funny joke, Jeff," I point out, gasping. "The waiter didn't get it, did he?"

"He wasn't very smart," Jeff says, looking a little grim.

"Just as I thought." I sigh. "You got it, didn't you?"

"Sure."

I gasp. "You totally didn't! It was fucking hilarious!"

"I did so get it."

"You're just saying that so I feel better. Am I being loud?" I whisper loudly.

"A little. What do you want to eat?"

I page through the menu, throw it on the table, pick it up again, page through, drink my water, nearly spitting it out as I remember my joke, and sigh. I stare at the menu. "This is totally overwhelming."

Jeff nods. "It's a long menu." He closes his and helps me decide. We eliminate everything on the menu except one thing, and I order the red curry with mock duck, which is what I order every time we come here; I have never ordered anything else.

"I'm exhausted," I say, and slump in my seat. "This is a totally weird day."

MY CONDO is perfect. I am never leaving it. Everything is perfectly clean. I have placed each book in its exact right place, the place where I understand that God intended it to be. Everything is a little bit magical, just enough so that I feel the vibrations of it (everything) in the palms of my hands. I follow the cat around with a vacuum cleaner in case she sheds. I think I will just vacuum the cat, but she protests. I crouch to look under the couch for dust bunnies. I cannot see any but I vacuum under there anyway, just in case. The vacuum cleaner makes a very satisfying roaring sound. My parents used to run the vacuum cleaner by my head when I was a baby and refused to sleep. For some reason the vacuum cleaner knocked me out. I wonder now if it also would have been effective to put me in a box with a blanket and a ticking clock, like you do with a puppy, which is so stupid it thinks the clock is its mother's heartbeat. This strikes me as *hilarious,* and I note out loud, "Hil*a*rious!" over the roar of the vacuum cleaner. I notice I am talking to myself, and turn off the vacuum cleaner so I can hear myself better.

"I'm talking to myself!" I remark to myself, as if I am my mother and remarking on a particularly endearing and/or cute thing I have done. "Is that odd?"

Myself and I continue to converse while I put the vacuum away in the hall closet. "You really should clean this closet," I say, wandering into the thicket of ball gowns and coats and suits as if I'm heading for Narnia. I pick my way over several suitcases and climb up a ladder and down the other side, having realized that it is important to find my bathing suit *right now,* but I trip on a broken television and land with a thud in a pile of boxes. "Oh, for *God's sake,* don't get me started," I shout, and crawl back out, finding my hiking boots on the way. I go down the hall to collect all my shoes. "The thing is, probably everyone talks to themselves now and then, don't they?" I sweep everything off the closet shelves and begin arranging my heels in order of color and height. "But perhaps they don't talk to themselves quite this *much*. Time to do the laundry!" Abandoning the shoes, I pull all the bedclothes off the bed, upending cats, and go out my back door and down the staircase of my condo, singing a little laundry song, and I trail through the basement with my quantities of linens, note that my laundry song has taken on a vaguely Baroque sort of air, and note further that, to my regret, I do not play harpsichord, though my first husband's mother did, but she was really fucking crazy, and once called me a shrew. "A shrew!" I cry. "Can you *imagine!* Who says *shrew?*" I laugh almost as hard as I did when she said it. I continue my efforts to stuff my very large, very heavy brocade bedspread into the relatively small washer. "Perhaps it won't fit," I murmur, concerned, but then realize that if I just leave the lid open, the washer will, in its eminent wisdom, *suck in* the bedspread in its chugging, *"obviously,"* I say, rolling my eyes at my own stupidity. I pour half a bottle of laundry soap over the bedspread and turn the washer on. I stuff the sheets and attendant cases, pillows, etc. in the other washer and wander back upstairs. "I've locked myself out," I say grimly. "Fucking idiot." I lean my forehead against the door and become curious as to whether I can achieve perfect balance by tilting myself just right, "On the *tips* of my toes, with the forehead just *so*, and she does it!" I cry, balancing there. "People, she does it again! Will she *never* cease to amaze!" I shake my head in wonder, and laugh riotously. "Probably time to stop talking," I murmur. My neighbor comes out his back door with a bag of garbage. Real casually, I lean my cheek against the door and sort of right myself with a shove of my face. *Hi!* I wave dramatically, as if he is far away. He smiles nervously. I can't decide if he smiles nervously because I am acting weird, or because he is getting his PhD in philosophy, which would make anyone nervous. His girlfriend makes me nervous. He makes me nervous. The only person in that condo who doesn't make me nervous is their dog. I am quite nervous now, and wish for him to go away. We stand there, having run out of things to say. Why isn't he leaving? *Leave!* I think. *Leave! Leave! Leave!* His beard is somewhat devilish. He hems a minute more. "Are you — locked out?" he asks gently. "No!" I say gleefully, and immediately regret it. "I was putting out the recycling," I say, and haul off down the stairs, calling, "Have a nice day!" "You too," he calls after me, sounding a little weirded out, but I'm probably just feeling self-conscious and he didn't think anything of our exchange at all. I dash into the laundry room, leaping like a little lord, green pajamas flapping, and shout, "Just in time!" for I have flooded the basement. My bedspread is emerging out of the washer in an enormous coil, burbling over the edges like some kind of disgusting tongue, which I remind myself it is *not,* is *not* a tongue, "now don't start with *that* shit, missy," I snap, and tiptoe through the pool of soapy water that swirls all over the concrete floor. I grab the bedspread and try to wrestle it out of the washer, which takes this opportunity — *"fuckers!"* — to hemorrhage vast quantities of water; water is surging up and out of the washer and all over me, drenching me and twisting the coil of the bedspread ever higher so it looks like a cobra dancing out of the washer (though it does not "look" in the traditional sense like a cobra, i.e., I do not *really* see a cobra, or anything other than a bedspread, which causes me to meditate for a split second on the nature of simile and metaphor), "ah yes!" I bellow, "I have you now!" I climb up on the washer, barefoot, skidding a little, and seize the bedspread with all my strength and begin to drag it out of the *"fucking bastard washing machine!,"* which, I will think later (as I am giving myself a "calming" bath), it does not occur to me to simply *turn off,* no, I hop down from the washer and, the soaking bedspread over my shoulder, lean forward with all my weight and begin a long, slow trudge across the basement, looking a little like Titian's Sisyphus, and I remind myself that this is merely laundry day, and not in any sense a Sisy-phean journey.

Having freed the bedspread at last, I lug its considerable wet weight over to the dryer, where I spend five minutes trying to shove it in before I succeed and turn it on. As I head back up the stairs, I hear the dryer make a sound of great mechanical distress, *nnnnnnneeeeeeeeeeee,* and I pause for only a moment before I decide that if I leave, I will no longer intimidate the machine, and it will then do its job very well without me.

I go upstairs, let myself in with the spare key, and get into bed, after first raising the blinds to make sure I do not get depressed because I am sitting in bed in the dark on a gorgeous Saturday afternoon in fall, because I am a *fucking wack job.* I tuck myself in neatly and survey the situation. I get out of bed and go get an apple and get back in bed. I munch on my apple, chattering like Johnny Carson's dummy, *A-yah yah yah yah yah.* I put the apple core in the ashtray and light a cigarette. My sheets are covered with burn holes. "I really ought to stop smoking in bed," I note briskly, and open my 938-page clinical tome *Manic-Depressive Illness,* from which I am learning many interesting things about brain chemistry, and which surely, somewhere, somehow, will explain to me precisely why the *fuck* I am like this.

I imagine what an outside observer would see if he stood at the foot of my bed: a woman with wild red hair and a pair of crooked glasses, an enormous book propped up on her lap titled, in gigantic letters, MANIC-DEPRESSIVE ILLNESS.

"Well." I sigh. I pop an Ativan and turn a page. "So it goes."

From the bowels of the building, the dryer screams in pain, makes a disturbing *chunk* sort of sound, and goes silent.

SOON THE HYPOMANIA morphs into something darker. The eating disorder has taken hold for real. It's no longer just a few symptoms I was using to try to control the moods. It's taken on a life of its own. I am eating next to nothing, spending hours every day at the gym, standing on the scale four, five times a day, consumed with the fear of gaining weight, with fear that the writing is going badly, with fear that Jeff and I aren't going to make it, with fear that I will always be alone, or go crazy again, or spend my life in an institution. So I channel all the vague, amorphous, all-encompassing fears that have come to rule my days and nights into a fierce desire to lose weight. And more weight. All bones, I clatter around my house, aimlessly, running this way and that, calling people and hanging up, starting projects and abandoning them, getting into bed in the middle of the day and then getting out. My brain is electric, no longer the beautiful network of perfectly connecting thoughts and ideas, but now the manic fritzing and spitting, so loud it feels like it's going to shatter my eardrums. I smoke three packs a day. Jeff and I get together and devolve into the same fight we've been having for months, and we walk away from each other, torn up a little more each time. I am intensely lonely, and the nights are endless.

The fleeting feeling of confidence I got from moving into my own place and doing everything right has been replaced with the familiar, violent self-hatred I know. I had everything, and I lost it. Instead of hating the illness, I hate myself.

Soon I am throwing up even the little I eat. I eat an apple, then throw it up. A few grapes, then throw them up. When I go out to lunch with Megan, I eat a salad, then disappear into the bathroom to throw it up. Megan is pleading with me to go to the hospital. She and all my friends and family are crazy with worry. I'm skeletal, jumpy, scared all the time. Jeff's petrified — he's never seen my eating disorder before, and he's not in any position to help me deal with it, so he just tries not to look at how ugly I've become. I see him less and less. I begin to hide out in my house. I begin abusing laxatives. I spend my days running from my kitchen to the bathroom. Some days I am brave enough to venture out of the house and spend hours at the gym; sometimes I am afraid I am being watched.

And for the life of me, I can't figure out why my meds aren't working.

RUTH GETS ME out of the house for coffee. I sit staring at the red Gerbera daisy in its little white vase on the table. It absorbs me completely. Ruth is talking. She sounds far away, as if my head is wrapped in cotton batting and the sound waves can't quite make it through. I watch her lips. I hear myself explain to her that my thoughts are getting weird, and while I know that, I can't seem to do anything to stop them.

"It feels like I am physically trying to hold my head on. It feels like it's about to fly off. I don't want to go to the hospital. I don't want to hurt myself. I don't want to do any of it, but I feel like I have no way to keep myself together. What happens if I really can't?" I start to cry.

Ruth puts her hands over mine on the table. I have twisted and shredded a number of napkins, and it looks as if the table is covered with snow. "Oh, honey," she says. "I'm sorry."

I pick up a shred of napkin and blot at the mascara running down my cheeks. "It's okay," I say. "I hate crying. It's not a big deal, anyway. It's just a little bit harder than seems really necessary."

"It is," she says. "Are you cutting yet?"

I shake my head, pulling petals off the daisy. "I think about it all the time. I can't think other things for more than a few minutes before I think about it all over again."

"You know that's crazy, right? You know cutting is not a realistic option?"

I nod and heave a sigh. "It just seems like such a good idea. The obvious idea."

"That's crazy."

"It would be so calm. It would be so clean. Such nice clean lines, if you have a good razor. A few neat slices, and then I'd stop."

"Marya, you don't stop after a few slices. You always mean to, but you never do."

"I guess so," I say, lining the red petals up in a row.

"So you can't start."

I nod again. "The only thing that really worries me, though, is that I keep having this idea to try making a nice, neat slice in my neck, to see if I can hit the jugular."

"Okay, you need to be in the hospital," Ruth says.

I look at the bald stem sticking out of the little white vase. My eyes start leaking again, to my serious dismay. I tip my head forward over the table so I don't mess up my mascara more. I drip.

"I'm okay," I say. "They're just thoughts. I don't have a plan." The doctors always ask if you're having suicidal ideation — thinking about death, fantasizing about killing yourself, even when you don't want to — which I am, and if so, whether or not you have a plan, which I don't. I know myself well enough to realize that if we went to the emergency room, I would miraculously get better. I would show no signs of madness. It's called plausible sanity. It's a product of what they call lack of insight: when you're very sick, you don't have any perspective. You truly believe you're well, so you report that you're well. You act cheerful, put-together, and completely sane. You're articulate and very persuasive, and you explain to them that there's been a terrible mistake — you're not really crazy, and this ridiculous trip to the hospital is just a friend overreacting, or your family trying to trap you, or your spouse trying to get back at you for something. Because you seem perfectly fine — plausibly sane — doctors are hard-pressed to believe that you are, in fact, crazy and in need of hospitalization, even in cases where you've wound up in their emergency room as the result of a suicide attempt.

For this very reason, I often show up in the emergency room

clutching a list of my symptoms. I make this list before I go, while I still have the insight to see that I'm crazy. I am aided in making this list by an objective observer — Megan, Jeff, Ruth, my mother, or my father — and when we get to the hospital and I immediately change my mind, feel fine, insist that I'm sane and want to go home, the objective observer can tear this list from my fat little fists and give it to the doctor as proof that I am not, in fact, *plausibly sane,* and need to be locked up. But when you don't have such a list, and you do seem plausibly sane, they send you home with alarming frequency. It's happened to me several times. And I've gone straight home and started doing all over again whatever it was that had gotten me to the hospital in the first place. It's not at all uncommon to find that a bipolar person had seen a doctor almost immediately before he or she committed suicide. What happened? the baffled, grieving family and friends and colleagues ask. He seemed perfectly fine. She didn't even seem depressed. Why didn't the doctor stop him? Why didn't they keep her at the hospital?

"What are you doing tonight?" Ruth asks me.

I stare at her blankly, horror rising in my chest. I don't know. I have no idea how I will make it through the night. I can't bear the idea of going home and floating around, alone with my wretched, spinning thoughts. My eyes start to leak again.

"All right," she says, standing up. "You're coming with me."

We pick up Christi and go in search of dinner. Christi has been having a rough couple of days. I am wildly relieved to see her, both for my own sake and because I know that if she's with us, she'll be all right. For the rest of the evening, Ruth herds us around like a couple of giant children. We are crazy. Ruth is sane, at least today. So she gets to be in charge. She takes our hands and leads us into the restaurant. She orders for us. We stare at her as if she will explain everything any minute now. If Ruth is here, then there is hope. If Ruth is here, we are safe. Until the thoughts start up again.

*

I DON'T KNOW how long I've been in my house. It's dark. Last I checked it was day. I think I've thrown up seven times today. I'm so dehydrated I can barely walk, and I'm crawling down the hall. The eating disorder has gotten too bad. It's not working. I see it for what it is: an attempt to control a self that I felt was completely out of control, a life that was falling apart. And it has done nothing but make the bipolar worse, and ruin my body in the process. I have taken an entire box of laxatives. I am throwing up and peeing blood. But I didn't mean for it to get this bad — I only wanted to feel a little better — it seemed like a good idea at the time — I had forgotten how ugly this was. But I still have a loose grip left on reality, and I know that the bipolar will only keep getting worse if this keeps up. The eating disorder is only the beginning. I am half dead already, and if I don't stop I will wind up really dead.

I call Ruth and tell her I need to go to the emergency room. She's at my door. Christi's with her. I'm dizzy, disoriented, sorry, scared. They drive me to the emergency room. Then it goes dark.

I WAKE UP on the eating disorders ward to find Megan standing over me, hands on her hips. She explains to me, none too cheerfully, that she has been trying to find me for three days.

"Do you remember calling me?" she demands.

"Vaguely." I do, very vaguely indeed; I remember laughing and whispering into the phone a really funny joke that I had just thought up, but I don't remember the joke.

"You told me you were in an undisclosed location and were being restrained."

"Aha! That's right." I start laughing all over again. "It was a good joke, wasn't it?"

"I thought you were in jail."

"Of course I wasn't in jail."

"Then I thought you'd been kidnapped. Then I realized, wait, she disappears *all the time,* you *freak,* and I started calling all the hospitals in town." She leans forward, looking fierce. "Of course, none of them would tell me if you were *there.*"

"Why not?"

"Because," she says, narrowing her eyes, "you're in here under a *false name.*"

"I am?" This is news.

"Yes. You are. You're in here under Mary Miller."

"Really?"

"Yes. Why, exactly, are you in here under Mary Miller when your name is *Marya Hornbacher?*"

"My name almost *is* Mary Miller."

"No it's not! Your name is not almost Mary Miller!" she shouts.

"It is! Marya is Russian for Mary, and —"

"Forget it. Why are you in here under a false name in the first place?"

I furrow my brow. "I guess I didn't want them to know who I am."

"Marya, they *know* who you are!"

I think, then remember. "That's right. I didn't want *you* to know I was here."

"*Why not?*"

"I didn't want you to worry."

"You didn't want us to *worry?* Your mother's hysterical. Your father is ready to have the lakes dragged. And you didn't want us to *worry?*"

"I hate it when you worry."

She stares at me some more. She heaves a sigh and flops down next to me, shaking her head. Then she brightens up and says, "So, how's the food?"

"HOW ARE YOU feeling?" asks the psychiatrist on the eating disorders ward.

"A little zippy."

"Not depressed?" As I've said before, the assumption when you've got an eating disorder is that you've also got depression.

"No."

"How is your depression?"

"I don't have depression. I have bipolar."

"Yes, but depression is part of that," she says, smiling tensely. She's getting irritated. She wants me to say I'm depressed. Right now I'm not, though, so we could be sitting here a long time.

"I'm bipolar type one," I say. "Mostly I have mixed episodes."

"So you're a little depressed."

"No," I say patiently. "I'm not depressed at all right now. I don't get depressed until February. At the moment, in fact, I'm coming off a *manic* episode."

"I think I'm going to increase your antidepressants." She turns to her desk and starts looking up meds in the pharmaceutical handbook. As far as I'm concerned, she might as well just page through it with her eyes closed and stab the page with her finger and say we're going to put me on . . . let me see here . . . lithium! Zoloft! Wellbutrin! Zyprexa! Why not!

"I think that's a very bad idea," I say, becoming quite cross. "My psychiatrist will have a fit if you mess with my meds."

"I'm sure he'll understand if I add a little Prozac. It should help with the anxiety. It's a good antidepressant."

"Are you joking?" I ask, almost laughing. "You can't give me Prozac, or any SSRI! It will make me completely insane! Christ!" I throw my arms up in the air. "Haven't you people figured out yet that not everyone with an eating disorder has depression? And I can't *believe* you'd do something as stupid as put me on an SSRI. That shit sends me through the roof! Leave me on the antidepressants I'm on. They don't make me crazy."

She sighs, writing the order in my chart. "I think you'll find the Prozac will help your depression a great deal. It has almost no side effects."

"Except the one where it makes a lot of bipolar people *psy-*

*chotic!*" I tie myself into a tighter knot in my chair and chew my knee in frustration.

"You know," she says, glancing up, shaking her head and looking concerned, "I read your first book. I am just *really* sorry that you had such bad experiences with therapy and psychiatry. That's really uncommon." She looks totally baffled.

I stare at her. "Right-o," I say.

"I see here you've been having trouble sleeping. Do you want something to sleep?"

"I take trazodone. It works okay."

"Why don't I put you on Ambien?"

"Because I'm an addict and I'll start abusing it. Doesn't it say that in my chart?"

"Yes. I'm sure you won't start abusing it." She writes an order for Ambien in my chart. Now I'll have everyone staring at me tonight while I argue with the nurse about whether or not I'm going to take my meds. I feel like throwing the *DSM-IV* at her and telling her to look up *Axis I: bipolar disorder; Axis II: substance abuse*.

"I won't take it."

"So you're saying you're going to resist treatment." She sighs dramatically.

"No. I'm saying I'm going to continue the treatment my doctor has laid out for me."

"What about your depression? I don't think he's really looking at your depression. Untreated depression is a terrible thing. In fact, I suspect your eating disorder may have reemerged because you are very depressed."

"I'm done now," I say. I untie my legs and shuffle out of the office and down the hall to *Snack*. I hate the world.

I GET DISCHARGED in December. I've broken the cycle of the eating disorder and remember how to go back to living without one. The mania, too, has broken. I feel like I'm broken myself.

But I do my best. I go home to my empty condo, buy some real food, and eat like a normal person. I pay the bills that have piled up, return the phone calls, get back to work. I write the lectures that I'm scheduled to give at a couple of universities in February and March.

It's winter. Winter brings the blues. I'm afraid of them coming, and I know they will. My only hope is that I can get through the winter without going back to the hospital. If I can do this, then maybe I can stop hating myself. I think, if I just keep going, keep doing what they say, take the meds, go to sleep, use the light box, get out of the house, get *some* exercise (as opposed to working out four hours a day), eat enough, try to avoid stress, then maybe I can do it.

They don't tell you how to manage grief. And I miss Jeff so much it's killing me.

But there's nothing I can do about that now. All I can do is keep going forward. Maybe this way I can make it to April. Just this once.


## Winter 2006

*Seven* A.M. I wake up in the dark. There are so few hours of daylight — the sun will start to fall at about three o'clock in the afternoon, and it will be fully dark by four. It is hard to want to leave the house, or work, or live, in Minnesota during the winter months. The suicide rate goes sky high. All over this snow-blanketed city, there are people who lie in bed well into the flat gray afternoon, turning this way and that, slogging in and out of sleep. They may drag themselves up around dinner, when a spouse or partner comes home; they may attempt to dress, or they may not. February is the worst for me, but it's not February yet, and to-day I am hoping to spend the hours of light at my desk, trying to pretend the lack of sun isn't pressing in at me, pushing me into catatonia, a failure of the will to live. And so:

*Eight A.M.* I go into my kitchen. Take my handfuls of meds. Take the supplements they tell me will help. Take anything they tell me to take. I eat the food they tell me to eat; a little protein, they say, takes the edge off the anxiety, the ever-present morning fears. I go into my office and turn on the light box, which blasts a blinding fluorescent light into the room. I stare at it, drinking my coffee, for the allotted half-hour — enough to block the depression, with luck, but not so much that it will trigger mania. The balance in winter is hard to strike. All these years, every winter I've slipped into a mixed episode, a devastating depression coupled with the frenzied, chaotic energy of mania. This is what we are trying to avoid. I am not certain I can. I doubt it. But I have a little hope. And so:

*Nine A.M.* I sit down at my desk to work. I'm not writing well, but I'm only writing for myself. This is to make me feel functional, a feeling I lost during those years of total disability, so that at the end of the day I can feel good about the fact that the day did not pass me by. They want me to be functional. My doctors' goal, ulti-mately, is for me to return to a normal life — well, not return, for I've never had such a life, but to build the skills that will help me function at a level acceptable to me. They know that my function-ing may have been damaged by the severity of the episodes over the past few years. I'm still holding out hope that I will return to those two good years when Jeff and I were first married — the constant parties, the spotless house, the boundless energy, the end-less, unstoppable work. They have tried to tell me that I might not have that, and even that it might not be desirable; they are trying to explain to me that such a life may be exactly what triggers the episodes. But I don't want to believe it. I believe *that* life is normal.

That, to me, is functioning. I don't listen when they say I might have to adjust my expectations for myself. To me, this sounds like *You will have to accept failure. You will never be good enough again.*

*Ten A.M. to six P.M.* I work like a demon. I work, and work, and work. At the end of the day, I don't know what I've written, or how much. It almost doesn't matter. What matters is that I am still writing. I am still able to get up and do my job every day. Every week the doctor asks me if I'm working. If I am, he's pleased. If not, he worries. For me, the first sign of oncoming madness is that I'm unable to write. I stare at the computer, type a few lines, delete them in increasing despair. I believe my mind has dried up, that I will never write again. Most people would call this writer's block, and that's partly what it is — if only it didn't also signal the beginning of something else, to wit, the loss of my ability to function. When my mind leaves the room, the words are the first things it grabs on its way out, leaving me at my desk, terrified, hating myself, dreading what's next. And so, today, I write as if my life depends on it, because right now it does.

*Six P.M.* I go to the gym. They tell me the gym will help stabilize my moods — the adrenaline and the dopamine rush that exercise triggers will level out the rises and falls, interrupt the cycles that can lead me into and out of episodes and extreme moods. They tell me it will make me happier. They tell me it will decrease the ever-present, crippling anxiety. And that's what it seems to do. The only trick is talking myself into leaving the house. I've been in here peacefully all day, maintaining my marginal grip on the world outside of my house and head; but now I have to get dressed and go out into the freezing cold dark. I force myself out of my chair, bundle up, and drive to the gym, skulk into the workout room, onto the treadmill, glancing around me to see if anyone's watching. On good days, they aren't. On bad days, I know they are, and I am terrified of them. Dr. Lentz says no one is watching. So I say to myself, chanting along with my footfalls as I run in place, *No one is watching, no one is watching, all's well, no need to worry, level the mood swings, increase self-image, protect against episodes, you need to be here,* and I finish my run — and I am elated, out of breath, feeling alive, feeling at peace. It works every time. When I do it every day, the peace builds up, and I go through the day not quite so crippled by anxiety as I usually am.

*Eight P.M.* I'm eating dinner when Jeff calls. My heart freezes in my chest when I hear his voice, then starts up again. I can hardly understand him. He's crying. Sobbing, really, hysterical. I drop my fork and it clatters on the floor. I stand up but then am paralyzed and can't move. My throat closes. I want to hang up. I want to help him. He's living in a hellhole, his — our — house is trashed, filthy, full of boxes and the detritus of the three renters who've moved in in my absence. He is hiding in a ten-by-ten room with windows that don't close all the way, and the icy wind gets in, and he shivers there, under the covers in bed in his clothes. His room is full of dirty dishes, he's compulsively spending money on things he doesn't need, things that arrive and are abandoned wherever they land, the kitchen, the bathroom, the hallway, towering stacks of boxes, a thick film of dust over it all. I've only been there twice since I left, and it made me incredibly sad and worried for him; he's slipped into the depression that has dogged him all his life and that was violently set off when we split, and now we are quite a pair, crazy as hell and deep in sorrow and fear. I stand frozen in my kitchen, waiting for him to take a breath, but he doesn't — *Jeff. Jeff, you've got to stop for a second, I can't understand you, what do you want? Are you all right?* And obviously he is not all right. *Can I come over?* he begs. And I say yes.

*Nine P.M.* Jeff is in a ball on my living room floor, rocking back and forth. I am terrified. I think he may be suicidal. I am numb. I cannot force myself to feel. I hate him for being like this. Finally, with an enormous effort, I make myself go over to him. I lie down on the floor at his back and curl my body around him. I say, *Let's get off the floor. Let's go to the couch. Is that okay?* And, his face tortured and red and wet with tears and snot, he nods and gets to his knees and crawls over to the couch. He lies down and I put his head in my lap. He is screaming in pain, incomprehensible strings of words pouring out of his mouth. *Can't take it* is all I hear him say. *Need you*, I hear. And then he loses the power of speech again and dissolves. I don't know if I should call an ambulance. I want him to be safe and I know if he leaves he will not be safe. But he won't let me call, and he won't let me take him to the ER. Finally I convince him to stay with me. His breathing slows. He nods. He falls asleep. I sit there with his heavy head in my lap, staring down at his face. I feel nothing. I know that I love him and want to help him, but we have grown so far apart. I don't know what to do.

*One A.M.* He sleeps heavily in my bed. I stand at the window, smoking, looking out. There is cloud cover — no stars, all black. I want to stay sane. We cannot both be mad. We can't end like this.

*Two thirty-four A.M.* I watch him sleep, his mouth open, peaceful at last. I don't know how, but right then I realize that we will make it. Our life will include mental illness, its absurdities and devastations, the laughter and destruction it causes, the level of functioning it allows. We will have to accommodate it. That is a great deal to ask. But it is the way it has to be. And I believe we are up for it.

Just not tonight.


MEGAN AND I have coffee. I ask her what it's like to have a friend with bipolar. She looks at me, then at her hands.

"It's unlike any other friendship I have," she says. "In most ways, there's nothing different about it. You're just the way you are, and I accept that absolutely, and I don't think of you as crazy, and I don't feel like you're a burden, for God's sake, like you always worry about." She thinks a minute. Then she says, "But there's the one difference. With other friends, I'm not constantly aware that they could very easily die. With you, I am aware of that. I am always aware that you have come so close to committing suicide, someday it might happen."

"I won't," I say.

"I know," she says. "But you might. You could. And so I have to try to understand how I feel about that. And this is how being friends with you is different. I would be devastated if you died. Completely devastated."

She thinks another moment, trying not to look away from me. She is trying not to cry.

"But I would understand," she finally says. "I don't mean that I'm giving you permission. I just mean that I really understand how deeply and painfully you struggle. I won't let you do it. But I would understand if you did."

But I won't.

I won't.

FEBRUARY AND MARCH are difficult. The depression deepens past the point where I can wrest myself out on my own. Dr. Lentz puts me in outpatient treatment for a few weeks, and I sit in my little groups, nearly comatose. All I know is that I'm going to stay out of the hospital if it kills me. Lentz changes my meds, changes them again, finally resorts to another round of ECT. Between that, the Herculean efforts of family and friends, and my own pigheaded refusal to give up, I manage to keep enough of a handle on reality to stay out of the psych ward. Finally, the snow begins to melt.

And Jeff starts to emerge from his own hell. As spring begins, somehow the two of us are able to build a little closeness, a tentative trust, enough that we can lean against each other, staggering around inelegantly, but somehow on our feet, and together.

I come bounding up the steps in front of our house: the lilac is blooming! I rush into it, fling my arms around it, bury my face in the heavy-scented flowers. I look over at the garden: the snow is gone, and the beds are bare but for the broken gray stalks and dead leaves that fall left behind, but the lawn is green, and a few bulbs have sent up tiny shoots, barely there, and there are two absurd yellow tulips, blooms bobbing in the soft spring breeze, leaves and stalks an urgent green. The tulips say it's spring, so I say it's spring. And with spring comes the joy that lives beneath the difficult times. The joy is an absurd yellow tulip, popping up in my life, contradicting all the evidence that shows it should not be there.

I open the door and walk through the house. Wide swaths of yellow-white light flood through the windows and fill the rooms. The groggy dogs glance up from their sun spot on the floor, glance at me, yawn, and flop their heads back down, exhausted by their miniature day.

This is my house again. We packed up the boxes and books from my condo and carted them back home. Jeff went on a mad cleaning spree to sweep out the dust, the boxes, the dirty dishes, the old newspapers, the broken stereos, the debris that filled the house while I was gone, and now it is clean, new, and there is room for us both. We circle each other, still uncertain, and laugh, startled, when we touch, when we speak. We are new. We do things this new way, a way we can't exactly describe, but a way in which we both seem to have enough space to exist. This is not another honeymoon. There is something serious underneath, a knowledge that things are fragile, incomplete, that things can be ruined and lost; and a knowledge that we will do anything to not let that happen again.

I wake up a little terrified every day. An old fear sends out shoots in my body that wind around my ribs, filling me with anxiety. But it will pass. As spring goes on, the fear will recede. I can almost remember a time in my life when the fear wasn't always there. I can almost imagine a life without it. The idea makes me a little dizzy; it seems so foreign, so unfamiliar, as if I wouldn't know how to live that way.

My new therapist tells me that I don't know how to live without crisis. She's right. I ask her questions: What do I do with my days if things are all right? How is it possible that one can get through a day without the rigid need for absolute perfection? What do you mean, "You let some things go"? How can I tolerate myself if I do something wrong?

"What do you mean, wrong?" she asks.

"Well, so, I almost had a perfect day the other day," I say. "I did everything right. I worked for hours. I paid all the bills as soon as they came. I unloaded the dishwasher right away. I picked up a piece of paper off the floor the minute I saw it. I went to the gym. And then it all went to hell." I flop back on her couch, defeated.

"How so?"

"I forgot to take the chicken out of the freezer!" I shout, flinging my hands in the air. "I totally fucked up!"

She laughs at me.

"Not funny!" I say.

"But it is," she says. "Do you know that normal people don't have to be perfect every day? I have never had a perfect day. I figure, at the end of the day, that I did pretty well, and that's fine."

"That's fine for *you*," I say. "But not for me."

"Why on earth do you get special rules? Are you so unique?"

"It's not that," I say. "It's that your *pretty good* is better than my *perfect*. I have to be perfect just to measure up. To be as good as someone normal. Just look at the last few years."

"You've been sick," she says.

"I've been a total fuckup. I couldn't do a single basic thing that normal people do every day without falling apart or having a nervous breakdown. Normal people just *do* things. It's not a big deal."

"So now you have to make up for it," she says.

"Yes!" I shout. "Exactly!"

"You don't, you know. You didn't do anything wrong. You were doing the best you could."

"And that wasn't good enough," I snap. "For example, I have this dentist, right? And he works downtown. But every time I have to go, I have a total meltdown and usually cancel. I've canceled my last four appointments. And then there was that day where I had a bunch of errands to run, and I got scared, so on the way here, I called you to cancel, because my meds were making me fall asleep, and I called to cancel the dentist, because I was giving up and going home. But then I felt better so I called you *and* the dentist to tell you I was coming after all. Then I went to get a manicure, but I fell asleep while she was painting my nails, so I called you and the dentist to cancel again. But then by the time I went out to my car I was feeling more awake, so I called you and the fucking dentist to tell you I was definitely coming. But then on the way to the dentist I got scared of downtown and the parking garage, so I had to turn around and go home because by then I was totally insane. Because I'm a complete idiot and I freak out over nothing. I don't like downtown. I don't like parking garages. I can't deal with a fucking *parking garage*."

She shrugs. "Have you thought about finding a new dentist?" she asks. "You could find one with a regular parking lot."

I stare at her, astonished.

"That's what a normal person would do," she says calmly. "If they didn't like going to one dentist, they would find another one that worked better for them."

"But there's no *reason!*" I shout. "I *should* be able to deal with downtown and a stupid parking garage!"

"Why should you?"

I slump back in my chair, stumped.

"See, the thing is, you've got this idea of normal that's not normal. Normal people don't do everything perfectly. You don't have to do everything perfectly to be normal. To be normal, you've got to kind of relax and let some things go. Your problem is that you're so used to being in crisis that your whole perception of yourself is as a fuckup, a permanent fuckup, never someone who gets to *not* be a fuckup, so you have to torture yourself and hate yourself just to be as good as everyone else. You're having a hard time realizing that you're not a fuckup anymore. You're entering a whole different period of your life where you *are* normal. And you're having a hard time getting used to it."

I gaze out the window. "But if you're not trying to be perfect, then how do you know if you're doing things right?"

"There is no *right*," she says. "There's the best you can do. And that's fine. That's normal."

"The best I can do is sometimes completely fail," I say.

She shrugs. "Fine," she says. "The rest of us do it all the time."

Bewildered, I wander out to my car.

I'M WEARING a pair of pants four sizes too big and there are nine half-full coffee cups on my desk. Some of the cups also hold cigarette butts, some have mold, and one has an apple core. I've been in my office since, I think, last Tuesday; it is either Friday or Saturday today, maybe. I just went into the kitchen to get something to eat and found we have only condiments. I will be eating frozen spinach, pesto, and caper berries for dinner.

Megan shows up. She wants to go to lunch. But I'm certain it is only seven o'clock in the morning.

"It's noon," she says, standing in my doorway. "Can I come in?"

"It isn't noon," I answer, opening the door wider and going down the hall. She closes the door and follows me to the kitchen. I stand there staring at the clock on the stove.

"It's noon," I tell her. "How is it noon?"

"Happens every day," she says.

"What in the hell have I been doing? Did I just get up?" I ask.

"I don't think so," she says. "You're dressed."

I look down. I *am* dressed, more or less. "I don't know what I've been doing," I say, baffled.

"Working," she says. "I called you at nine. You were working."

"What was I working on?"

"The book," she says.

I stare at her blankly.

Megan has her own weirdnesses. She has some issues with disorder and dirt, and occasionally has her rabid fixations. So, just as a special treat for some unsuspecting waitress, Megan and I sit down at a table in a new restaurant we're giving a try. We have been having lunch at the same restaurant every week for the past five years; we thought we'd venture a change.

"I would like a cup of coffee with skim milk," Megan says to the waitress, smoothing her napkin.

"We only have two-percent," the waitress says.

Megan stares at me without expression for a good long while in silence.

"Okay," she says finally, and picks up her spoon and squints at it.

The waitress goes away. Then I remember I want coffee too, so when she comes back with a plate of bread, I order a cup, and we order lunch. She leaves.

"Is it Friday or Saturday?" I ask Megan, scooting myself into the far corner of the booth, where I can keep an eye on the room.

"Thursday," she says. "The day we always have lunch."

"Right," I say, nodding.

"When was the last time you left the house?"

"Last week sometime." I crane my neck around the high-backed booth.

"There's nobody there," she says mildly. I turn back around, fold my legs up under me, tuck my hands between my thighs, and cross my feet so that I am pretty much in a knot, my back pressed against the wall. I like to feel compact.

Megan goes to the bathroom. When she comes out, she walks over to our table and stands there. I have switched to her side of the booth. I look up at her.

"What was wrong with that side?" she asks.

"It made me anxious."

"Okay," she says, and sits down. "Can I wash my hands at your house?"

"Of course," I say.

"I forgot my wet wipes," she explains.

The waitress comes back with my coffee and then leaves again. I spread my napkin out on the table, take a piece of bread, tear it into three pieces, lay them out on the napkin, and butter them with exactly one-third of a pat of butter apiece. It makes me calm to do this. Megan watches me. "I need a little plate," she says, and flags down the waitress.

"Yes?" the waitress says.

"I would like a little plate and an extra napkin. Please."

"We're lots of fun," I remark.

"I tip well," Megan says, lining up the pepper with the salt.

We discuss the new series of paintings she is working on, work she's doing on the Iraq war, the sources of light and color so saturated they seem to bleed. We talk about the chapter that's driving me bananas, and my very weird writing process. We discuss the war, and our husbands, and how very odd it must be to be married to us, for we are, as Shakespeare said, passing strange.

Our lunch arrives.

Megan takes the top piece of bread off her sandwich, reorganizes the lox with her fork, cuts her cornichon into four pieces, takes a spoonful of soup, and says severely, "They should have put these beans through a food mill. They're disgusting this way. They have those things."

"What things?"

"Those *skins*." Megan proceeds to spoon every bean out of her white-bean soup.

We agree that we like this lunch place, the Bakery on Grand. We agree that it is safe, and that we will come here again, and this will be our new place, and the decaf's pretty good. We are immensely relieved.

Megan comes over after lunch, decides she can't wash her hands in my bathroom because there's a cat box in it, washes her hands in my kitchen sink, reaches her arms around me to give me a hug, keeping her hands in fists so as not to touch me, bangs me on the back, and goes.

A fine time was had by all.

When she leaves, I phone Medicare. For two hours — that's how long the call lasts — I try to make myself focus on and understand at least some small part of what they are saying, becoming increasingly convinced that they are making it harder on purpose. There is some snafu in my insurance coverage, and for the moment, no one will cover anything. So I have to enroll in a new plan. I have been staring at the booklets all week, these booklets that surely someone must be able to translate for me, because I can't make heads or tails of what they say *at all*, and every time I look at them I get overwhelmed and want to weep, and I flip pages frantically and make obscure notations in the margins, which confuse me even more, so I am doing what the doctors tell me — I am *asking for help!* I am on the phone with Medicare in the hopes that they'll help me figure out what the hell I am doing, and I listen intently while the person on the phone speaks some other language at me in a steady drone.

"I have to say," I cut in.

"Yes, ma'am?"

"It seems a little silly to me that the whole reason I have Medicare is because my brain doesn't work, which means I can't understand a word you're saying, let alone what's printed in these massive manuals you send me, where one page refers to another page, which refers to some other booklet, which tells me to call you, whereupon I get an automated answering service that confuses me more, and now that I've got you, you tell me to call back on the fifteenth, which I will forget and will not therefore get myself enrolled in whatever program I am supposed to enroll in, which is supposed to cover my drugs, but apparently does not cover Pap smears because they are not 'medically necessary,' and now my other insurance won't pay for anything because they figured out I have a mental illness, and you won't pay for anything because you think the other insurance is supposed to be paying, and I am pretty sure someone is in fact supposed to be covering my medical expenses, which are in excess of five thousand dollars a *month,* so I am pretty well just shit out of luck, is that what you're saying?"

There is a little pause. Cautiously, the voice says, "Noooo . . ." And we start again.

Eventually I give up and hang up the phone. I have done this every day for a week. I will keep doing it until one day, suddenly, it all makes sense. Surely, someday, it will.

THE PHONE RINGS. *"What!"* I shout into it. I pace in circles in my office.

"Hey, sweetie!" It's Jeff, with his interminable cheeriness. Son of a bitch. I hate him. I wish he were here so I could work. I wish he would go away so I could work. "How's the writing going?"

"Horrible." I plunk down in my desk chair and spin around in circles.

"I'm sure it's fine. I'm sure it's *great.*"

"It isn't. It's crap. I spent three hours writing and then I read it and it was crap."

"So what are you doing now?"

I look at my computer screen. I am in a bidding war on eBay, attempting to acquire a purple silk smoking jacket with black satin lapels. I intend to wear it as a robe. I am also bidding on a gold ball gown that I have realized I cannot live without. "Research," I say.

"Well, that's great! You've been avoiding research for days!"

"Shut up. I have not."

"Oh. My mistake."

I have been avoiding research. He is only humoring me in my delusions of competence.

"I'm never going to write again." I heave a sigh.

"Yes you will."

"No I won't! I haven't written all week! I might as well just sit around eating truffles."

"Maybe so. But I think you're stewing something. You're just about to write."

"About to write! Always about to write! Never writing! I am a waste of human space," I say glumly and slump in my chair. I raise my bid on a standing ashtray without which my life will be completely incomplete. "I think I'm depressed," I say. "But maybe I'm just sick." I can never tell if I'm depressed or just sick. I don't believe in being sick. I drive myself crazy trying to work when I can't because I'm sick. "Do you think I'm sick?" I ask, feeling my forehead.

"No."

"You see? I'm just being lazy!" I crow, triumphant, and pound the desk with my fist. "And I'm never going to write again! Do you want a new set of golf clubs?"

"What? No." I bid on them anyway. They look sort of retro. I decide I'm into retro, and type in *retro*. "Are you on eBay?" he asks.

"No," I say. "Yes. I haven't bought anything yet."

"Try not to."

"What do you care? It's my money."

"What are you buying?"

"Ball gowns."

"Oh," he says.

"I'm not writing."

"You'll write tomorrow. I can tell."

"How can you tell? Yes!" I yell, having just won a bid for a child's antique desk. Next: find child's chairs.

"Maybe I'm manic. Maybe that's why I can't concentrate."

"Maybe you're a complete lunatic."

"I'm going to buy you a pair of plaid pants. What?" I ask, distracted.

"Nothing. Keep at it. Good job."

"Thank you. I will." I win the bid for a kilt.

I hang up and reach for my cigarettes. Remembering that I've quit, I go down the back stairs and fetch them out of the garbage can, hoping that no one is watching me dig through the trash while only very marginally dressed.

I don't write for a week. I'm driving both myself and everyone who knows me totally insane. Half the time I'm hysterical and pacing, half the time I'm in bed. I keep books there with me; it makes me feel more productive. I hate myself. I get horribly depressed. I lie in bed, trying to decide how I will kill myself. One thing is for sure — I can't hang myself because Jeff would find me and would be upset and I would feel terrible. I will drown myself instead.

I wake up in the middle of the seventh night.

I have it. There it is. The thing I've been trying to write. I creep down the hall to my office. I emerge three days later. The chapter is done.

And then it's evening, and Jeff's home, and we're sitting on the deck looking out over the wildly blooming world, and the sun is making its way lazily down the sky, not in any hurry to end the day. I go up to bed eventually, read, take my handfuls of pills, turn out the light, and sleep.

Well, sleep off and on. Lately the sleep has gotten a little messed up. I'm sure it means nothing. I don't have time for things like that. So I ignore it.

May flows into June and summer's arrived. I feel human again. A little superhuman, really. I can do anything. I'm unstoppable. All that craziness — it's over, and it's never coming again.

Except that it is. The rest of them see it before I do. My mood goes up and up, bobbing above me, and I dangle by its string, going higher every day.

Maybe, though, this time I can come down easy, like I did this winter. Maybe it won't be too bad. I've worked so hard. In the brief instants of insight when I feel this coming on, I feel so helpless and frustrated that I want to scream. I did what they said. I tried. I did my best. And it wasn't good enough.

But that's the way it goes.

## Summer 2007

When it comes, it comes quietly enough. One morning I am suddenly, acutely aware that I am *extremely* happy. It's a fine, bright day, and I'm feeling rather grand. I fling my arm out before me, which admittedly is a little odd, in a gesture intended to signify my magnanimous state of mind. Sally forth! I am overcome with a sense of possibility — which clearly means that I should go shopping.

Entirely possessed of my senses, and in a *very* good mood, I buy nine Coach purses, twelve Coach scarves, and six identical Coach hats, items I obviously need immediately, *urgently*. (Though of course one *can* overaccessorize, and in certain regrettable moments one has in fact *vastly* overaccessorized, wearing for example more than one hat, a winter scarf around the neck, a silk head scarf, Gibson Girl short pants, black bug-eyed sunglasses, earrings in only the *left* ear, and a totally inappropriate baby-doll T-shirt one has impulsively purchased which reads *Hot Buns*.) It is important not to look *cluttered*.

However, now possessed of this fine, fine collection of hats, I make a trip to all the vintage and antique stores in the Twin Cities in search of a *hat rack*, which rack should be *pewter*. While at these stores I become distracted by and violently attached to: a curiously tiny writing desk, several large buffets, an entire set of *spectacular* crystal glasses (for white wine, red wine, martini, highball, lowball, cordial, brandy, and aquavit) (I haven't had a drink in years), a deeply significant dining room set, a somehow Dutch-looking and incredibly tacky tureen, a green velvet couch with broken springs and wear marks on the arms, several fake diamond rings, a horrid red paste choker I intend to wear "to the *theatre*," and a number of florid lamps. I buy them all.

This is good. This is life. I am brilliantly, thrillingly, violently *alive*.

I'D BEEN DOING fine. My medication was working beautifully. And then I went on vacation. The flight back was a redeye, and that was the trigger, something that small: one night without sleep, the tiniest bit of jet lag — two hours' time difference — and I was off to the races.

So of course I'm not the least bit tired, and spend the day running around, fixing, cleaning, planning to save the world next week. I don't have the slightest idea that I'm spinning off into the stratosphere — lack of insight, one of the first signs that hypomania is morphing into full-blown mania. You have no idea that your symptoms are symptoms; they seem like completely reasonable behavior to you. Today, you think, is a good day to get things done, and indeed you get things done.

I wake up in a splendid mood, the sleep deprivation bothering me not at all. I sit down to write for eighteen hours and nearly wrap up an entire section of this book, about seventy pages. Jeff comes home at some point. I ignore him, keep typing, obsessed, my cheeks flushed, fingers flying, heart pounding in my chest. "Out!" I shout at him without looking up from my computer. "Writing! Can't stop now! Almost done!" He goes away.

A minute later I simply *must* talk to him. I pound down the stairs and find him in the kitchen, looking surprised. "We're moving to New York!" I shout, turning and sliding around the hardwood floor in my socks. The dogs bark wildly, as excited as I am, clearly getting it completely. Jeff loosens his tie. "Okay," he says, turning back and continuing to chop whatever it is he is chopping. I crash into him, pulling on his shirt. "I've decided to start a public relations company! Sorry to be so loud! I'm just extremely, extremely excited!" I hop onto the kitchen counter and wiggle my feet. "Have you eaten anything?" Jeff asks, putting a pot on the stove. I roll my eyes and sigh loudly. "Pain in the ass!" I cry. "Completely boring!" I fly out of the room and up the stairs into my office and get back to work.

Eventually I come tearing out of my office, cackling with glee. "I finished it!" I shriek, sliding down the hall, crashing into the wall, heading into the bedroom. "Finished!" I shout. Jeff looks up from his book. I dive headfirst onto the bed, flip onto my back, and kick my legs. "I'll finish the book by Friday! Isn't that *marvelous*?" I demand, sitting up. "Let's watch *Law and Order*. Quick!" I climb under the covers, fully dressed and wearing shoes. "Hurry! We must watch it right now! Is there any chocolate?" He passes me the box and turns on the TV. I gaze at it intently, becoming totally absorbed in seconds flat.

Somewhere between scenes, I start sobbing. Startled, I look at Jeff. "It is *so fucked up!*" I wail, putting my head in my hands. I sob terribly, as if someone close to me has died. The odd thing is, I'm not even slightly sad. Between gasps and snorts and sobs, I explain this to Jeff, who is perfectly cheerful. "I know," he says. Handing me the box of Kleenex, he says, "I think you wrote a little too long today." "Noooooooo!" I wail, sliding down onto my back and flipping over on my front. Pounding the bed with my fists, I bury my face in the pillows, sobbing even harder. Jeff puts his hand on my head and says, "Anything I can do? Do you need me to sit on you?" (Sometimes I feel uncontained, and he does that. It works very well.) "No," I sob. "I'm fine. Nothing wrong. Had a perfectly nice day. Sorry about this." "No problem," he says, and keeps watching TV. I sob myself silly, then abruptly stop. "Better?" he asks as I sit up. "Just fine," I say brightly, wiping off my face. We settle in and continue as before.

He falls asleep around the fifth hour of reruns, and continues to sleep though I bat at him to wake him up. Eventually I turn off the television and the light and lie down and try, uselessly, to sleep.

I feel my mouth filling with words, words I need to write down right now, and my mind begins to race, words whirling in circles, a cyclone of words. I force myself to try to rest. I breathe slowly, in through the nose and out through the mouth, as instructed by the many books on breathing and "being in the moment" that I've been given over the years. I imagine myself in a beautiful place, on a beach, or in the mountains. I count sheep. Somewhere around two thousand, I fall asleep, thinking gleefully of how much I will write the next day, what with all these wonderful words.

But I don't write the next day, or the next or the next after that. Because sometime during that night, the words scattered. The whirl-wind of words, beautiful strings of sentences, which I pictured as a net of letters, strands of words spun into a kind of silver sugar cone inside my head, whirl away from me, phrases and snatches of words now seething all over my brainpan like a pit of snakes.

Never mind that. I am alive. I'm full of ideas, ideas I know I will string together again, any second now, but while I wait I become a tiny Tasmanian devil, tearing through my days. The ideas disappear in my wake, one after another, words flying through the air, *hitching post, emperor's elbow, hats off to the watchers, the watchers who watch and wait, the whispering watchers who watch and wait and wiggle and writhe,* madly alliterating. Flight of ideas — it happens in the early stages of mania. Ideas fly past and I chase them in all directions, but they elude my grasp, a flurry of butterflies that twitch away just as I close my hand.

At the urging of everyone, I give Lentz a call.

I feel like I have been sitting in Lentz's office for the past ten years. Jeff is there too. I am slouched in my chair, practically horizontal, madly wiggling my foot. I raise it above my head and watch it wiggle with incredible speed.

"Have you seen my socks?" I ask Lentz, holding out my foot.

He glances up. "Very nice," he says. He is looking at his computer, scrolling down through my chart. He tips his head backward and peers down his nose.

I have been seeing Lentz since I was twenty-three. He has seen me as batty as I've ever been, from florid manias to catatonic depressions. And he has seen me utterly sane. He reads my books and articles faithfully. It seems to matter not a bit to him whether I show up wearing a tailored suit or a pair of grotty pajamas, an old torn coat, and a pair of gardening shoes. To him, I'm not crazy. I'm just the way I am.

He looks down at his little notepad and says, "Looks like you're feeling a little speedy."

"A little. Only a very little. A very little bit," I say, holding my fingers about an inch apart. "But I have to get my things done. I can't stop now. I'm on a roll."

He nods, and says to Jeff, "How would you say she's doing?"

"She's bats," Jeff says. This bothers me not at all. I have learned to take Jeff with me to the doctor when I am feeling off, since I have no perspective. He sits across from me on the little couch. He's watching me, looking worried. This irritates me gravely. I sigh at him and become more fully involved in the incredible speed of my foot.

"Marya?" Lentz breaks into my thoughts. I focus now on the tips of my fingers, which feel tingly.

"I bought a canary!" I announce, looking up.

"Oh?"

"She didn't buy a canary," Jeff says with a sigh.

"I see," Lentz says. "Have you been sleeping?"

"Not really. I don't like to sleep. Sleep is a monumental waste of time. Sleep is irrelevant in the face of my things. Which I have to get done."

"She's sleeping about two hours a night," Jeff adds. "Total. She's up and down."

"I'm up and down," I concur. I pause in my study of my fingers and stare at Lentz intently. "But you have to understand, I need to get my things *done*."

"I know you do," Lentz says, poking at his little Palm Pilot, which has the pharmaceutical handbook on it. "It's important that you get them done."

"It's very important," I say.

"I know it is. We don't want to break your focus."

"Very important," I repeat, when suddenly my foot takes off again.

"How much Geodon are you on?"

"Eighty milligrams," Jeff says.

"I'm going to up your Geodon," Lentz says.

I look up, worried. "Will it make me fat?"

"No."

"Will it make me stupid?"

"No. It should just make you a little less edgy."

"I can't lose my edge," I say to him sternly.

"Of course not. How much is she working?" Lentz asks Jeff.

"All the time. She even works when someone's talking to her. She won't change her clothes because she says it would interrupt her 'things.'"

"I wrote fifty pages yesterday," I tell him, quite smug.

"Good for you. Are you eating?" Lentz asks.

"She's not eating," Jeff says.

"I'm eating," I say, rolling my eyes.

"She's only eating fruit."

"Marya, you have to eat more than fruit."

"No, I do not," I snap.

"Are you cutting?"

"I took all the razors," Jeff says.

"Totally unnecessary," I snap again, and get up and stroll in circles around the room.

"Do you need to be in the hospital?" Lentz asks.

"Absolutely *not!*" I say, hopping once in protest. "How am I supposed to get any work done? They never let me bring my computer. I can't very well work on *construction paper!*"

"I think she needs to be in the hospital," Jeff says.

I spin around and jab my finger into his chest, hopping again and kicking him once in the shin. "I certainly do not! They don't let me have my *cell phone! Which is crucial!*"

"Marya, you're really quite speedy," Lentz says.

I sit down in the chair and grip the arms to prove a point. "No I'm not."

"Okay," he says. To Jeff, he says, "Call me if she's still like this tomorrow."

"I'm going to get *lots* of work done," I say, very pleased.

"What are you writing?" Lentz says, standing up and shaking Jeff's hand.

I tick them off on my fingers. "A play, a novel, an article, and a new series of poems."

"I look forward to reading them," says Lentz. "Take a Zyprexa."

"Absolutely I will *not*," I say in a huff. "It makes me stupid and fat."

Lentz sighs.

Jeff goes out the door. I hop after him like a baby chick.


SO THIS MORNING, I trot downstairs to start the day. "How are you this fine morning?" Jeff asks, handing me a cup of coffee.

"I'm good! Well, I felt a little funny this morning — anxiety, a little blue — so I increased my Wellbutrin." I sit down in an armchair. The day is sunny and beautiful. I will feel better in no time at all. This habit of fucking with the dosages of your meds is common among bipolar people; since we don't trust the doctors, we figure our ideas are better than theirs, and so we add and subtract pills all the time. This rarely has good effects.

That's why Jeff stares at me for a minute, then picks up the phone and dials the emergency nurse line.

"Oh, for God's sake!" I shout at him. "You are such an over-reactor!"

He waves his hand at me to shut me up. "Yes, hello? My wife has bipolar. She decided to take" — he glares at me and hisses, "How much did you take, you idiot?" and I cheerfully say, "Thirteen hundred and fifty" — "she took triple her regular dose of Wellbutrin. Thirteen hundred and fifty milligrams. Isn't that an overdose, more or less? What should I do? All right. All right. I'll call right away." He hangs up the phone and dials again.

"You might have a stroke," he snaps. "I completely can't believe you. This is serious. Why did you do it?"

I say, "I thought it would help," but he's on the phone. "Hello?" he's saying. "Yes, my wife has overdosed. I need an ambulance right away."

"This is ridiculous!" I'm shouting, slamming through the house. "I only took three extra!" He's ignoring me. The ambulance shows up. I'm sitting in the parlor with my legs crossed, perfectly presentable, and the EMTs stand around the room, looking a little ridiculous.

"I'm perfectly fine," I tell them.

"She took an overdose," Jeff says from the doorway.

"It was hardly an overdose," I say, rolling my eyes. "I took a few extra."

"She's having a manic episode," Jeff says. "She could have a stroke."

"Well, I'm obviously not having a stroke," I say. "Really, you can leave."

They don't leave. They escort me, indignant, out to the ambulance. The ride to the hospital is excruciatingly slow. Arriving at the hospital, I am put in a little room with a security guard outside. I lean out the doorway.

"Do you have to stand there?" I ask the guard. He looks alarmed, as if he didn't know crazy people could talk. After a panicky minute, he nods.

"I won't run," I say, and go back into the room. I'm irate. Also a little dizzy, a sort of vertigo. All I did was take three extra Wellbutrin on the theory that perhaps they would cheer me up. Admittedly, I should have looked up the possible side effects of overdose before I took them, rather than after, but still, what a ridiculous fuss they're making about all this. I start to pace around the room.

I pace faster. Then faster. I want to know where Jeff is. I start to cry. This won't look good. I'm trying to come off as perfectly sane, but this pacing and crying makes me look crazy. I realize this with a touch of surprise — why would I be acting crazy? And I suddenly understand that, in fact, somewhere in my reptilian brain, I honestly don't *see* myself as crazy. Which, I realize, means I definitely am. I want to go home. Why isn't Jeff here? I'm whipping around the room, holding my head in my hands. I have brought my tome *Manic-Depressive Illness* with me as reading material while I wait, which I am supposed to be doing *calmly*, which I am not, and I pick up the book and go stand in the doorway again. I'm sobbing now. The guard is horrified. "Would you find me a nurse, please?" I sob. "Really, if you could find someone who could come talk to me, that would be great." I go back in the room and keep pacing. Seconds, hours later, I don't know, there's a young nurse in the room, *What's wrong, how can I help?* and I'm explaining that I have bipolar disorder, and I offer her the book in case she doesn't know much about it, and where is my husband,

and could she please find my husband, and I didn't mean to commit suicide, I just wanted to feel a little better, and she is making all the right soothing noises — there are some amazing nurses in the world — and assuring me that the doctor will be here soon, and she leaves and returns with Jeff, on whom I fling myself, hysterical, apologizing for making such a fuss, and Jeff pretends he doesn't mind.

The psych ward people come down and talk to us. The woman says, very earnestly, that I have to learn to take my illness *seriously*, and I tell her I *do* take it seriously, but in this case I just want to go home. She tries to talk me into coming upstairs with her, but I'm having none of it. Finally I talk my way out of the emergency room and ride home with Jeff, my forehead on the window, watching the trees flash past.

"I'm really sorry about that," I say.

"You're damn right," he says.

"Really," I say. "I know that was shitty."

We ride home in silence.

NEW MEDICATIONS, increases, decreases. I am trying in my muddled way to manage this — I take whatever meds Lentz tells me to take, I try to keep track of my swinging moods on my mood chart, and the rotation of friends and family comes to my house every day — my mother or father in the mornings, Megan or my aunt and uncle in the afternoon, sometimes other friends. The schedule changes every day, and every day I'm surprised again when someone shows up, and I apologize for needing them there.

When they leave, the agitation grows, and I pace from room to room, trying to escape the thoughts, the powerful impulses to run away, hurt myself, do something dangerous and extreme. These states scare me, and I know I am crazy, and I don't know if it's going to stop. The hope I felt in the spring eludes me now, seems like a lifetime ago, and at night I curl up in bed, pressing my head between my hands.

One night, when Jeff joins me there, curling his huge body around me, I tell him, chattering wildly, that I can't take this anymore, not the side effects, not the mood swings, not the terror or manic elation or dull, pressing pain. Screaming in bed, I rock, my body clenched into a fist. *I can't take it, I can't live like this anymore,* and Jeff rubs my back, *I know, I know,* he says, *we'll go see Lentz tomorrow, okay?* I gasp and howl in response, *What the fuck for? He's just going to change my meds again. And then the side effects will get worse, and he'll change the meds again, and the side effects will change but they won't go away. Jeff,* I gasp, *I cannot take it anymore, I want to be dead —*

*Don't say that!* Jeff sits up and starts to cry.

The magic words. I'm not supposed to say them, never say them, never say them to Jeff. If I say them, I might believe them, and then what? *No, no,* I say, uncurling my body and taking his face in my hands and wiping it off. *I didn't mean it. I swear I didn't mean it. I'm sorry, honey —* I smile brightly. *See? I'm right here. I promise.*

*Promise me you won't go away.* Jeff falls face first onto the bed, his arms wrapped around himself. I rub his ears. He likes that. His mother did it to him when he was little. It makes him feel safe.

*I promise,* I say. *I swear.*

Sometimes I believe, with every fiber of my being, that I truly can't take it, that I've reached the end of my rope, I've had it, I'm done.

I'm not done. I will never be done. It will never go away.

*I will never go away,* I tell Jeff, and we are quiet, wet-faced, snotty, and I rub his ears.

AT THE FRONT desk of the emergency room, Jeff says, "My wife has bipolar," and immediately they press the button to open the door and Jeff ushers me in. Here's a trick: if you ever want to get into the emergency room fast, tell them you're bipolar or schizophrenic. Works every time. They take my vitals — my pulse is racing, my blood pressure is about twenty points higher than it usually is — and show us to a room, assuring us that the doctor will be there soon.

We're sitting in the triage room — well, Jeff is sitting, and I'm in the corner, having crawled on top of a cabinet behind a tangle of medical equipment, agitated and talking a mile a minute until the doctor comes in, at which point I snap my mouth shut and become mute.

"Why are you up there?" the doctor asks me, baffled. Jeff and I stare at him. Finally Jeff says, "Because she's *crazy*."

The doctor raises his eyebrows. "Ah," he says, still not quite getting it. He asks me a series of questions — what brings me in here today, am I suicidal, do I have a plan. With every question, I look at Jeff. He repeats the question to me, and I nod or shake my head. In this way, we establish for the doctor that I'm nuts and need to be hospitalized. The doctor disappears and is replaced by someone from the psychiatric staff. The man walks in, takes one look at me, and says, "Would you feel better if the lights were off?"

"Yes!" I shout, then shut up again. He switches off the lights and takes a seat.

"Tell me what's going on," he says, and Jeff does.

"This happens every summer," he says. "Around June, she gets hypomanic, in July she's manic, and by August she's gone completely around the bend. It happened again this year. It started with her working around the clock and not sleeping. Then the anxiety set in, about a month ago. She's seen her doctor a bunch of times, and he's been trying to switch her meds fast enough to keep up with the episode, but obviously it hasn't worked. In the last week, she's been afraid to leave the house, just running around being compulsive for days, talking constantly, and then today I came home and she'd been cutting."

The man is writing on his clipboard. "Is she suicidal?"

"Yes."

"Does she have a plan?"

"She says she doesn't, but she's lying."

The man looks at me. "Does all this sound about right?"

"I don't have a plan," I say.

"She's lying," Jeff says.

"The point is that you're not safe to be at home, is that right?"

I nod. By the time we get to the hospital, I'm no longer under the impression that I'm sane. Once I've started cutting, I know I'm not likely to stop until I've done some serious damage, and I don't want that any more than anyone else does. The last place I want to be is the hospital, but I'm not stupid. I know when it's time to go in. I am so terrified of myself and of the vast, frightening world, that the psych ward, with its safe locked doors, sounds like a relief.

"All right," the man says, and then suddenly we're interrupted by another doctor, who walks in the room and switches on the lights. I flinch and shade my eyes. The second doctor goes through the same questions as the first doctor — what brings me here today, am I suicidal, do I have a plan — and Jeff goes through the same answers — she's having an episode, she's suicidal, she has a plan. Satisfied that the psych staff has it under control, the doctor leaves, and the first doctor switches off the lights again.

"Sorry about that," he says. "Well, listen. You've obviously done everything you can at home, and we don't want to make you wait when you've already made a serious effort to stay out of the hospital. Give me a minute and I'll get you upstairs." Soon he comes back to get us and escorts us up to Unit 47, where they know me well.

AND THEN all of a sudden, it's day. I open my eyes and squint in the white light pouring in through the windows. I assess the situation: I am in a room. Upon further consideration, I am in my room at home. I am in bed, probably my bed, unless they've moved someone else's bed in here, though I can't imagine why they would do that, so, I think, very groggy, probably not.

My head feels like it's wrapped in cotton batting and weighs a ton. I'm clearly drugged. I have no idea what day it is, or even what season of the year. I dimly remember a hospital, but I can't remember if I was in it yesterday or if I am remembering the last time, or the time before that. I wonder how long I've been gone. Surely somebody around here knows.

I crawl out of bed, unsteady on my legs. I make my way down the hallway, holding on to the wall. I wander into the kitchen and stand there in my gross pajamas, weak, filthy, hungry, cold. Looks like summer. The afternoon light spills in through the long wall of windows. All is white light. I begin to get confused, my mind spooling out in front of me, and then I snap out of it and look around the room.

There they are, lounging around. Megan and my mother are having a chat at the kitchen table. My father is making a turkey. Christi and Jeff are paging through *Vogue* and discussing the importance of the excellent handbag. (Jeff has exceptional taste.) My aunt and uncle are reading the paper. Everyone looks up and sees me and stops.

The front door opens and Ruth comes in. She stops. There is a long silence. No one knows what to say, because they don't know yet if I'm totally mad or suddenly sane, or what strange sequence of words will come rolling out of my mouth this time. We wait.

"I brought éclairs," Ruth finally says, absurdly. She gestures vaguely with a bakery box.

I think this over, weaving side to side. "Okay," I croak. I look at my husband. "Hello," I say. I think a minute more, looking at the assemblage of people in my living room. "How long was I crazy?" I ask no one in particular.

Jeff shrugs, turning a page. "Couple of weeks."

"What day is it?" I try to shake the fog out of my skull.

"Saturday."

"What month?"

"August. Do you remember the hospital?"

"Sort of. When did I go in?"

"Last month. They changed your meds. You got zapped."

"Oh," I say, and fall over. Ruth comes over and picks me up. She gives me a plate with an éclair. I look at it for a while.

"Now sit down," she instructs.

I look at the chair she is holding out. "Right," I say. I sit.

"Now eat," she says.

I take a bite. Everyone sighs in relief. I'm back. Time begins again.

That's what madness looks like: a small woman in baggy red pajamas sitting on a kitchen chair, her feet dangling above the ground, trying to figure out how to eat an éclair while everyone she knows and loves watches her closely, as if she's a rat in a cage, to see what will happen next.

And soon I will go upstairs, peel off the filthy pajamas, get dressed, and come back down to sit with them. They will know I am well as soon as I laugh.

I always do.

# EPILOGUE

· ══════ ·

I wake up, roll over in bed, prop up on an elbow, and start tossing back pills like they're candy. Twenty-one of them — they add up to 450 mg of Wellbutrin, 600 mg of Lamictal, 800 mg of Tegretol, 200 mg of Geodon, and a handful of supplements that are supposed to improve the mood. This, of course, is only the latest combination of meds, and will doubtless be adjusted and readjusted soon. In about an hour, I'll take a milligram of Ativan, a tranquilizer that will help (a little, anyway) press back the raging anxiety that hits the minute I get out of bed.

There's a cup of coffee with Jeff and we get our day all planned: what we'll do, when we'll be home, how long I'll be alone, what's stressing me (or us) out, any tasks that will take me out of the house, what we're having for dinner. We get the schedule straight so there's no room for me (or him) to go spinning off in the tornado of thoughts that can kick in when there is too much unscheduled time.

Time for the mood chart. I open my notebook. First, on the left side of the page, is the column that reads TREATMENTS — so I record what meds I took and how many, and check off if I've gone to therapy. In the middle of the page, I make any relevant notes — that I'm sick, on vacation, someone's died — whatever external factors might be contributing to my moods. Then I note the number of hours I slept last night. Then I rate my level of IRRI-TATION and ANXIETY. Typically, I'm not irritated, and I'm pathologically anxious. But there you are. Then come the moods: there's DEPRESSED first, then ELEVATED, each with several options: *Without Impairment, Significant Impairment but Able to Work, Significant Impairment and Not Able to Work,* and *Psychosis.* Personally, I have always wondered how many people are sitting down to do their mood charts while in *Psychosis.* So if I am ELEVATED and write on the chart that I am *Fanfuckingtastic!* and write down *YES!!!* next to *Able to Work,* I would still note that there was a degree of impairment — the idea is to be something milder, like *happy* or even *fine.* And if instead I am DEPRESSED, and write that I am *in despair,* and that I am *Not Able to Work* . . . you get the picture. The ideal day is when I am *Without Impairment — No Symptoms.* So far, I haven't written that more than a few times, but lately, the impairment is mild, and I'm able to work. Which is more than good enough. It's fanfuckingtastic, if you ask me.

Then I make a few notes in my journal — what's up with work, goals small and large — and do whatever amount of talking myself down off the ceiling I need to do. I try to Change My Thoughts. I Shift My Perception. I Choose Peace of Mind. And as stupid and cheesy and self-helpy as all that sounds, it *does* help — I change my thoughts from bracing for a terrible day to expecting a lovely one; shift my perception from seeing myself as a fuckup to seeing myself as capable and doing my best; and choose peace of mind over rigidity, terror, and all the rest. And they tell me to keep a mood chart. So I do it.

That's today — and tomorrow, and next week, and next month, and for how long? I'm trying to picture what a day will be like, what my life will be like, a couple of years from now, when you're reading this book. The future, and even the past and the present, are blurry concepts when you're mentally ill. Maybe a few years from now, I'll have left my senses entirely, abandoned my life as if it were a couple of books and some socks lying on the floor. But that's not what I believe. How could I?

I know some things will be the same, no matter what year it is. I'll start the day with a mouth full of pills. I'll stagger around for an hour, dizzy with the onslaught of chemicals coursing through my brain, rerouting errant neurotransmitters, herding neurons into their proper rows, creating connections that need to be there and blocking reactions that don't. Maybe it will be one of the really entertaining days when I've just had my meds changed, and we'll have a little Fun with Side Effects, one of the meds interacting with another in such a way that I'm walking into walls and seeing double until two in the afternoon. Or maybe not. Maybe my chemistry will sort itself out quickly and start chugging along like a good fellow. Maybe (hopefully) science and medicine's recent surge of interest in the brain will result in the development of medications that will make a difference in the daily lives of people like me.

Is it possible? Maybe I won't dread the days. Maybe I won't wake up with my chest clenched in terror. Even now, already, the morning panics that have been with me for so long are starting to lessen. Even now, madness sometimes holds off a little while, allows me to watch the sunrise before anyone else in the world is awake, when I can imagine that it's just me and the rising purple light and the chattering birds. Maybe I'll be lucky, and every day I'll wake up and find only Jeff and the dogs in the bed. Not the heavy, breathing body of madness, attached to my left leg, that I drag behind me wherever I go.

I want to think that the impossible can happen — I will no longer need to spend so much time devoted to the daily micromanagement of my moods, the constant monitoring of my thoughts, the second-guessing of everything I do. What if everything that went through my head wasn't inflected with the arbitrary whims and twitches of a broken brain? What if the madness wasn't always trying to speak through my mouth, manipulate my emotions and perceptions, pull the levers like the Wizard of Oz? What if my husband, friends, parents, didn't have to ask me again and again if I am all right — watching me, fearing that every minor shift in mood, every moment of excitement, every gloomy sigh is a sign that I'm flying or falling again? What if I could just have a bad day? A good one? Be in a regular old mood? What if, one day, the illness was not immediately present, right behind my eyes, right at the front of my brain, but had backed off a little, so that my thoughts were my own, my moods were just moods?

The promise of that freedom almost makes me dizzy — the freedom to stop thinking about my illness, to speak for myself, decide for myself, just go about my day. Maybe I would trust myself to do the right thing. Maybe I would trust my mind not to suddenly defect.

Sometimes, even now, I can. Sometimes, I feel as if the world has opened up around me, as if I have been staring at my feet for years and now have lifted my eyes, and there are sunshine and trees and days of rain, and there are people in my life. I am greedy for connection. All of a sudden, there are possibilities everywhere. I could leave my house. I could wake up unafraid. I could write a new book. I could plan for the future. I could travel, see all the theater I want, listen to jazz for days on end, read all the books in the world. I could live a very long time. I could be free of this monster.

I could be normal.

But I know this illness. I know its cycles. My days will always be different from your days; my idea of stability isn't your idea. The things I do, the choices I make, the places I go are limited to an extent by this illness — I can't stay up all night, cross many time zones, work too much, cram my calendar with things I'd love to do, hold a regular job, though some people with bipolar certainly can. I can't have the insane professional life I dream of — I can't write books *and* do journalism *and* academia *and* get a PhD *and* give lectures *and* teach college all at once, and some of those things I'll never do. I'll never backpack around Southeast Asia or hike through the Middle East — I can't go anywhere far from a hospital with modern meds. I could have had children — there are people with bipolar who do — but I didn't. Some of the things I won't do are things you take for granted; many of them are things I want to do, but can't. This isn't the end of the world. It's just the way things are. Managing mental illness is mostly about acceptance — of the things you can't do, and the things you must.

I wonder if I'll ever lose the anger at having bipolar, or the sorrow I feel for all the memories I've lost or never made. What about the years I can't remember at all? What about the moments with my family or with Jeff that I should be able to treasure but can't, because they are lost to inaccessible parts of my brain? What about the times my friends needed me and I wasn't there? There is grief for the years that slipped by, guilt at having hurt people, and for having needed so much and given so little for so long, regret about the goals I never attained.

But there is hope too. It's been a long time since I've felt hope. I might have been mad, but in spite of it I did things, heard things, was inspired by things, wrote things, held conversations, worked, loved, even if I can't remember it all. The episodes come less often these days, and I have more time to build memories in between. Now, I am finally able to piece together some semblance of a coherent life.

So I am there at Megan's gallery in New York. I am there in a fabulous leopard-print dress. There are people everywhere. Megan is luminous, astonished at what is happening to her life. Her work is beautiful, the colors overwhelming, and everyone walks around talking about it, blown away. I am here to see it. I am here with her. I am present in a moment in her life. I am here with Ruth as she sits on my couch at two A.M., her skinny legs tied in a knot, smoking my cigarettes and crying in frustration when her partner Christi has to go back to the psych ward. Ruth wants to know if Christi will ever improve, if her madness will lift long enough for them to build a life. I tell her it will. And I know that it will. I am here when Jaime, recovering from the breast cancer that smashed into her life when she was only twenty-four, finally breaks down years after the surgery and starts realizing what she has been going through. I listen to her on the phone and I want to fix it and I know I can't so I listen some more. I am there when Lora gets laid off and spends the next six months buried in a dark place, unable to write, compulsively listening to music, and I am there when we go running through New York in the middle of the night in search of Italian pastries, and I am there when she's finally laughing, and I don't miss a minute of it. I am there with my father up at the lake, listening to the loons call and playing Scrabble and getting my ass kicked by my aunt. I am there with him at lunch, with his white hair and shorts with knee-high socks and his roaring laugh. I am there with my mother when she curls up in my reading chair and tells me about her latest adventure, about Italy, Russia, Transylvania, Vietnam, the Mexican ruins in the west. And I am there with Jeff when we take a road trip, the wheels humming, looking out the windows at the cornfields and the thickets of pines, both together doing something we love, talking about the lives we have and the lives we want, and it all helps me learn him again, brings him closer to me. The madness leaves me alone for long enough to be with the people who make my life my life. And in the years that are coming, I will have the great gift of watching these astonishing people become who they are.

How do we know who we are or what we can become? We tell ourselves stories. The stories we tell are what we know of ourselves. We are a creation, a product of our own minds, a pastiche of memory, dream, fear, desire. My memory looks like a child's collage, or a ransom note, incomplete and full of holes. All I have is today, this moment, to work with. I am writing my story as I go. I am inventing myself one moment, one experience, at a time.

And that's all right. It means I can choose who I become. It means I can write my future. I can create a person, write a story, full of hope.

The mind is the seat of all that we are, the source of all we create. As strange and imperfect as mine may be, I also owe my career and passions to it. It is the source of all we think and feel — and while I feel and think, as Byron said, a bit too wildly at times, I also delight in the workings of the intellect and imagination, the ways that people are able to feel with and for one another, the deep experience of feeling at all. My brain sometimes departs from the agreed-upon reality, and my private reality is a very lonely place. But in the end, I'm not sure I wish I'd never gone there. I find value in having been to the places I've been. While there are days when I wish to God I could trade brains with someone else, just for a minute, just long enough to get some peace, I wouldn't exchange the life of my mind for the life of another.

I am who I am. This is the way it is: a balance, maybe an uncomfortable one. It's about doing all the necessary, frustrating, boring, exasperating, annoying, banal everyday tasks to keep the episodes at bay, but accepting that they'll come at some point anyway; structuring my life tightly in order to function well, but being flexible enough to deal with the unexpected; embracing the bizarre notion that sometimes things might go wrong — but other times they might not. I try to build a future out of contradictions; madness is only a small part of my life, yet sometimes it completely takes over and tries to destroy me.

Both things are true. That's all right. It has to be.

And it is. I relish my life. It is a life of which I am fiercely protective. I have wrested it back from madness, and madness cannot take it from me again. I will not throw it away. So what if it isn't a normal life? It's the one I have. It's difficult, beautiful, painful, full of laughter, passing strange.

Whatever else it is, whatever it brings — it's mine.

# BIPOLAR FACTS*

• ━━━━━━━━━━━━━ •

- American adults who have bipolar disorder: 5.8 million (2.8% of the U.S. population)
- Position of bipolar on the World Health Organization's scale ranking causes of disability worldwide: 7
- Year the Surgeon General gave his first report on mental illness: 1999

- Life expectancy of an adult with serious mental illness: 25 years shorter than that of a person without
- Bipolar patients who have attempted suicide: 25%
- Bipolar patients whose suicide attempts have been lethal: 15–20% (This is the highest suicide rate of any psychiatric disorder, and more than 20 times higher than the rate of suicide in the general population. About half of all suicides in the U.S. can be attributed to bipolar.)

*

---

*These figures are drawn from a number of sources — medical and psychological periodicals, policy reports and budgets, books published within the past seven years (most listed in the bibliography), and other sources. The numbers I've used are those most consistently cited across the literature; there is some variation between sources, and different studies come up with a range of conclusions. However, these numbers are representative of common conclusions in the research. By the time this book is published, the precise percentages may have changed, but they all indicate consistent trends.

- Year the term *manic-depressive insanity* was first used in medical texts: 1896
- Year the term *bipolar* was first used: 1980
- Year the first medication (lithium) was discovered to have an effect on manic patients: 1948
- Year the first medication designed specifically to treat bipolar was developed: still waiting

- Average age of onset: 23
- Average age of correct diagnosis: 40
- Average number of years from the onset of symptoms before a bipolar person or his/her family seeks treatment: 10
- Number of bipolar sufferers who have been misdiagnosed at least once: 70–75%
- Bipolar people who are not receiving treatment at any given time: approximately 50%

- Bipolar patients taking mood stabilizers who go off their medications because of side effects, the desire for manic energy, or impaired insight: 50%
- Number-one risk factor for relapse into a bipolar episode: going off meds

- Odds that a person with bipolar I will also struggle with substance abuse: 60:40
- Odds that a person with bipolar II will: 50:50
- Rate of alcoholism in bipolar men: three times higher than in the general population
- Rate of alcoholism in bipolar women: seven times higher than in the general population
- First-marriage divorce rates for people with bipolar disorder: twice as high as that of people with any other psychiatric dis-

order; three and a half times higher than the rate of divorce in the general population

- Annual direct and indirect costs of bipolar disorder in America: $45 billion
- Number of visits to the emergency room between 2000 and 2003 by people whose primary diagnosis was mental illness: four times that of all other emergency room visits
- Major reasons for this difference: lack of effective treatments and coordination of care for people with mental illness; inaccessibility of treatments for patients without insurance
- Bipolar and schizophrenic people who have no health insurance: 50% (The diagnosis of mental illness makes it far more difficult to get, and keep, insurance, and most insurance plans offer only limited coverage for mental health services and medications.)
- Primary cause of a lack of effective treatments: insufficient research funds
- Projected breakdown of research funding for the 2008 National Institutes of Health:
  - Bipolar: estimated at below $250 million (not included in NIH's 2008 report)
  - Diabetes: slightly over $1 billion
  - Depression: $334 million
  - Schizophrenia: $363 million
  - Other brain disorders (not including Alzheimer's, which receives $642 million): $4.7 billion

- Current medications: Lamictal, Tegretol, Geodon, Wellbutrin, trazodone, Ativan, and a number of supplements that are thought to support mood stability, including a high dose of fish oil and a strong vitamin B-complex
- Some habits that help me: a structured schedule, including daily mood charts, keeping a journal, yoga (I'm serious), cardiovascular exercise, meditation, baths, massage, going out of my house and interacting with another human being at least once a day, long periods of sunshine, and, during the winter, my light box. Also, seeing my doctor and therapist frequently, seeing my family and friends several times a week, and, critically, staying sober.
- Weekly cost of my meds: around $300, one third of which is out of pocket
- My side effects last week: double vision until 2 P.M., dizziness, poor balance, headaches, nausea, digestive problems, low blood sugar, anxiety, shaking hands
- Weekly cost of therapy: $217, out of pocket
- Cost of psychiatric visits: $300 per session (at least two a month, sometimes more), only partially covered by my three forms of insurance
- Cost of my last hospitalization: $45,000 covered by insurance; $10,000 paid out of pocket

# USEFUL WEBSITES

● ══════════════════════ ●

## GENERAL INFORMATION

American Academy of Child and Adolescent Psychiatry — *aacap*.org
American Psychiatric Organization — *psych*.org
American Psychological Association — *apa*.org

## DIRECTORIES OF LINKS

*directory.google.com/Top/Health/Mental_Health/Disorders/Mood/*
  *Bipolar_Disorder* — Google's list of websites about bipolar disorder
*dmoz.org/Health/Mental_Health/Disorders/Mood/Bipolar_Disorder*
  — the Open Directory Project's bipolar disorder link list
*mentalhealth.com/dis/p20-md02.html* — the Internet Mental Health site's comprehensive and helpfully organized list of links to more sites on bipolar disorder
*mhselfhelp.org* — National Mental Health Consumers' Self-Help Clearinghouse site
*psycom.net/depression.central.bipolar.html* — list of bipolar links

## OTHER SITES

*a-silver-lining.org* — chat rooms, bulletin boards, articles, newsletter, bookstore, and links to related resources *bipolarchild.com* — based on Demitri Papolos's book *The Bipolar Child*, the site offers a sample IEP (individual education plan), links, a free newsletter, and a FAQ sheet

*bipolarworld.net* — offers general information on bipolar, message boards, an art gallery, a place to post poetry, and an "ask the doctor" forum

*bpchildresearch.org* — Juvenile Bipolar Research Foundation (JBRF) is "the first charitable foundation devoted solely to the need for further awareness, education, and research in childhood-onset bipolar disorder." It funds research into the causes, treatments, and prevention of the disease.

*bpkids.org* — the website of the Child and Adolescent Bipolar Foundation (CABF), a nonprofit that gives a great deal of information to visitors about early-onset forms of the disease

*bpso.org* — stands for "bipolar significant others." Offers general information and a peer-support mailing list.

*citizen.org/eletter/* — sponsored by the Public Citizen's Health Research Group and the Treatment Advocacy Center, which do not accept pharmaceutical company support, this site provides up-to-date, unbiased information on medications used to treat bipolar and other psychiatric disorders.

*crazymeds.org* — a private website run by someone with a mental illness, this site is incredibly helpful. It provides ongoing reviews of a large number of meds, which are written by people who actually take them. The site is informational, gives all the details of what it's like to take the meds and what they do, and gives readers a wide range of experiences from mentally ill people on meds. This is not an official site sponsored by any pharmaceutical company and does not claim to be a scientific resource.

*dbsalliance.org* — Depression and Bipolar Support Alliance (DBSA) is probably the most comprehensive resource around for individuals with bipolar disorder. It includes information on signs and symptoms; help for people just diagnosed; articles on the latest research; extensive information on all the mood disorders; excellent material about how to get involved with advocacy; suggestions on becoming a peer-group leader or a grassroots organizer; where to go for online support groups and discussion boards; how to contact local DBSA chapters and other support groups in your area; tools for recovery and management; information about how to help a loved one; a bookstore; and more. This is a fantastic site for people with mood disorders, their families and friends, and anyone who wants to get involved.

*electroshock.org* — The site is maintained by a psychiatrist and offers information about ECT.

*harbor-of-refuge.org* — online peer support for people with bipolar and their families

*manicdepressive.org* — The website of the Harvard Bipolar Research Program at Massachusetts General Hospital offers general information, as well as a useful downloadable mood chart, and has a nationwide database to help you find bipolar specialists in your area.

*mcmanweb.com* — This privately run site for people with mood disorders offers chats, discussion boards, basic information, and ideas for managing your illness. The moderator is the author of *Living Well with Depression and Bipolar*.

*med.jhu.edu/drada/other_org.html* — website of the Depression and Related Affective Disorders Association (DRADA), associated with the Department of Psychiatry at the Johns Hopkins University School of Medicine

*medscape.com/pages/editorial/resourcecenters/public/bipolardisorder /rc-bipolardisorder.ov* — An enormous source of information on bipolar, this site is primarily aimed at clinicians but is definitely worth a look if you want to expand your knowledge about the scientific and clinical aspects of the disease.

*medwebplus.com/subject/Bipolar_Disorder* — MedWeb does free searches of health and science information.

*mental-health-matters.com/articles/print.php?artID=550* — A free online booklet put together by bipolar sufferer Shay Villere, this resource offers answers from someone who deals with the disorder.

*mental-health-matters.com/research/bipolar.php* — an extensive source of links to information on bipolar for supporters, professionals, and individuals with bipolar *mentalhealth.samha.gov* — site maintained by the Center for Mental Health Services under the U.S. Department of Health and Human Services

*mental-health-today.com* — An excellent resource dealing with many forms of mental problems, it offers information on medication (and how to get free meds), a therapist search engine, a bookstore, articles, online communities, bulletin boards and chats, tests you can take, exercises you can do, information on stigma, an e-mail-the-volunteer page, opportunities to volunteer, information for clinicians, and more.

*mentalhelp.net* — A free service that offers a search engine for finding therapists and a section on bipolar disorder that also provides general information on a number of bipolar topics, including symptoms and treatments, psychiatric classification information, bipolar news, and links to other Web resources.

*mhsanctuary.com/bipolar* — a clearinghouse for information on bipolar disorder, as well as support groups for people who have it and their families, bulletin boards, chat rooms, mental-health-related blogs, personal stories and articles written by people with bipolar, a file of frequently asked questions, and ideas for self-help

*mhsource.com/bipolar* — Part of the Mental Health InfoSource site, this Web source offers clinical treatment information, an electronic newsletter, and other materials to help consumers stay abreast of what's afoot in the clinical world. See also *mhsource.com/interactive/chat.html,* where you can find consumer and clinical chat rooms.

*mhsource.com/narsad/html* — The website for the National Alliance for Research on Schizophrenia and Affective Disorders (NARSAD) (see Research Resources, below)

*moodgarden.org* — popular support forum for people with bipolar and depression

*nami.org* — Formerly the National Alliance for the Mentally Ill, this organization calls itself, and really is, "the nation's voice on mental illness," providing the most comprehensive network of support, opportunity for involvement, and information on mental illness available. The organization is a major national presence, and the website keeps visitors up to date on NAMI's advocacy efforts and how to get involved. It also has a wide range of online support and discussion groups for people with a variety of mental illnesses. The organization has more than 1,200 affiliates nationwide, and this site enables you to search for a local chapter, get legal support, and more. It also publishes the useful twice-monthly newsletter *NAMI Advocate*.

*nimh.nih.gov* — The website for the National Institute of Mental Health (NIMH) states that its mission is "to reduce the burden of mental illness and behavioral disorders through research on mind, brain, and behavior." This is a good site to visit if you are interested in advocating for improved and expanded research on bipolar and other mental illnesses. To look at the page specifically on bipolar research and resources, go to *nimh.nih.gov/publicat/bipolarmenu.cfm*.

*nmha.org* — National Mental Health Association (NMHA) is a nonprofit organization dedicated to addressing many aspects of mental health and illness. It has 340 affiliates nationwide that work to improve mental health through education, research, and advocacy. The website offers general information and access to its affiliate directory.

*obad.ca/main.htm* — Organization for Bipolar and Affective Disorders Society (OBAD), based in Alberta, Canada, aims to help people with a range of affective disorders, offering downloadable material on those disorders, an "ask the experts" column, and information about resources.

*oreilly.com/medical/bipolar* — Part of the Patient-Centered Guides organization, which publishes a number of books and other literature on a number of disorders including bipolar disorder, this site provides support to parents of bipolar children and adolescents, offering resources such as advocacy and support groups and links to other websites. It also offers information on related conditions and symptoms, special-needs parenting and sibling issues, special education, health care and insurance, medications and complementary treatments, medical facilities, and public mental health agencies.

*patientcenters.com/bipolar* — Gives links to publications, related websites, advocacy groups, material about medication and special issues related to bipolar disorder, and articles excerpted from Mitzi Waltz's book *Bipolar Disorders: A Guide to Helping Children and Adolescents*.

*pendulum.org* — Far-reaching website that includes information on medications and complementary treatments, stress management strategies, and diagnostic criteria, as well as an online bipolar support group, writing by people with the disorder, and resources to help you get more support.

*psychcentral.com* — Run by mental health professionals, the site claims to be the largest mental health social network. It offers information on a broad spectrum of mental disorders, as well as blogs, chats, quizzes, information on medication and treatments, an "ask the therapist" link, links to reports on mental illness in the news, and information about further resources.

*psycheducation.org/index/html* — An educational site that offers articles on a wide range of mental health subjects, particularly all types of bipolar; a therapist search engine; an "ask the doctor" link; and information about medications and other treatments.

*psychlaws.org* — The website for the Treatment Advocacy Center (TAC), a legal advocate for the improvement of mental health treatment, is an extremely helpful site that focuses on problems associated with the failure to treat people with bipolar and other severe psychiatric conditions. Much of this information is unavailable elsewhere. (See Useful Contacts for information on TAC.)

# USEFUL CONTACTS

**NAMI** (formerly the National Alliance for the Mentally Ill)
Colonial Place Three
2107 Wilson Blvd., Suite 300
Arlington, VA 22201-3042
703-524-7600
Helpline: 800-950-6264
*nami.org*

See website listing for more information about this organization.

**DRADA** (Depression and Related Affective Disorders Association)
Johns Hopkins University Medical Center, Meyer 3-181
600 N. Wolfe St.
Baltimore, MD 21205
410-955-4647
*med.jhu.edu/drada*

Education and support groups for people with affective disorders.

**TAC** (Treatment Advocacy Center)
3300 N. Fairfax Dr., Suite 220
Arlington, VA 22201
703-294-6001
*psychlaws.org*

A legal advocacy organization founded to bring attention to the failing mental illness treatment system and correct its consequences. TAC's special focus is on people with bipolar, schizophrenia, and other severe mental illnesses who are being victimized, are homeless or jailed, are at risk of suicide, or are a danger to others because they are not being treated. TAC works to reform legal systems that prevent mentally ill people from getting treatment. It is a resource for individuals trying to reform treatment laws in their own states. Its free bimonthly newsletter *Catalyst* can be ordered by mail or online.

# RESEARCH RESOURCES

*Stanley Foundation Research Programs*
5430 Grosvenor Lane, Suite 200
Bethesda, MD 20814
301-571-0770
*stanleyresearch.org*

*NARSAD (National Alliance for Research on Schizophrenia and Affective Disorders)*
60 Cutter Mill Rd., Suite 404
Great Neck, NY 11021
516-829-0091
*narsad.org*

Outside of the U.S. government, these are the two largest providers of funds for research on mental illness; the Stanley Foundation also funds brain research. Both organizations work to make up for the significant shortfall between what's provided by the federal government and what's still needed, and both welcome donations.

# BIBLIOGRAPHY

━━━━━━━━━━━━━━━

Akiskal, Hagop S., Juan Jose Lopez-Ibor, Mario Maj, and Norman Sartorius, eds. *Bipolar Disorder*. West Sussex, UK: John Wiley and Sons, Ltd., 2002.

Akiskal, Hagop S., and Mauricio Tohen, eds. *Bipolar Psychopharmacotherapy*. West Sussex, UK: John Wiley and Sons, Ltd., 2006.

Anglada, Tracy. *Intense Minds: Through the Eyes of Young People with Bipolar Disorder*. BC, Canada: Trafford Publishing, 2006.

Anonymous. *The Dual Disorders Recovery Book*. Center City, MN: Hazelden Publishing, 1993.

Atkins, Charles. *The Bipolar Disorder Answer Book*. Naperville, IL: Sourcebooks, 2007.

Aubrey, Jean-Michel, Francoise Ferrero, Nicolas Schaad, and Mark Bauer. *Pharmacotherapy of Bipolar Disorders*. Hoboken, NJ: Wiley, 2007.

Basco, Monica Ramirez. *The Bipolar Workbook: Tools for Controlling Your Mood Swings*. New York: Guilford Press, 2005.

Behrman, Andy. *Electroboy: A Memoir of Mania*. New York: Random House, 2003.

Bennett, Bob. *Mental Illness: A Guide to Recovery*. BC, Canada: Trafford Publishing, 2006.

Bentall, Richard P. *Madness Explained*. New York: Penguin, 2005.

Birmaker, Boris M. *New Hope for Children and Teens with Bipolar Disorder*. New York: Three Rivers Press, 2004.

Bloch, Jon P., and Jeffrey Naser. *The Everything Health Guide to*

*Adult Bipolar Disorder: Reassuring Advice to Help You Cope.* Cincinnati: Adams Media Corp., 2006.

Burgess, Wes. *The Bipolar Handbook.* New York: Penguin, 2006.

Carter, Rosalynn. *Helping Someone with Mental Illness: A Compassionate Guide for Family, Friends, and Caregivers.* New York: Three Rivers Press, 1999.

Castle, Lara R. *Finding Your Bipolar Muse: How to Master Depressive Droughts and Manic Floods and Access Your Creative Power.* New York: Marlowe and Company, 2006.

Castle, Lara R., and Peter C. Whybrow. *Bipolar Disorder Demystified: Mastering the Tightrope of Manic Depression.* New York: Marlowe and Company, 2003.

Corrigan, Patrick W., ed. *On the Stigma of Mental Illness.* Washington, D.C.: American Psychological Association, 2005.

Corrigan, Patrick, and Robert K. Lundin. *Don't Call Me Nuts!: Coping with the Stigma of Mental Illness.* Tinley Park, IL: Recovery Press, 2001.

Daley, Dennis C., and Roger F. Haskett. *Understanding Bipolar Disorder and Addiction.* Center City, MN: Hazelden Publishing, 2003.

Dally, Peter. *The Marriage of Heaven and Hell: Manic Depression and the Life of Virginia Woolf.* New York: St. Martin's Press, 1999.

DelBello, Melissa P., and Barbara Geller, eds. *Bipolar Disorder in Children and Early Adolescence.* New York: Guilford Press, 2003.

Fast, Julia, and John Preston. *Loving Someone with Bipolar Disorder.* Oakland, CA: New Harbinger Books, 2004.

———. *Take Charge of Bipolar Disorder: A Four-Step Plan for You and Your Loved Ones to Manage the Illness and Create Lasting Stability.* New York: Wellness Central, 2002.

Fawcat, Jan, Bernard Golden, Nancy Rosenfeld, and Frederick K. Goodwin. *New Hope for People with Bipolar Disorder: Your Friendly, Authoritative Guide to the Latest in Traditional and Complementary Solutions.* 2nd ed. New York: Three Rivers Press, 2007.

Foucault, Michel. *Madness and Civilization: A History of Insanity in an Age of Reason.* New York: Vintage, 1988.

———. *Mental Illness and Psychology.* Berkeley: University of California Press, 1987.

Gershon, Samuel, and Jair C. Soares, eds. *Bipolar Disorders: Basic*

*Mechanisms and Therapeutic Implications.* New York: Marcel Dekker, 2000.

Goodwin, Frederick K., and Kay Redfield Jamison. *Manic-Depressive Illness: Bipolar Disorders and Recurrent Depression.* 2nd ed. New York: Oxford University Press, 2007.

Hershman, D. Jablow, and Julian Lieb. *Manic Depression and Creativity.* Amherst, NY: Prometheus Books, 1998.

Hinshaw, Stephen P. *The Years of Silence Are Past: My Father's Life with Bipolar Disorder.* New York: Cambridge University Press, 2002.

Isaac, Rael Jean, and Virginia C. Armat. *Madness in the Streets.* New York: Free Press, 1990.

Jacobsen, Nora. *In Recovery: The Making of Mental Health Policy.* Nashville, TN: Vanderbilt University Press, 2004.

Jamison, Kay Redfield. *Exuberance: The Passion for Life.* New York: Vintage, 2005.

———. *Night Falls Fast: Understanding Suicide.* New York: Vintage, 2000.

———. *Touched with Fire: Manic-Depressive Illness and the Artistic Temperament.* New York: Free Press, 1996.

———. *An Unquiet Mind: A Memoir of Moods and Madness.* New York: Vintage, 1997.

Karp, David A. *The Burden of Sympathy: How Families Cope with Mental Illness.* New York: Oxford University Press, 2002.

———. *Is It Me or My Meds? Living with Antidepressants.* Cambridge, MA: Harvard University Press, 2006.

Ketter, Terrence A. *Advances in Treatment of Bipolar Disorder.* Arlington, VA: American Psychiatric Publishing, 2005.

Lederman, Judith, and Candida Fink. *The Ups and Downs of Raising a Bipolar Child: A Survival Guide for Parents.* New York: Fireside, 2003.

Lombardo, Gregory T. *Understanding the Mind of Your Bipolar Child.* New York: St. Martin's Press, 2006.

Lyden, Jacki. *Daughter of the Queen of Sheba.* Boston: Houghton Mifflin, 1997.

MacCarthy, Fiona. *Byron: Life and Legend.* New York: Farrar, Straus and Giroux, 2002.

Mariani, Paul. *Desert Song: The Life of John Berryman.* Amherst: University of Massachusetts, 1986.

———. *Lost Puritan: A Life of Robert Lowell.* New York: W. W. Norton, 1996.

Marneros, Andreas, and Frederick K. Goodwin. *Bipolar Disorders: Mixed States, Rapid Cycling and Atypical Forms.* New York: Cambridge University Press, 2005.

Martin, Emily. *Bipolar Expeditions: Mania and Depression in American Culture.* Princeton, NJ: Princeton University Press, 2007.

McManamy, John. *Living Well with Depression and Bipolar Disorder.* New York: HarperCollins, 2006.

Middlebrook, Diane. *Anne Sexton: A Biography.* New York: Vintage, 1992.

Miklowitz, David J. *The Bipolar Survival Guide: What You and Your Family Need to Know.* BC, Canada: Guilford Press, 2002.

Miklowitz, David J., and Michael J. Goldstein. *Bipolar Disorder: Family-Focused Treatment Approach.* BC, Canada: Guilford Press, 1997.

Mondimore, Francis Mark. *Bipolar Disorder: A Guide for Patients and Families.* 2nd ed. Baltimore, MD: Johns Hopkins University Press, 2006.

Nettle, Daniel. *Strong Imagination: Madness, Creativity, and Human Nature.* New York: Oxford University Press, 2001.

Oliwenstein, Lori. *Taming Bipolar Disorder.* New York: Penguin Group, 2004.

Ortman, Dennis. *The Dual Diagnosis Recovery Sourcebook: A Physical, Mental, and Spiritual Approach to Addiction with an Emotional Disorder.* Columbus, OH: McGraw-Hill, 2001.

Papolos, Demitri, and Janice Papolos. *The Bipolar Child: The Definitive and Reassuring Guide to Childhood's Most Misunderstood Disorder.* New York: Broadway Books, 2002.

Phelps, Jim. *Why Am I Still Depressed? Recognizing and Managing the Ups and Downs of Bipolar II and Soft Bipolar Disorder.* Columbus, OH: McGraw-Hill, 2006.

Porter, Roy. *Madness: A Brief History.* New York: Oxford University Press, 2003.

Post, Robert M., and Gabriele S. Leverich. *Treatment of Bipolar Ill-*

*ness: A Casebook for Clinicians and Patients*. New York: W. W. Norton, 2007.

Ralph, Ruth O., and Patrick W. Corrigan. *Recovery in Mental Illness: Broadening Our Understanding of Wellness*. Washington, D.C.: American Psychological Association, 2004.

Sexton, Linda Gray. *Searching for Mercy Street: My Journey Back to My Mother, Anne Sexton*. Boston: Little, Brown and Company, 1994.

Solomon, Andrew. *The Noonday Demon: An Atlas of Depression*. New York: Scribner, 2002.

Sorenson, John. *Relapse Prevention in Bipolar Disorder: A Treatment Manual and Workbook for Therapist and Client*. Hertfordshire, UK: University of Hertfordshire Press, 2006.

Styron, William. *Darkness Visible: A Memoir of Madness*. New York: Vintage, 1992.

Torrey, E. Fuller. *Out of the Shadows: Confronting America's Mental Illness Crisis*. New York: John Wiley and Sons, 1997.

Torrey, E. Fuller, and Michael B. Knable. *Surviving Manic Depression*. New York: Basic Books, 2002.

Wahl, Otto F. *Media Madness: Public Images of Mental Illness*. New Brunswick, NJ: Rutgers University Press, 2003.

———. *Telling Is Risky Business: Mental Health Consumers Confront Stigma*. New Brunswick, NJ: Rutgers University Press, 1999.

Waltz, Mitzi. *Adult Bipolar Disorders: Understanding Your Diagnosis and Getting Help*. Sebastopol, CA: Patient-Centered Guides, O'Reilly Media, 2002.

Weineck, Silke-Maria. *The Abyss Above: Philosophy and Poetic Madness in Plato, Hölderlin, and Nietzsche*. Albany: State University of New York Press, 2002.

Whybrow, Peter C. *American Mania: When More Is Not Enough*. New York: W. W. Norton, 2005.

———. *A Mood Apart: Depression, Mania, and Other Afflictions of the Self*. New York: HarperCollins, 1997.

———. Whybrow, Peter C. *A Mood Apart: The Thinker's Guide to Emotion and Its Disorders*. New York: HarperCollins, 1998.

# ACKNOWLEDGMENTS

My deepest thanks to:

Ruth Berger, Lora Kolodny, Erica Crowell, Marlee MacLeod, and Jaime Kleiman, for reading the early and late drafts, providing invaluable insight and advice, filling in the blanks, and for the ineffable much. As always, yours.

Megan Rye, who can probably recite the thing. For stretching and pushing, correcting and demanding, inspiring and challenging, and occasionally lying. For all the rest. No way to say thank you for that.

My family, which survives it and accepts it and never-endingly gives. Jay, Judy, Steve, Gayle, Andy, Roger, Christie, and everybody out west. You are my greatest gift.

My agent, Sydelle Kramer. Constant, certain guidance on far more levels than are really required of you. For getting this book and all the others out of me in the first place, for my career and much of my sanity, thank you.

My brilliant editor at Houghton, Deanne Urmy. This book is ours, not mine. If it's any good, that's your fault.

And Jeff. Not enough words for you. Ask me sometime.

**P.S.**

Ideas,
interviews
& features...

# About the author

# About the book

# Read on

# Q & A with Marya Hornbacher

**When you write, do you have an imagined reader in mind? Is there a particular person you imagine writing to, or for?**
My imagined reader varies – I do not write specifically for a male or female reader, young or old. I have a vague image of someone curling up with a book, opening it, and diving in. When I'm writing, I'm very aware of how my particular voice will reach a reader in their private thoughts, and I want my voice to be one they can connect with, identify with, and hear clearly speaking to them.

**How does your family feel about your representation of them and of their relationship with each other and with you in your writing? Have they ever objected to anything they felt was unfair, or have they been supportive throughout?**
I could not have been luckier in the family I got. They have been adamantly supportive. When I was writing, I felt it was extremely important to portray them as accurately as I could, and to that end I interviewed them extensively, in person and in letters, so that I could be sure they felt involved in the process, and thought that their characters clearly represented what happened and who they are.

**You write with a voice utterly lacking in self-pity or any form of sentimentality. In fact, there's often a wry tone to your descriptions of yourself in a manic or**

depressive state which makes your writing very funny. I caught myself laughing out loud at some parts – for example, your conversation with your neighbour when you locked yourself out after flooding your basement – but then I felt a bit uneasy when I reflected that the source of amusement was a description of the effects of mental illness. Are you after a particular effect when you use humour in these episodes? Is it okay to laugh? What do you think about these mixed reactions readers might have to some parts of your work?

It is my sincere hope that people feel like they can laugh when it's funny. And my experience of mental illness is both funny and serious; I hope that that mixture of feelings comes through in the book, and that the reader experiences it as they read.

In *Madness*, you often say that when in the grip of an episode you 'write and write and write'. What kind of material would you produce in those times? Did you write creatively, or was it more a catharsis, or a confessional, diary-kind of writing?

It's not quite either. Overall, it's garbage; in order to write well, I need a sharp clarity of thought and an ability to shape my words and stories, whereas when I'm manic I'm just pouring out the first things that come to mind. It's not really cathartic diary-style writing; it's usually very cerebral, scattered, and very much evidence of how the manic mind works, flying from thought to ▶

Marya Hornbacher is the author of two memoirs and an acclaimed novel. She was born in California in 1974, but grew up in Minnesota. She now lives in Minneapolis.

## Q & A with Marya... *(continued)*

◄ thought so quickly it makes little sense to anyone else. In short – what I write in those periods that many people imagine must be very creative is easily the worst stuff I have ever produced in my life.

**How much do you prepare before you write a novel? Do you write a plan to guide you, or do you write spontaneously and edit later?**
I usually go into a book with a loose outline or synopsis of the plot, sketches of the characters, and a lot of notes on what I want to do in the book; I use these as reference, but not as a specific plan I need to stick to. Writing has a nasty habit of taking you where you never knew you'd go, and there's really no choice but to follow it.

**Who has been the biggest influence on your writing? Are there any particular writers you go back to time and time again for inspiration or encouragement?**
I read and re-read Virginia Woolf, Jeanette Winterson, Shakespeare, Chekhov, and Beckett, in prose; in poetry, I'm all over the map. I read prose to teach me story, and poetry to teach me language. The number and variety of influences that play a part in what I think about, and what I want to write about, is enormous; I think all of us are influenced in some way by virtually everything we read. We seem to store it away in some corner of our brains and draw on it even when we don't know we're doing so. It's sort of wonderful.

> ❝ It is my sincere hope that people feel like they can laugh when it's funny. And my experience of mental illness is both funny and serious; I hope that that mixture of feelings comes through in the book, and that the reader experiences it as they read. ❞

**Were there any parts in *Madness* you found especially difficult to write? If so, how did you overcome this?**

It was difficult to write the sections in the hospitals, because my memory of them is so much pieces and bits here and there. So I wrote it that way – recorded the bits I remember in a very abstract way, which mirrors my memory of it. Accuracy in memoir is essential; accuracy of memory that is not linear or complete needs to be represented as incomplete. So that's how I handled it.

**And finally, if you could give one piece of advice to aspiring writers, what would it be?**

Read! The best education you will ever get in writing lives in the books of the writers who came before you. Never think you're done evolving as a writer. Keep reading, keep learning, your whole life long, and your writing will be enlivened and enriched. ∎

6 Never think you're done evolving as a writer. Keep reading, keep learning, your whole life long, and your writing will be enlivened and enriched. 9

# Top Ten Writers of All Time

William Shakespeare

Anton Chekhov

Toni Morrison

Joan Didion

Virginia Woolf

Samuel Beckett

Anne Sexton

Robert Lowell

C. S. Lewis

Jeanette Winterson

# Top Ten Musical Artists of All Time

Tom Waits

David Bowie

Gabriel Fauré

John Coltrane

Pablo Jones

Bob Dylan

Simon & Garfunkel

Lucinda Williams

The Magnetic Fields

Iron & Wine

# Lives Too Often Kept Dark

*Marya on Memoir*

WRITING A MEMOIR is a funny thing. The two questions people ask me most often are these: *Is it hard having people know so much about your life?* and *Was it cathartic to write your memoirs?* The answers, respectively, are yes and no. Let me explain.

Writing a book about a period in my life is not the same as telling the story of my life, or myself – that's autobiography, not memoir. And there is a difference. The former really is the story of someone's life, presumably written when they're older, and presumably written by someone who's had a particularly interesting life. The latter is just a story, like I said, of something *about* someone's life – a period, or a particular event. My memoirs – about eating disorders and bipolar disorder – are about specific subjects. The story of my *whole life* would be a drastic bore. My life is pretty regular; I mostly read books and write, which doesn't make for much of a book. But I've had some interesting experiences, and I wrote memoirs about them for one reason: they are actually *common* experiences, but ones that aren't written about very often, because they're experiences we consider somehow secret. The fact that we consider them secret, though, leads to misunderstanding, and, for the people who share those experiences, too often leads to shame.

We hide our stories of mental illness and eating disorders. And hiding them means they eat away at us. What I wanted to do, in telling stories about the way these things have impacted me, is shed some light on areas of our lives that are too often kept dark. That darkness is lonely and damaging. I wanted to do something to change that if I could.

So I wrote about my own life. And when people ask me if it's hard to have people know so much about it, I have to say yes. But not so hard that I'd rather keep it a secret. It's important to me that people feel they can tell *their* stories. I wanted to open a door that would allow people to do that. I wanted people to sit down with my memoirs, open them up, and feel that they were reading not so much my story as their own.

But when people ask if it was cathartic to write these things – the answer is a definite no. I don't really believe that good books are pure 'self-expression'. I have a diary and a therapist if I want to express myself. What I'm trying to do with memoir is tell a story – and as a writer, it's awfully important to me that I tell it well. Accurately, truthfully, and well. To do this in memoir, you do have to dig deep; you have to reach a level of understanding with yourself that brings the most honest voice to the surface. But writing about yourself isn't always particularly comfortable. Catharsis is a process of getting something out of your system; I didn't feel I had to do that with these issues. I felt I did ▶

6 What I wanted to do, in telling stories about the way these things have impacted me, is shed some light on areas of our lives that are too often kept dark. That darkness is lonely and damaging. I wanted to do something to change that if I could. 9

## Lives Too Often Kept Dark *(continued)*

◀ have a story to tell that might reach people, and in order to tell it I had to look inside myself for what I knew, examine memories, think carefully about what it was I was trying to say. But that isn't getting something out of your system. That's just reporting. I approached writing my memoirs like a reporter: I interviewed the people in my life who knew the stories from all angles, went over hospital records, re-read letters and journals from years ago, nagged everyone who was close to me – *Is this how you remember it? What did you think at the time? Is this accurate?* – for more details and more points of view, and had seven different people read drafts of the books throughout the process for accuracy. It was absolutely critical to me that my memoirs represent situations and people correctly. It wasn't about getting myself down on paper, or recording every thought that went through my head. It was about telling a story that other people could connect with.

And I hope that people can. We all have a story to tell. The reason they are important is that they connect us to other people – we find similarities, we hear echoes of something we ourselves know to be true. The human condition is a weird state of affairs. Without each other, we're just up a creek. It's by story that we connect – I tell mine, you tell yours, we find the places where our stories cross paths and intersect. Memoir is not me telling a story to hear myself talk. It's talking, as best I can, directly to you. I hope I've said something you can use. ■

❝ It's by story that we connect – I tell mine, you tell yours, we find the places where our stories cross paths and intersect. ❞

# A Writer's Life

**When do you write?**
Odd hours – generally from 4–6 a.m., then I break for yoga, then write from 8–2, then in the evenings usually 6–8.

**Where do you write?**
In my office at home or in coffee shops.

**Do you prefer using a pen or a computer?**
Computer. I do notes for what I'm writing in a notebook, but compose on a computer.

**Do you write to silence or music?**
Music.

**What started you writing?**
It never occurred to me not to. I think it was getting a blank notebook for my fourth birthday and being very unnerved by the fact that there were no words on the pages. So I filled it up.

**Can you remember the first thing you wrote?**
A 'short story' called 'Clouds'. It was largely a commentary on how I liked them.

**Do you have any writing rituals or superstitions?**
Nope.

**Could you tell us a bit about your tattoos?**
I have four. One on each arm (an orchid and a calla lily), the Chinese character for 'literature' on my hip, and a large Russian firebird on my back, with a series of ▶

### A Writer's Life *(continued)*

◄ Chinese characters down my spine. They all mean different things to me, and all have been done at sort of transitional points in my life. I like them. ■

# Have You Read?

*Other books by Marya Hornbacher*

### Wasted: Coming Back from an Addiction to Starvation

Fearful of 'fat' from just five years of age, Marya Hornbacher became embroiled in a vicious battle with food that very nearly destroyed her. In this stunning, courageous and raw memoir, she recounts her struggle with anorexia and bulimia, and explores the psychological compulsion towards eating disorders so often neglected by doctors and 'experts' more concerned with treating symptoms than examining causes. Hers was a life of madness – whirlwind emotions, drugs and promiscuous sex, secrecy, lies, and cunning. Marya learned every trick in the book to keep doctors and family in the dark about her weight, eating habits, and state of mind. She was hospitalised countless times and at her worst, given just one week to live. But her survival instinct eventually won out over her equally fierce desire for self-annihilation. *Wasted* is a testament of one woman's struggle with herself – a story of a journey to the very edge of life, and back again.

'Hornbacher describes eating disorders with a stark candour that captures both their pain and underlying purposes. She is wise beyond her years'

*New York Times Book Review*

## Have You Read? *(continued)*

### *The Centre of Winter*

Kate Schiller is only six years old when her beloved father goes into the garage and shoots himself in the head. She doesn't yet understand her father's demons, and the utter despair that drove him to take his own life. Now, as a cruel Minnesota winter curls around the Schillers and seals them into their grief, Kate's mother Claire must find hope again for the sake of Kate and her twelve-year-old son Esau – who is already showing signs of the same black despair that plagued his father...

'Hornbacher succeeds marvelously. She constructs a kaleidoscope of speakers at times beautiful and often disturbing...An adroit first novel'

*Los Angeles Book Review*

# If You Loved This,
## You Might Like...

*Notes from an Exhibition*
by Patrick Gale
Rachel Kelly is a gifted artist with bipolar
disorder. She's a whirlwind of creative highs
and anguished, crippling lows, which takes
its toll on her family – especially her
wayward daughter Morwenna, who has
inherited her mother's demons...

*The Cornstalk Man*
by Daniel Crocker
Missouri, 1970. One woman struggles with
bipolar disorder at a time when the illness
was not understood at all, and people
thought she was just plain mad...

*Blue Sky* (1994)
Starring Jessica Lange and Tommy Lee Jones.
The story of an army major and his stunning,
unusual wife, who has bipolar disorder.

# Find Out More

**Marya Hornbacher's official website:**
www.maryahornbacher.com

........................................................................................

*Bipolar Disorder: The Ultimate Guide*
by Sarah Owen and Amanda Saunders
A sensitive and compassionate guide to
bipolar disorder. Clear, informative, and
comprehensive.

........................................................................................

*My Friend Paul* (1999)
(documentary)
A moving account of a man's struggle with
bipolar disorder, as recorded by his best
friend.

# What's next?

Tell us the name of an author you love

| Marya Hornbacher | Go ▶ |

and we'll find your next great book.